T0305221

Central Banking, Monetary Policy and Social Responsibility

THE ELGAR SERIES ON CENTRAL BANKING AND MONETARY POLICY

Series Editors: Louis-Philippe Rochon, *Full Professor, Laurentian University, Canada, Editor-in-Chief,* Review of Political Economy *and Founding Editor Emeritus,* Review of Keynesian Economics, Sylvio Kappes, *Assistant Professor, Federal University of Ceará, Brazil and Coordinator, Keynesian Economics Working Group, Young Scholars Initiative* and Guillaume Vallet, *Associate Professor, Université Grenoble Alpes and Centre de Recherche en Economie de Grenoble (CREG), France*

This series explores the various topics important to the study of central banking and monetary theory and policy and the challenges surrounding them. The books in the series analyze specific aspects such as income distribution, gender and ecology and will, as a body of work, help better explain the nature and the future of central banks and their role in society and the economy.

Titles in the series include:

The Future of Central Banking
Edited by Sylvio Kappes, Louis-Philippe Rochon and Guillaume Vallet

Central Banking, Monetary Policy and the Environment
Edited by Louis-Philippe Rochon, Sylvio Kappes and Guillaume Vallet

Central Banking, Monetary Policy and Social Responsibility
Edited by Guillaume Vallet, Sylvio Kappes and Louis-Philippe Rochon

Future volumes will include:

Central Banking, Monetary Policy and the Future of Money
Edited by Guillaume Vallet, Sylvio Kappes and Louis-Philippe Rochon

Central Banks and Monetary Regimes in Emerging Countries
Theoretical and Empirical Analysis of Latin America
Edited by Fernando Ferrari Filho and Luiz Fernando de Paula

Central Banking, Monetary Policy and Income Distribution
Edited by Louis-Philippe Rochon, Sylvio Kappes and Guillaume Vallet

Covid 19 and the Response of Central Banks
Coping with Challenges in Sub-Saharan Africa
Salewa Olawoye-Mann

Central Banking, Monetary Policy and the Political Economy of Dollarization
Edited by Sylvio Kappes and Andrés Arauz

Central Banking, Monetary Policy and Gender
Edited by Louis-Philippe Rochon, Sylvio Kappes and Guillaume Vallet

Central Banking, Monetary Policy and Financial In/Stability
Edited by Louis-Philippe Rochon, Sylvio Kappes and Guillaume Vallet

Central Banking, Monetary Policy and Social Responsibility

Edited by

Guillaume Vallet

Associate Professor, Université Grenoble Alpes and Research Fellow, Centre de Recherche en Economie de Grenoble (CREG), France

Sylvio Kappes

Assistant Professor, Federal University of Ceará, Brazil and Coordinator, Keynesian Economics Working Group, Young Scholars Initiative

Louis-Philippe Rochon

Full Professor, Laurentian University, Canada, Editor-in-Chief, Review of Political Economy *and Founding Editor Emeritus,* Review of Keynesian Economics

THE ELGAR SERIES ON CENTRAL BANKING AND MONETARY POLICY

Cheltenham, UK • Northampton, MA, USA

Published by
Edward Elgar Publishing Limited
The Lypiatts
15 Lansdown Road
Cheltenham
Glos GL50 2JA
UK

Edward Elgar Publishing, Inc.
William Pratt House
9 Dewey Court
Northampton
Massachusetts 01060
USA

A catalogue record for this book
is available from the British Library

Library of Congress Control Number: 2022938986

This book is available electronically in the **Elgar**online
Economics subject collection
http://dx.doi.org/10.4337/9781800372238

ISBN 978 1 80037 222 1 (cased)
ISBN 978 1 80037 223 8 (eBook)

Printed and bound by CPI Group (UK) Ltd, Croydon, CR0 4YY

Contents

About the editors

Guillaume Vallet is an Associate Professor of Economics at the University of Grenoble Alpes, France and a Research Fellow at Centre de Recherche en Economie de Grenoble.

He holds two PhDs, one in economics earned from the University Pierre Mendès-France (Grenoble, France) and the other in sociology obtained at the University of Geneva (Switzerland) and at the École des hautes études en sciences sociales (Paris, France).

Guillaume was awarded a Fulbright Award, in 2021, to explore the development of the social sciences during the Progressive Era (1892–1920), especially in light of economists' and sociologists' treatment of income inequality.

His research focuses on monetary economics, the political economy of gender and the history of economic thought during the Progressive Era. He is the author of 47 articles in peer-reviewed journals and books, and has written nine books. His work has appeared in several distinguished academic journals, such as *Revue d'Economie Politique, Economy and Society*. His work on Albion W. Small has appeared in *Business History* and the *Journal of the History of Economic Thought*. He has been invited to give talks by many institutions, such as the New School for Social Research (New York, USA), the Bank of Ecuador, the Bank of Hungary, the Bank of Israel, the Swiss National Bank and the United Nations in Geneva.

Sylvio Kappes is Assistant Professor of Economic Theory at the Federal University of Ceará, Brazil. He has a PhD in Development Economics from the Federal University of Rio Grande do Sul, Brazil. His main areas of research are Central Banking, Monetary Policy, Income Distribution and Stock-flow Consistent models. His work has been published in a number of peer-reviewed journals, such as the *Review of Political Economy*, the *Journal of Post Keynesian Economics* and the *Brazilian Keynesian Review*. Sylvio is a co-editor of The Elgar Series on Central Banking and Monetary Policy, together with Louis-Philippe Rochon and Guillaume Vallet. He is the Books Review Editor of the *Review of Political Economy*, and sits on the editorial boards of the *Review of Political Economy* and the *Bulletin of Political Economy*. He is also a co-coordinator of the Keynesian Economics Working Group of the Young Scholars Initiative (YSI) of the Institute for New Economic Thinking (INET).

Louis-Philippe Rochon is Full Professor of Economics at Laurentian University, Canada, where he has been teaching since 2004. Before that, he taught at Kalamazoo College, in Michigan. He obtained his doctorate from the New School for Social Research, in 1998, earning him the Frieda Wunderlich Award for Outstanding Dissertation, for his dissertation on endogenous money and post-Keynesian economics.

In January 2019, he became the co-editor of the *Review of Political Economy* and its Editor-in-Chief in 2021. Before that, he created the *Review of Keynesian Economics*, and was its editor from 2012 to 2018, and is now Founding Editor Emeritus. He has been guest editor for the *Journal of Post Keynesian Economics*, the *International Journal of Pluralism and Economics Education*, the *European Journal of Economic and Social Systems*, the *International Journal of Political Economy*, and the *Journal of Banking Finance and Sustainable Development*. He has published on monetary theory and policy, post-Keynesian economics and fiscal policy.

Louis-Philippe is on the editorial board of *Ola Financiera*, the *International Journal of Political Economy*, the *European Journal of Economics and Economic Policies: Intervention*, *Problemas del Desarrollo*, *Cuestiones Económicas* (Central Bank of Ecuador) and *Bank & Credit* (Central Bank of Poland), the *Bulletin of Political Economy*, *Advances in Economics Education*, *Il Pensiero Economico Moderno*, the *Journal of Banking, Finance and Sustainable Development* and *Research Papers in Economics and Finance*.

He is the Editor of the following series: The Elgar Series of Central Banking and Monetary Policy; and Elgar's New Directions in Post-Keynesian Economics series.

Louis-Philippe has been a Visiting Professor or Visiting Scholar in Australia, Brazil, France, Italy, Mexico, Poland, South Africa and the USA, and has further lectured in China, Colombia, Ecuador, Italy, Japan, Kyrgyzstan and Peru.

He is also the author of 150 articles in peer-reviewed journals and books, and has written or edited close to 35 books.

He has received grants from the Social Sciences and Humanities Research Council in Canada (SSHRC), the Ford Foundation and the Mott Foundation, among other places.

Contributors

Massimo Amato teaches Economic History, History of Economic Thought and History of Financial Crises at Bocconi University. He is co-director of the MINTS (Monetary Innovation, New Technologies, and Society) Research Unit at the Baffi Carefin Research Centre at Bocconi. Among his books are *Le radici di una fede* (2008), *L'énigme de la monnaie: à l'origine de l'économie* (2015), and with L. Fantacci, *The End of Finance* (2012), *Saving the Market from Capitalism* (2014) and *A Fistful of Bitcoins* (2020). His research activity focuses on the functioning, crisis and possible reforms of the monetary and financial system, both local and global. Recently he elaborated with co-authors a proposal for reforming the management of eurozone public debt ("Europe, public debts, and safe assets: the scope for a European Debt Agency", *Econ. Polit.*, 2021).

Maqsood Aslam is a Post Doctoral Fellow at the University of Lille. He has vast research and teaching experience. His research combines extensive historical archival data, theory and rigorous empirical analysis to explain how natural and man-made shocks affect decision-making and preferences in short and long run. His areas of research include natural experiments, religion, farm productivity, education, economic development, political economy, finance, social preferences and central banking. He has published in reputed peer-reviewed journals such as *Kyklos*, *Cliometrica* and *Finance Research Letters*. He holds a PhD in Economics from the University of Lille, and completed an MPhil in Econometrics from the Pakistan Institute of Development Economics, Islamabad. He obtained an MSc in Economics as well as a Post Graduate Diploma in Applied Economics (PGDAE) from the University of the Punjab, Lahore. He has worked as research lead with international organizations. He has participated and presented in several international workshops and conferences.

François Claveau holds the Canada Research Chair in Applied Epistemology and is a professor in the Department of Philosophy and Applied Ethics at Université de Sherbrooke. He is also director of two labs in computational humanities and social sciences. His research is mainly on knowledge claims of expert organizations such as central banks and think tanks. He mixes conceptual analysis as practiced in contemporary philosophy with computational methods from natural language processing and social network analysis. He co-authored *Do Central Banks Serve the People?* (2018); co-edited *Experts, sciences et sociétés* (2018); and co-wrote numerous articles, including "Macrodynamics of economics: a bibliometric history" (*History of Political Economy*, 2016) and "Appraising the epistemic performance of social systems: the case of think tank evaluations" (*Episteme*, online 2020).

Marie Cuillerai is Full Professor of Philosophy at the University of Paris, Institute Humanités et Sciences Sociales (HISS), and a member of the Laboratory of Research on Social and Political Change (LCSP, EA 3537). Her first works paved the way on research on the relationship between economics and political philosophy, by questioning the Regulation Theory in particular, through the institutionalist theory of money. Likewise, she focuses on criticisms of capitalism through the lens of the French contemporary philosophical current, including Michel Foucault and Gilles Deleuze, Georges Bataille and Pierre Klossowski. Her latest published article is "Extension du domaine de la dépense", in M. Cuillerai and F. Rambeau (eds), *Tumultes*, 57, *Violences: Histoires, théories, experiences* (Kimé éditions, 2021).

Peter Dietsch is a professor in the Department of Philosophy at the University of Victoria. His research focuses on issues of economic ethics, notably on tax justice, normative dimensions of monetary policy and income inequalities. Dietsch is the author of *Catching Capital: The Ethics of Tax Competition* (2015), co-author of *Do Central Banks Serve the People?* (2018) and a co-editor of *Global Tax Governance: What Is Wrong with It and How to Fix It* (2016). He has published numerous articles, and is a regular contributor in the media on debates in his field. Dietsch received the Friedrich Wilhelm Bessel Research Award from the Humboldt Foundation in 2021 and was nominated to the College of New Scholars, Artists and Scientists of the Royal Society of Canada in 2017. Dietsch has held visiting positions at the Wissenschaftszentrum Berlin and at the European University Institute in Florence.

Jérémie Dion is a PhD student in Science, Technology and Society at Université du Québec à Montréal, and a member of the Canada Research Chair in Applied Epistemology at Université de Sherbrooke. Using methods borrowed from social network analysis, bibliometrics and natural language processing, he works on central banking research and science funding. He co-wrote *Quantifying Central Banks' Scientization: Why and How to Do a Quantified Organizational History of Economics* (2018).

Etienne Farvaque is Full Professor of Economics at the University of Lille. He is also Fellow Associate at the CIRANO (Québec). He received his PhD in Economics from Lille 1 University in 1997 and his habilitation degree from the same university in 2006, and has held visiting positions at, for example, Kochi University of Technology, Kwansei Gakuin University and the EUIJ (Japan), and at the Center for Research on European Integration (ZEI) in Bonn. He has taught in many universities, including the University of New Caledonia, Polytechnique Montréal and Cracow University of Economics. He is an expert for several research assessment agencies (HCERES, FNRS, etc.). His research and teaching interests include European economics, European integration, political economy, fiscal rules and central banking. He is the author of four books (including one on the European Central Bank and one on the economics of democracy), and has published in journals such as the *European Journal of Political Economy, Economic Modelling, German Economic Review, Journal of Economic Dynamics and Control, The World Economy, Kyklos, Journal of Macroeconomics* and *Public Choice*.

Clément Fontan is Professor of European Economic Policy at UCLouvain and Saint-Louis University, Brussels. He is a co-director of the journal *Politique européenne* and coordinator of the political economy research section of the French Political Sciences Association. He has published in many academic journals his research on political economy, European studies, financial ethics, central banking and financial crises. He co-authored *Do Central Banks Serve the People?* (2018) and often presents his research in front of policymakers and in media outlets.

Lucio Gobbi holds an MA in Economic and Social Sciences from Bocconi University and a PhD in Economics and Management from Trento University, and is currently a postdoc researcher in Political Economy at Trento University, where he teaches Financial Markets and Economic Activity. He has published several articles in scientific journals, such as the *Cambridge Journal of Economics* and the *Journal of Macroeconomics*. He co-edited the *Moneta e Credito* special issue "Development paths and currency areas: alternative options and structural constraints". He is co-author of "Europe, public debts, and safe assets: the scope for a European Debt Agency" (*Econ. Polit.*, 2021). His research focuses mainly on macroeconomic and monetary policy, systemic risk and public debt.

Charles Goodhart was appointed to the Norman Sosnow Chair of Banking and Finance at the London School of Economics (LSE) in 1985, until his retirement in 2002, when he became Emeritus Professor of Banking and Finance. He was elected a Fellow of the British Academy in 1990, and awarded the CBE in 1997 for services to monetary economics. In 1986, he helped to found the Financial Markets Group at the LSE. For the previous 17 years he served as a monetary economist at the Bank of England, becoming a chief adviser in 1980. Following his advice on overcoming the financial crisis in Hong Kong in

1983, he subsequently served on the HK Exchange Fund Advisory Committee until 1997. Later in 1997 he was appointed for three years, until May 2000, as one of the four independent outside members of the newly formed Bank of England Monetary Policy Committee. He became an economic consultant to Morgan Stanley in 2009, until he resigned, at the age of 80, in 2016. It was during this period that he began work on the subject matter of his recent book, *The Great Demographic Reversal* (2020), with his colleague there, Manoj Pradhan. He has written widely on matters relating to monetary policy, especially central banking, and macroeconomics. Goodhart is the author of Goodhart's Law: "that any observed statistical regularity will tend to collapse once pressure is placed upon it for control purposes".

Rob Macquarie writes as an independent researcher working on the intersection of environmental crises, economic policy and democratic institutions. His research on central banks and monetary policy is rooted in theoretical political economy, and has covered the growing legitimacy gap following the Global Financial Crisis as well as policy options for responding to climate change, in particular at the Bank of England. He is a policy analyst at the Grantham Research Institute on Climate Change and the Environment at the London School of Economics, where he has worked on government strategy for net zero, international development and carbon markets. Through earlier research tracking global climate finance at Climate Policy Initiative, he has contributed data to the Intergovernmental Panel on Climate Change's Sixth Assessment Report and the Biennial Assessment of the United Nations Framework Convention on Climate Change Standing Committee on Finance.

Manoj Pradhan is the founder of Talking Heads Macroeconomics, an independent research firm, and co-author of the bestseller *The Great Demographic Reversal* (2020). Pradhan was most recently Managing Director at Morgan Stanley, where he led the Global Economics team. He joined Morgan Stanley in 2005 after serving on the faculty of George Washington University (Washington, DC) and the State University of New York. Pradhan works on thematic global macroeconomics, with a focus on emerging markets. He has a PhD in economics from George Washington University and a Master's in Finance from the London Business School.

Jong-Un Song is a board governor of the Korean Association for Political Economy. He holds a BA in International Relations from the University of Hanshin, an MA in Politics from Seoul National University and a PhD in Economics from Kyungsang National University. He was Visiting Professor at Baesok Art University. His research is on macroeconomic and monetary theory and policy, and the Federal Reserve's history and policy.

Piotr Stanek, PhD (hab.), is an Associate Professor in the Department of International Economics at the Cracow University of Economics (CUE). He obtained his doctorate at the University of Lille 1 in 2007, defending a dissertation on the effectiveness of decision-making in central banks; and a habilitation degree at the CUE in 2020, based on a series of publications on the assessment and determinants of debt sustainability and price stability. His research and publications focus on decision-making in central banks and on the issues of the global financial and economic crisis and, consequently, threats to the stability of public and foreign debt of the euro area countries. He has published in such journals as the *Journal of Economic Dynamics and Control, Journal of International Money and Finance, Economic Modelling, The World Economy, Business History, Kyklos, Eastern European Economics, German Economic Review* and *Portuguese Economic Journal*. He has also authored one book and many chapters in collective works, edited two of them and served as associate editor (2013–2020) for *Entrepreneurial Business and Economics Review*, an international journal published by the CUE.

Timo Walter is a faculty member at the Institute of Political Studies of the University of Lausanne. Having earned a PhD in International Political Economy from the Graduate Institute of International and Development Studies in Geneva, his post-doctoral research has led him to Copenhagen Business School, the University of Erfurt, the Max Planck Institute for the Study of Societies in Cologne and the University of Edinburgh. His contribution to this book is part of a project examining how the formalization and technization of economic valuation has transformed the nature of economic coordination and made possible the financialization of global capitalism. His publications include "How central bankers learned to love financialization" (with Leon Wansleben, *Socio-Economic Review*, 2019) and "Formalizing the future: how central banks set out to govern expectations but ended up (en-) trapped in indicators" (*Historical Social Research*, 2019).

John H. Wood, Reynolds Professor of Economics, Wake Forest University, has also been at the universities of Birmingham and Pennsylvania (Wharton School), Northwestern University (Kellogg School), the Federal Reserve Board, and the Federal Reserve Banks of Chicago, Philadelphia and Dallas. He has written *A History of Central Banks in Great Britain and the United States* (2009), and is working on *Whose Monetary Policy?*, an expansion of his chapter in this book.

Acknowledgements

In the making of this book, we would like to thank all the authors who contributed a chapter, and therefore their time and energy. Written and put together during the worst of COVID-19, we appreciate it more knowing that many of the authors had urgent family commitments, and we all had to navigate more difficult work conditions.

We would also like to acknowledge, as always, Alan Sturmer and the rest of the team at Edward Elgar Publishing for their continued and enthusiastic support of our work.

Introduction to *Central Banking, Monetary Policy and Social Responsibility*

Guillaume Vallet, Sylvio Kappes and Louis-Philippe Rochon

INTRODUCTION

Since the 2007/08 financial crisis, central banks have been waking up to new realities concerning both the limitations of conventional policies, and the impact conventional and unconventional policies may have, only to face the possibility of aggregate demand secular stagnation. The task currently facing central banks is in identifying the challenges ahead and to respond to them with the right tools and policies.

This is a far cry from the Goldilocks years of the Great Moderation when central bankers and policymakers celebrated, thinking they had finally got things right. Business cycles had been vanquished, we were told, with huge and obvious implications for monetary policy. Keynes was a relic of a bygone era. However, this illusion was short lived.

With the financial and then the pandemic crises, central banks tested the limits of monetary policy. They pushed interest rates to near zero in many countries, but the results were disappointing as the policy had very limited or even no success in generating economic growth, thus disapproving neoclassical theory. It would appear that consumption and investment decisions rely on variables other than the rate of interest. Real interest rates were pushed to negative territory in the hope of stimulating demand. However, this was an instance of imposing a theory where the empirical evidence was clearly showing otherwise. As Storm writes, 'As the real interest [rate] *increased* from 1.6% in 1980 to 8.1% in 1984, the investment rate *increased*' (Storm 2019, n.p., original emphasis).

Nevertheless, there was still a belief in the loanable funds theory: if only real rates were pushed low enough, investment would pick up. This was how some, such as Lawrence Summers, interpreted secular stagnation: not as much as a crisis in aggregate demand, but instead as a crisis in loanable funds, easily solved by lowering interest rates.

This approach corresponded, for the past few decades, with the rise of the Austerian philosophy, where central banks have been made to carry most of the economic-policy burden, thereby contributing to the age of monetary policy dominance, during which fiscal policy was given up to the pursuit of economic growth. Governments, it was assumed, overburdened us and future generations with piles of public debt. They had to assure balanced or sound finances, and leave the challenge of fine-tuning economic activity to independent central bankers.

An important conclusion we can draw from the pair of crises is that central banks are unable to carry the whole burden of recovery. With the failure of both conventional and unconventional policies, many central banks resorted to asking governments to inject stimulus, given that they 'had done their job'. As Bernanke testified in front of Congress, on 5 June 2012, 'Monetary policy is not a panacea. … I would feel much more comfortable if Congress would take some of this burden from us and address these issues.'

It was the return of Keynes, or rather, the 'Return of the Master' (Skidelsky 2009). Although Keynes did make an appearance in 2009, it was short lived as, by 2010, many countries had resorted back to sound finance. But the Master did return in a big way during the COVID crisis, when unprecedented fiscal stimulus, including in some countries the quasi-nationalization of private-sector wages, proved so historically important. Around the world, governments embraced deficit spending on a large and unprecedented scale: once again, Keynes rescued aggregate demand.

Central banks also went through a rethinking process of their own. Strict adherence to inflation targeting, which has been around since the early 1990s, started to wane, as some central banks started to adopt either dual mandates, for example, New Zealand which was ironically the first bank to inflation target, or a looser version of inflation targeting – average inflation targeting.

Of particular note, and following in the footsteps of a number of countries such as Canada, the Federal Reserve abandoned reserve requirements in 2020, in a further attempt to update their monetary framework. This is a clear statement that reserve requirements do not work in giving central banks control over the supply of credit by commercial banks. That is, the money multiplier is dead, and as a recently published paper by the Federal Reserve states, 'RIP money multiplier' (Ihrig et al. 2021).

THE OLD MODEL OF CENTRAL BANKING

Despite these seemingly positive changes over the past decade, has there been real change in monetary thinking, or has it been more cosmetic than anything else? The answer may be a little of both.

To answer this question, let us begin with a discussion of what we call the old model of central banking, most associated with Friedman's monetarism, pre-dating the new consensus model. Such an old model, we argue, is based on the following nine fundamental arguments:

1. Central banks control the supply of high-powered money or reserves.
2. Central banks exert control over the growth of monetary aggregates, the money supply.
3. Central banks control reserve requirements.
4. The money multiplier is at the core of the transmission mechanism.
5. Debate over rules versus discretion, favouring the former.
6. The natural rate of interest is a relevant variable for policy.
7. Money and inflation are linked.
8. Central banks must be independent.
9. The long-run neutrality of money.

Accordingly, central banks can control the money supply given their control over high-powered reserves and reserve requirements, a key element in the money multiplier. It is assumed that the money multiplier is stable. If central banks want to rein in money supply growth, they need only to either decrease the supply of high-powered money or increase reserve requirements. In both instances, the supply of money is assumed exogenous and therefore independent of whatever occurs in the economy, by definition. In accordance with the quantity theory of money, assuming stable velocity, the rate of growth of the money supply should be set according to the long-run, natural growth of the economy, also known as Friedman's rule.

According to this model, commercial banks are mere financial intermediaries, and their lending activities are at the mercy of central banks: they are severally constrained in their ability to lend – by the availability of reserves and deposits. Central banks can influence lending by increasing or decreasing the availability of high-powered money to the banking system and, through the (stable and predictable) money multiplier, will impact the supply of bank loans. That is, deposits create loans.

However, if the central bank can influence the supply of loans, this is only a short-run phenomenon. Indeed, monetary policy only has short-run effects. In the long run, money is neutral and has no impact on real variables. Money only affects prices in the long run. This is the standard way of reading the quantity theory of money equation: from left to right and, if money supply growth is appropriately set, then in the long run the price level remains constant.

This is an important function of central banks, and is seen as crucial given the notion that inflation is influenced by all things monetary: inflation is 'always and everywhere a monetary phenomenon'. Control of the growth of the money supply therefore becomes of paramount importance: if central banks cannot control the money supply, then they must as well give up on trying to control inflation.

The idea that inflation and money are linked was considered – and still is – a universal truth. This led Friedman to propose his monetary rule. There were in fact two main reasons for favouring rules over discretion: Friedman had a deep mistrust of central bankers, and in this sense always opposed the notion of independent central banks. At least, were they so independent, rules would ensure that central bankers would follow proper monetary policy etiquette.

THE NEW MODEL OF CENTRAL BANKING

In recent years, central banks themselves have come a long way in leaving at least parts of the monetarist story behind, and many have gone so far as to embrace some version of the post-Keynesian theory of endogenous money (even though post-Keynesian works and authors are seldom, if ever, cited). If the old model of central banking owed a debt to Friedman, the new approach owes a great deal to the work of Wicksell.

In this new model, most now readily admit that it is the rate of interest that is the control instrument, not some monetary aggregate, and that the setting of interest rates is independent of the quantity of reserves in existence – what Borio and Disyatat (2010) have termed the 'decoupling' effect. Former Bank of Canada Governor Gerald Bouey famously stated in 1982, 'We did not abandon the monetary targets: they abandoned us' (Dodge 2010). It is perhaps because of this that central banks turned to another monetary framework, careful, however, not to stray theoretically too far from orthodox monetary thinking. Indeed, 'the main change is that it replaces the assumption that the central bank targets the money supply with an assumption that it follows a simple interest rate rule' (Romer 2000, p. 154).

With that in mind, central banks then looked for a more suitable model to build, and turned to inflation targeting, a concept that goes back at least to Keynes (1923). This elegant, three-equation model (see Romer 2000; Taylor 1993; Woodford 2003) contains a Taylor rule, and well-behaved IS and Phillips curves. New Zealand was the first country in the world to adopt the new model, in 1990, followed by Canada the following year.

The model was widely popular with central banks and academics. Indeed, Goodfriend (2007, p. 59) claimed that 'the Taylor Rule became the most common way to model monetary policy', and Taylor (2000, p. 90), heralded that 'at the practical level, a common view of macroeconomics is now pervasive in policy-research projects at universities and central banks around the world'.

The inflation target itself became the anchor for inflation, and in Wicksellian fashion, we find embedded in the model the inescapable natural rate of interest determined by productivity and thrift, and a market-determined benchmark rate set by the central bank. The model was also based on some fine-tuning: whenever the rate of inflation was above target, central banks, via a Taylor rule, would raise the benchmark rate, hoping the economy would slow down just enough to bring inflation back down to target, via the well-behaved IS and Phillips curves. Without these, of course, the model falls apart.

The adoption of this new model corresponded also to the period of the Great Moderation, leading some to argue that 'In the years prior to August 2007, central banks had appeared to have almost perfected the conduct of monetary policy' (Goodhart 2011, p. 145).

Yet, with the financial crisis, the model began falling apart and a new search for a new monetary policy framework was under way. This model was confronted with the problem of the lower bound, where central banks were unable to push nominal interest rates below zero. Here, central banks were convinced the natural rate was below zero and hence why they needed to push the benchmark rate to such low levels. However, in their model, even a zero nominal rate was still too high: real rates were still above the natural rate given low levels of inflation. Interestingly, the secular stagnationist view was based precisely on this view: our economies were stagnating because the natural rate had fallen below zero; austerity had nothing to do with it. As stated previously, stagnation was interpreted as a crisis in loanable funds, not a crisis in aggregate demand per se. Owing to this, fiscal policy was not seen initially as a possible solution; austerity made sense, according to this view.

In the continued absence of fiscal policy, central banks were struggling to be seen as still relevant, and turned to unconventional means to foster economic growth – means that proved as uninspiring as the more conventional policies. Yet, the financial crisis would eventually reveal the degree to which the monetary new emperor had no clothes: the limits of this new view were starting to emerge. In a startling new paper, 'Whither central banking', Summers and Stansbury (2019) were now admitting 'the impotence' of the model: 'Simply put, tweaking inflation targets, communications strategies, or even balance sheets is not an adequate response to the challenges now confronting the major economies ... Central banks cannot always set inflation rates through monetary policy'.

THE HUMPTY-DUMPTYING OF THE NEW MODEL

There is no denying that the new consensus model has come under criticism in the past decade, since the financial crisis, and not just from post-Keynesians, but from a growing number of analyses from within central banks themselves.

The question remains as to whether all the central banks' guards and horses can put the model back together again.

In a Bank of England paper now almost a decade old, McLeay et al. (2014) go to great lengths to dispel some old myths surrounding monetary creation, and clarify the misconceptions of money creation from the reality. In particular, they argue that lending creates deposits: 'In the modern economy, those bank deposits are mostly created by commercial banks themselves' (McLeay et al. 2014, p. 15). More crucial, we believe, is the explanation of why reserves are not an important component of bank lending, and cannot 'be multiplied into more loans' (McLeay et al. 2014, p. 14).

In a second paper published at the Bank of England, Jakab and Kumhof (2018) argue that 'loans come before deposits' and that 'a new loan involves no intermediation. No real resources need to be diverted from other uses, by other agents, in order to be able to lend to the new customer' (Jakab and Kumhof 2018, p. 4), which they claim is a 'more realistic framework' which is 'supported by a long and growing list of central bank publications' (Jakab and Kumhof 2018, p. 1). Moreover, they specify that this view 'has always been very well understood by central banks' (Jakab and Kumhof 2018, p. 7).

The Bundesbank, of all banks, also contributed to this new central bank model, in 2017, with a paper entitled 'The role of banks, non-banks and the central bank in the money creation process'. A reference to the 'money creation process' is a very telling rejection of the exogenous money story where this process is absent, in the notion of helicopter money. The paper argues that:

> Sight deposits are created by transactions between a bank and a non-bank (its customer) – the bank grants a loan, say, or purchases an asset and credits the corresponding amount to the non-bank's bank account in return. Banks are thus able to create book (giro) money. This form of money creation reflects the financing and portfolio decisions of banks and non-banks and is thus driven by the same factors that determine the behaviour of banks and non-banks. (Deutsche Bundesbank 2017, p. 15)

In a 2018 speech, Christopher Kent, Assistant Governor of the Reserve Bank of Australia, discussed whether money was 'born of credit?' He makes clear that 'Money can be created, however, when financial intermediaries make loans. Accordingly, the concepts of money and credit are closely linked in a modern economy ... The process of money creation requires a willing borrower ... [and the bank must] satisfy itself that the borrower can service the loan' (Kent 2018, p. 4).

These are familiar themes for post-Keynesians, who will recognize the notion that loans create deposits, and that they are demand-determined by creditworthy borrowers; that is, money is seemingly endogenous.

Moreover, two papers recently published by the Federal Reserve show a very different side to the central bank model. In the first, Rudd (2022) argues that inflationary expectations are no ground for predicting future levels of inflation. According to the author, such an idea rests on 'extremely shaky foundations' (Rudd 2022, p. 25). The conclusions are devastating as anticipations of inflation certainly are a core principle of central banking today. The 'pugnacious paper' created a firestorm, leading *The Economist* (2021) to declare the paper 'a social-media sensation'.

In the second paper, by Ihrig et al. (2021), with the provocative subtitle 'R.I.P. money multiplier', the authors explain the changes to monetary policy in the USA, following the financial crisis and COVID. The paper is worth noting for a few reasons. First, in light of the Federal Reserve's elimination of reserve requirements in 2020, the authors warn professors of mistakes they still make when teaching money and banking. Second, the authors admonish textbooks for still teaching the ways of the old model. The subtitle of the paper is meant to be a definitive statement (and perhaps even a warning) to economists that they are doing a disservice to students by not correctly representing (or understanding) what central banks do. Both reasons are summarized by the title to one section of the paper: 'Make sure your teaching is current'.

Finally, in celebrating the twenty-fifth anniversary of the publication of Moore (1988), Bindseil and König (2013) – Bindseil works at the European Central Bank (ECB) – have acknowledged that 'the last 25 years have vindicated the substance of his thinking [Moore's] in a surprising way that could hardly have been anticipated in 1988. Central bankers have by now largely buried "verticalism", at least when it comes to monetary policy implementation' (Bindseil and König 2013, p. 385). This is an acknowledgement that the old model of central banking is dead.

Or is it? While many of the above quotes (and we could have cited a number of other papers) certainly appear, at least on the surface, as indicative of important changes in monetary thinking, we are not convinced. While there is no doubt that central banks have come a long way in repudiating some of the elements of the old model, we argue they have not successfully done so in their entirety. What is left is perhaps best described as a hybrid model. We agree with Fiebiger and Lavoie (2020, p. 78) who have argued that 'The NCM replaced money supply targeting with inflation targeting while preserving monetarist results.' This is exactly what Lavoie (2006, p. 167) meant when he wrote, almost two decades ago, that new consensus models 'simply look like old wine in a new bottle'.

Let us once again refer to the nine arguments above:

1. Central banks control the supply of high-powered money or reserves.
2. Central banks exert control over the growth of monetary aggregates, the money supply.
3. Central banks control reserve requirements.
4. The money multiplier is at the core of the transmission mechanism.
5. Debate over rules versus discretion, favouring the former.
6. The natural rate of interest is a relevant variable for policy.
7. Money and inflation are linked.
8. Central banks must be independent.
9. The long-run neutrality of money.

We can conclude that arguments 1–4 have been abandoned by many central banks, and in new consensus models as well. However, despite these advances, welcome as they are, we are still not entirely in agreement with the idea that mainstream thinking is any closer to the post-Keynesian story of endogenous money. That is, the new model of central banking certainly leaves behind a number of assumptions of the old model, but from a post-Keynesian perspective, it does not go far enough. Five elements still remain at the core of the model.

Argument 5: as regards the debate over rules versus discretion, we can summarize that it has evolved, but perhaps not by much. The old model contains a monetary rule, while the new model contains an interest rate rule. However, Taylor (1993, p. 195) defines his approach as akin to 'a responsive rule'. Indeed, Taylor (1993, p. 196) claims that 'Policymakers do not, and are not evidently about to, follow policy rules mechanically', therefore leaving some room for discretion, and warns about making Taylor rules 'too complex'. So, in many ways, central banks use fine-tuning to adjust interest rates in response to inflation shocks.

Argument 6: as regards the natural rate of interest, it is still at the heart of new consensus models. In a Wicksellian manner, it acts as an anchor to short-term benchmark rates. The purpose of the central bank is to set the rate and to move it up or down until it reaches an inflation target, corresponding presumably with the natural rate.

The question is whether we can have a theory of endogenous money while also espousing a natural rate of interest. Rochon (1999) and Smithin (1994) have always rejected the claim that a theory of endogenous money can accommodate a natural rate of interest. If post-Keynesians believe the benchmark rate is truly exogenous, then that would rule out a natural rate that acts as an anchor for central bank rates. At best, as Palley (2006, p. 80) writes, the new consensus 'is a conception of endogeneity that is fundamentally different from the Post Keynesian conception, which is rooted in the credit nature of money'. Palley names the new consensus (NC) approach as 'central bank endogeneity'. In a similar vein, we would argue that the new consensus lacked a '*theory* of endogenous money'. As Setterfield (2004, p. 41) arrives at the same conclusion: 'whereas the stock of money is endogenous in practice in NC macroeconomics, it is endogenous in principle in PK macroeconomics'.

Argument 7: in addition, inflation is still thought to be linked to monetary policy. Only central banks are equipped to regulate economic activity efficiently in order to influence inflation and achieve its target, with minimal damage to the economy. Inflation, we can say, is always and everywhere a monetary policy phenomenon.

Argument 8: central bank independence is still considered a sine qua non of mainstream monetary policy. Advocates claim that it is at the core of current monetary thinking, especially now (at the time of writing this introduction) as inflation is starting to increase around the world. According to Goodhart (2021), if inflation persists, central banks must move to swiftly increase interest rates or risk losing credibility. Central bank independence is tied to notions of credibility: 'It is important to have in place adequate mechanisms to "guard the guardians" of monetary and financial stability' (Goodhart and Lastra 2018, p. 49).

There is also a staunch defence of the long-run neutrality of money. This is particularly so in current research on the links between monetary policy and income distribution. While some central banks recognize the income distributive impact of monetary policy, it is said to be small and temporary (see Rochon 2022). For instance, Romer and Romer (2001, p. 910) claim that 'It is certainly true that expansionary policy can generate a boom and reduce poverty temporarily. But the effect is unquestionably just that: temporary.' In a recent survey,[1] Colciago et al. (2019, p. 1224) argue that 'Over the longer horizon, the distributional impact is likely to die out given the temporary nature of the effects of monetary policy shocks.' This is a required conclusion to a theory that insists on long-run neutrality.

The new model is thus not too far from Friedman (Fiebiger and Lavoie 2020), well evidenced in the following quote by Bernanke (2003, online speech): 'I am ready and willing to praise Friedman's contributions wherever and whenever anyone gives me a venue … We can hardly overstate the influence of Friedman's monetary framework on contemporary monetary theory and practice … both policymakers and the public owe Milton Friedman an enormous debt'.

THE POST-KEYNESIAN MODEL OF CENTRAL BANKING

While mainstream economists have had to face new realities and come to some realizations about how central bank policy operates, post-Keynesians have also made some changes in the way they perceive central banks and monetary policy. Endogenous money is still the copingstone of post-Keynesian theory, where the rate of interest is set by central banks in a total disconnect with the natural rate, which is rejected. Loans make deposits, and banks are never constrained by a lack of deposits or reserves, but only by a lack of creditworthy borrowers. While Kaldor (1970) and Moore (1988) are central to this view, the ideas were present in many of Joan Robinson's writings, especially *The Accumulation of Capital* (1956).

Post-Keynesians have pushed the boundaries of central banking by advocating against the use of fine-tuning, and by linking monetary policy to income distribution. As regards the first of these, the concept of fine-tuning consists of incrementally increasing and decreasing interest rates until the correct rate of interest is found, which delivers an inflation consistent with its target. However, a great deal is assumed here. In new consensus models, this fine-tuning is based on well-established IS and Phillips curves: central banks change interest rates in an effort to generate just the right amount of change in output, which in turn will generate just enough change in unemployment and inflation. However, these are empirical relationships that need to be tested, and thus far the empirical evidence is weak.

Both Keynes and Robinson rejected fine-tuning. Keynes is famous for having said that fine-tuning 'belongs to the species of remedy which cures the disease by killing the patient' (Keynes 1936, p. 323). In a similar vein, Robinson, in a greatly underappreciated essay, argues that 'The regulating effect of changes in the rate of interest was at best very weak' (1943, p. 26), and again in 1952, where she describes as a 'false scent' the use of counter-cyclical monetary policy, and rejects:

> the conception of an economy which is automatically held on a path of steady development by the mechanism of the rate of interest ... But it is by no means easy to see how the monetary mechanism is supposed to ensure how that the rate of interest actually assumes its full employment value ... The automatic corrective action of the rate of interest is condemned by its very nature to be always too little and too late. (Robinson 1952, pp. 73–4)

While recognizing this, post-Keynesians further argue that monetary policy is foremost about income distribution. While the mainstream is starting to recognize this, as stated previously, there is nevertheless a stark difference with post-Keynesians. While for the mainstream, monetary policy may have income distributive effects in the short run, for post-Keynesians, monetary policy is income distribution. It is for both of these reasons that Lavoie (1996, p. 537), in rejecting fine-tuning, concludes that:

> It then becomes clear that monetary policy should not so much be designed to control the level of activity, but rather to find the level of interest rates that will be proper for the economy from a distribution point of view. The aim of such a policy should be to minimize conflict over the income shares, in the hope of simultaneously keeping inflation low and activity high.

PURPOSE OF THE CENTRAL BANKING AND MONETARY POLICY SERIES

In early 2018, we decided to organize a small gathering on 'the future of central banking', and applied for a financial grant from the Social Sciences and Humanities Research Council (Canada) as they have a wonderful programme for that purpose.

The three of us had been having discussions around this topic for a few years previously, noticing what appeared to be important changes in central banking and monetary policy, from 'unconventional policies' such as quantitative easing and lower-bound policies, to discussions over income distribution, the environment and the quasi-embrace of at least some version of endogenous money by some central banks.

It was in this spirit that we gathered in Talloires (France), on the shores of Lake Annecy, over a few days on 26–28 May 2019. We invited some well-known heterodox scholars, such as Elissa Braunstein, Gary Dimsky, Juliet Johnson, Marc Lavoie, Dominique Plihon and Mario Seccareccia, but also some more mainstream scholars, such as Etienne Farvaque and Ulrich Bindseil, in an effort to encourage a dialogue of sorts on central bank-related topics. We also partnered with the Young Scholars Initiative, from the Institute for New Economic Thinking, which funded the travel and accommodation of 11 young scholars. This partnership has proven rewarding for all those involved.

By all accounts, it was a huge success and it was from this gathering that the idea of a book on the same topic was born. The ensuing book went well beyond the initial plan, as we expanded its scope and breadth. *The Future of Central Banking* is the first book of this series, and we divided it into several sections, each dealing with the relationship between central banking, monetary policy and various themes, such as the environment, gender, income distribution, macro-prudential policies, structural change and central bank independence.

While we are very proud of this book, and it remains in many ways ground-breaking, it soon became apparent that there was more to be said on each of these topics, and so we began discussions with Edward Elgar Publishing to create a series dedicated to all aspects of central banking. While we signed the contract for the book in July 2019, by November we signed a contract to create the series. That first book would then anchor the rest of the series.

From there, we felt that many of the topics from the first book needed to be developed, so we decided to do entire books on each of these themes. We agreed on the next four titles – income distribution, the environment, social responsibility and the future of money – and quickly contacted some possible contributors.

This then launched us in new directions, and new reflections, with the aim of moving forward the critical discussion over the future of central banking, and pushing the boundaries of heterodox thought. In many ways, the mainstream was 'out-researching' us on some of these topics, and heterodox economists had to return to monetary policy and push forward. This was also the rationale for creating the Monetary Policy Institute, which we all direct.

The overall goal of this new series is to contribute to a new research agenda on central banking and monetary policy. Note, the title of the series is not simply 'monetary policy' as we understand it, that is, interest rates and their impact on the economy. While there is still a great deal of work to be done in this respect, for instance, understanding the impact of incremental changes in interest rates on income distribution and social classes, on gender, on the environment, and so on, we need to go beyond a mere discussion over interest rates, and consider central banks as institutions. This remains a gravely under-developed area of research in economics, though sociologists have considered this topic with great promise. In this context, economists have much to learn from sociology, and their emphasis on power, for instance.

Sociological studies on central banking highlight that, as institutions, central banks produce rules that 'coerce' individuals and shape their lives through their policies. In that, central banks exert what Susan Strange termed 'structural power' on the economy and society. This 'structural power' is personally concentrated in central bankers' hands, whose sociological profile should be put in relation to the distributive nature of monetary policy: do central bankers really serve the people? This crucial argument demonstrates that central banks reciprocally need people's confidence in order to gain social legitimacy: central banks' power needs to be 'socially embedded'. Central banks are undoubtedly non-neutral institutions, and for that reason, economics has a lot to learn from other social sciences.

Finally, the crucial question is whether central banks serve the interests of the people (see Fontan et al. 2018). This opens up a Pandora's Box of questions and more, about central banking, monetary policy and social responsibility, democracy, gender, income distribution and structural change. One by one, these themes are covered in the books in this new series which aims to push the boundaries of how we currently analyse, reflect and write about central banks.

THE STRUCTURE OF THE BOOK

This book is dedicated to a burning issue, namely that of central banks' social responsibility. Indeed, in the age of massive quantitative easing programmes implemented by central banks, the latter supposedly politically independent from governments, grappling with the issue of central banks' social responsibility is very timely. Such an issue is also crucial with respect to the on-going changes impacting both the economies and the democracies in every corner of the globe, since there are calls for central banks to cope with new concerns such as climate change or social inequalities.

The book contains 10 chapters by leading economists and social scientists.

In the opening chapter, Charles Goodhart and Manoj Pradhan explain that the widespread framework of independence for central banks was initially set up to separate the politics from monetary policy: politicians, for political reasons and in accordance with the central bank, could be tempted to defer or avoid increasing interest rates. Such an expectation did not occur, and in fact quite the opposite took place: we have experienced a general decrease in the level of interest rates, especially in developed countries, for the last past 10 years. Against this backdrop characterized by disinflationary forces that the authors attribute mainly to a combination of globalization and demography, governments benefited from the drop in interest rates, through the falling of debt services ratios. However, the authors argue that a change in this process has recently started, accentuated by the COVID-19 pandemic, in the sense that an inflation turn is in progress. Specifically, the likelihood of a soar in inflation is high, bringing about wage inflation in particular. Therefore, since the Central Bank Independence (CBI) model is challenged, the authors propose three possible scenarios that the readers will discover while reading the chapter: the 'Strict' scenario, the 'Accommodative' scenario and the 'Conflictual' scenario.

Chapter 2, by John H. Wood, focuses on the relationships between central banks, monetary policies and government policies, through the examples of key periods of the histories of the United Kingdom and United States (the post-French-wars resumption, the post-Civil War resumption, the Great Depression, the Great Recession, etc.). All these episodes exemplify that monetary policies and central banking must be political. Depending on the context, monetary policies are influenced by the compositions and experiences of central banks, and the power of the government or even that of the private sector (particularly the banking and financial sector). Reviewing the different types of relations of central banks with the other key economic and political actors of the United Kingdom and United States, John H. Wood sheds light on the distinctions between the actions of central banks when they interact with the government or the key economic actors. The chapter is particularly relevant for questioning the burning issue of the book, and of today's central banking, namely central banks' social responsibility.

The issue of central banks' social responsibility is also a concern of Chapter 3, which makes a connection between legal principles and operational accountability related to central banks' independence. In this chapter, Maqsood Aslam, Etienne Farvaque and Piotr Stanek, like the authors of Chapter 1, start by reminding us of the "why" of central banks' independence. The authors link this issue with legitimacy, democracy and, more broadly, the social order of a given society. Indeed, legal and formal independence go hand in hand with social accountability, transparency and disclosure requirements, and more generally with the understanding of monetary policy by the "markets" and the people (reachable through central banks' communication policies particularly). This is key for institutions such as central banks, exerting an "unelected power".

The issue of the relations between central banks and democracy, through the focus on the ECB, is also the purpose of Chapter 4. In this chapter, Marie Cuillerai analyses the nature of power that the ECB exerts over the eurozone's economies and societies. To that aim, she borrows Marx's concept of "bancocracy" to emphasize the extent to which this central bank regulates but also rules the life of economic actors but more generally of lay people. This was particularly conspicuous during the so-called "Greek crisis" in the early 2010s, when the ECB succeeded in framing European countries' fiscal policy at the expense of democratic values. In sum, the ECB's "bancocracy" challenges the sovereignty of the eurozone's states and thus calls for an alternative horizon linked to the democratization of money.

In Chapter 5, François Claveau, Clément Fontan, Peter Dietsch and Jérémie Dion present a critical analysis of the stance taken on inequality by two central banks since 2015: the Bank of Canada (BoC) and the Federal Reserve (Fed). Indeed, the authors point out that central banks' monetary policies are not neutral in their economic and social consequences, which drag them out of their usual official – and narrow – mandate. This is the case when the issue of inequality is at stake, which can conflict with their mandate at first sight. However, the authors remind us that central banks' massive interventions in response to COVID-19 have demonstrated that the target of the reducing of inequality is possible and even desirable, since a growing body of literature demonstrates that monetary policies have clear and identifiable distributional effects. Once again, this chapter leaves the floor open to discussions on the crucial issue of central banks' social responsibility.

Chapter 6 is dedicated to the social role of central banks in creating the conditions for a socialization of both infrastructure investments and their financing. The two authors, Massimo Amato and Lucio Gobbi, start their demonstration focusing on the basic structure of financial markets and the stabilizing role of central banks, in connection with fiscal policy and public debt. The authors remind us that with the COVID-19 pandemic, and contrary to the financial crisis of 2007–2009, fiscal policy was the first economic instrument put in place to try to stabilize the economy. This involved the use of discretionary spending and the activation of automatic stabilizers to an unprecedented extent. This required massive intervention from central banks, especially through the use of the so-called "unconventional" monetary policies.

Moreover, these different episodes of crisis challenge the role of financial markets in the context of radical uncertainty. Resting on Keynes' crucial analysis, the authors mention the "dilemma of financial markets": on the one hand, financial markets are supposed to promote investment, but on the other, they can engender instability. In order to both prevent instability from arising and recover faster in case of crisis, to promote public investment appears to be the adequate public policy.

With this in mind, the authors deal with the European case, where the response to the pandemic crisis has taken the form of a recovery plan, alleged to support a European Green Deal. The latter will need new types of financing as well as a reassessment of public debt management in the eurozone. Together with the ECB, a European Debt Agency (EDA) could be in charge of the management of previous, new and future European common debt for European Union-wide infrastructure investments. In order to demonstrate the benefits of the cooperation between the ECB and the EDA, the authors explain how the operational structure of the EDA could manage green investment financing.

Chapter 7, by Louis-Philippe Rochon and Guillaume Vallet, focuses on the power and social responsibility of both central banks and central bankers in a democracy. The chapter opens by reminding us of a crucial characteristic of monetary policy already mentioned in this introduction: monetary policy has distributional consequences on the economy and society, in both the short and long run. This has particularly been evidenced with respect to the income-distributive nature of monetary policy, contrary to mainstream economists' statements.

Therefore, such a distributive component of monetary policy raises important questions about the power of central banks and of central bankers, and their rightful place within a democracy. Since through their policies central banks have the power to shape economies and societies, they must be legitimate institutions to the people as they are supposed to serve the common good. Likewise, such a statement applies to central bankers, who are unelected but alleged "efficient" experts serving democracy.

The two recent crises (the Global Financial Crisis and COVID-19) have exemplified the need to reframe the relationship between central banks, central bankers and their social responsibility, through the designing of a new framework. At stake is the relation between central banks, central bankers and the political will of the people, who are at the core of the dynamics of democracy. The political will of the people, embodied by their specific culture (implying specific norms and values), materializes itself in a tangible way through economic and social policies until the common good is reached.

To that aim, after having underlined the cruciality of the combination of monetary and fiscal policies, the authors explain why we should seriously question the independence model and rules "à la Friedman". Finally, the authors address an issue of utmost importance: are central bankers sufficiently controlled, and if not, should the democratic control exerted over monetary policy be redesigned?

In Chapter 8, Jong-Un Song reminds us of the extent to which the two recent crises have shaken economies as well as the traditional framework of central banks and monetary policy. Central banks even seem to have sometimes "lost control" over the "real" consequences of their monetary policy, and also the functioning of financial markets. This explains why the issue of social responsibility is paramount, especially in times of turmoil, as the author sets out: the public's interest in central banks' social responsibility increases during social confusion or economic downturn.

The chapter points out that such a need is particularly visible in the United States, with the Fed, whose model is undergoing a significant change. Through its "unconventional" monetary policies implemented since the Global Financial Crisis of 2007–2008, the Fed has radically changed the size and composition of its balance sheet. But such policies have also changed the structural conditions of the social compromise accumulated by American capitalism. More problematically, the author puts forth that the Fed has lost control over financial markets, preventing the institution from reaching its dual mandate (price stability and full employment). For that reason, the Fed's social responsibility has been challenged, which is evidence of the need to fundamentally redesign its current system.

In Chapter 9, Rob Macquarie deals with "precautionary" monetary policy and democratic legitimacy, in relation to the issue of climate change. The author begins the chapter by reminding us that central banks have been called to action to manage the impact of environmental risks on economic and financial stability, and to help mobilize capital for the transition. In the context of climate change, central banks should first follow a "precautionary approach" consisting of recognizing the key role of uncertainty in the decision-making process of central banks. Second, in accordance with the previous statement, the environmental imperative challenges central banks' exercise of authority as well as their legitimacy in democracy.

Indeed, the author argues that a reassertion of central banks' democratic authority and legitimacy over aspects of monetary policy related to a just and sustainable transition to a "new" economic world would probably create tensions. In order to prevent these tensions from arising or spreading, Rob Macquarie advances propositions of pro-democratic institutional reforms. These reforms could help central bankers to take into account the "blind spots" in monetary policy – both social and environmental – and thus to improve democratic legitimacy at both ends of the input–output binary. By the same token, the author suggests a theoretical proposition with respect to the legitimacy of monetary policy operations, in order to move beyond that binary. The underlying idea is to question the process by which decisions are reached, since to reach the common good imposes on central banks a need to reframe their decision-making process under radical uncertainty.

Finally, in the last chapter Timo Walter claims that the two recent crises have made central banks indispensable to the economies and societies. The massive quantitative easing policies are evidence of this great role. Symmetrically, such a great role has conferred upon the banks great power, but also great responsibility. Against this backdrop, there have been calls to reframe central banks' monetary policies toward several new problems and challenges, beyond the mere objective of price stability. Therefore, their status of independence is now challenged, and more broadly, the author reminds us that some are pushing now for the democratization of monetary policy.

Resting on a sociological approach, Timo Walter sheds light on the need to reframe central banks' "technical power" and agency. However, this is a difficult task, since the banks are embedded in global finance, deeply rooted in the infrastructures of market-based finance. For this reason, principally, the author warns that the idea of a multigoal mandate for central banks has a side effect: it can erode the very basis of their "infrastructural power". Therefore, Timo Walter advocates for preserving a healthier ecology of policy tools and infrastructures of central banks.

NOTE

1. For a survey following a post-Keynesian perspective, see Kappes (2021).

REFERENCES

Bernanke, B.S. (2003), 'Remarks by Governor Ben S. Bernanke', at the Federal Reserve Bank of Dallas Conference on the 'Legacy of Milton and Rose Friedman's Free to Choose', Dallas, TX, 24 October, accessed 23 March 2022 at https://www.federalreserve.gov/boarddocs/speeches/2003/20031024/default.htm.

Bernanke, B.S. (2012), 'Five questions about the Federal Reserve and monetary policy', speech at the Economic Club of Indiana, Indianapolis, IN, 1 October, accessed 23 March 2022 at https://www.federalreserve.gov/newsevents/speech/bernanke20121001a.htm.

Bindseil, U. and P.J. König (2013), 'Basil J. Moore's horizontalists and verticalists: an appraisal 25 years later', *Review of Keynesian Economics*, **1** (4), 383–90.

Borio, C. and P. Disyatat (2010), 'Unconventional monetary policies: an appraisal', *The Manchester School*, **78** (September), 53–89.

Colciago, A., A. Samarina and J. de Haan (2019), 'Central bank policies and income and wealth inequality: a survey', *Journal of Economic Surveys*, **33** (4), 1199–231.

Deutsche Bundesbank (2017), 'The role of banks, non-banks and the central bank in the money creation process', Monthly Report, April, accessed 23 March 2022 at https://www.bundesbank.de/resource/blob/654284/df66c4444d065a7f519e2ab0c476df58/mL/2017-04-money-creation-process-data.pdf.

Dodge, D. (2010), '70 years of central banking in Canada', remarks to the Canadian Economic Association, accessed 23 March 2022 at https://www.bankofcanada.ca/wp-content/uploads/2010/06/dodge.pdf.

Fiebiger, B. and M. Lavoie (2020), 'Helicopter Ben, monetarism, the new Keynesian credit view and loanable funds', *Journal of Economic Issues*, **54** (1), 77–96.

Fontan, C., F. Claveau and P. Dietsch (2018), *Do Central Banks Serve the People*, Cambridge: Polity Press.

Goodfriend, M. (2007), 'How the world achieved consensus on monetary policy', *Journal of Economic Perspectives*, **21** (4), 47–68.

Goodhart, C. (2011), 'The changing role of central banks', *Financial History Review*, **18** (2), 135–54.

Goodhart, C. (2021), 'What may happen when central banks wake up to more persistent inflation?', VOX EU, Centre for Economic Policy Research, London, 25 October.

Goodhart, C. and R. Lastra (2018), 'Populism and central bank independence', *Open Economies Review*, **29** (1), 49–68.

Ihrig, J., G.C. Weinback and S.A. Wolla (2021), 'Teaching the linkage between the banks and the Fed: RIP money multiplier', Economic Research, Federal Research Bank of St Louis, September, accessed 23 March 2022 at https://research.stlouisfed.org/publications/page1-econ/2021/09/17/teaching-the-linkage-between-banks-and-the-fed-r-i-p-money-multiplier.

Jakab, Z. and M. Kumhof (2018), 'Banks are not intermediaries of loanable funds: facts, theory and evidence', Bank of England Staff Working Paper No. 761, Bank of England, London.

Kaldor, N. (1970), 'The new monetarism', *Lloyds Bank Review*, July, 1–17.

Kappes, S. (2021), 'Monetary policy and personal income distribution: a survey of the empirical literature', *Review of Political Economy*, June, doi:10.1080/09538259.2021.1943159.

Kent, C. (2018), 'Money – born of credit', remarks at the Reserve Bank's Topical Talks Event for Educators, Sydney, 19 September.

Keynes, M. (1923), *A Tract on Monetary Reform*, London: Macmillan.

Keynes, M. (1936), *The General Theory of Employment, Interest and Money*, London: Macmillan.

Lavoie, M. (1996), 'Monetary policy in an economy with endogenous credit money', in G. Deleplace and E.J. Nell (eds), *Money in Motion: The Post Keynesian and Circulation Approaches*, Basingstoke: Macmillan, pp. 532–45.

Lavoie, M. (2006), 'A post-Keynesian amendment to the new consensus on monetary policy', *Metroeconomica*, **57** (2), 165–92.

Introduction 19

McLeay, M., A. Radia and R. Thomas (2014), 'Money creation in the modern economy', *Bank of England Quarterly Bulletin*, Q1, accessed 23 March 2022 at https://www.bankofengland.co.uk/quarterly-bulletin/2014/q1/money-creation-in-the-modern-economy.

Moore, B.J. (1988), *Horizontalists and Verticalists: The Macroeconomics of Credit Money*, Cambridge: Cambridge University Press.

Palley, T. (2006), 'A post-Keynesian framework for monetary policy: why interest rate operating procedures are not enough', in C. Gnos and L.P. Rochon (eds), *Post-Keynesian Principles of Economic Policy*, Cheltenham, UK and Northampton, MA, USA: Edward Elgar, pp. 78–98.

Robinson, J. (1943), 'The problem of full employment', Workers' Educational Association & Workers' Educational Trade Union Committee, London.

Robinson, J. (1952), *The Rate of Interest and Other Essays*, London: Macmillan.

Robinson, J. (1956), *The Accumulation of Capital*, London: Macmillan.

Rochon, L.P. (1999), *Credit, Money and Production: An Alternative Post-Keynesian Approach*, Cheltenham, UK and Northampton, MA, USA: Edward Elgar.

Rochon, L.-P. (2022), 'The general ineffectiveness of monetary policy or the weaponization of inflation', in S. Kappes, L.-P. Rochon and G. Vallet (eds), *The Future of Central Banking*, Cheltenham, UK and Northampton, MA, USA: Edward Elgar, forthcoming.

Romer, C.D. and D.H. Romer (2001), 'Monetary policy and the well-being of the poor', in J. Rabin and G.L. Stevens (eds), *Handbook of Monetary Policy*, London: Routledge, pp. 887–912.

Romer, D. (2000), 'Keynesian macroeconomics without the LM curve', *Journal of Economic Perspectives*, **12** (2), 149–69.

Rudd, J.B. (2022), 'Why do we think that inflation expectations matter for inflation? (And should we?)', *Review of Keynesian Economics*, **10** (1), 25–45.

Setterfield, M. (2004), 'Central banking, stability and macroeconomic outcomes: a comparison of new consensus and post-Keynesian monetary macroeconomics', in M. Lavoie and M. Seccareccia (eds), *Central Banking in the Modern World: Alternative Perspectives*, Cheltenham, UK and Northampton, MA, USA: Edward Elgar, pp. 35–56.

Skidelsky, R. (2009), *Keynes: The Return of the Master*, London: Allen Lane.

Smithin, J. (1994), *Controversies in Monetary Economics: Ideas, Issues and Policy*, Aldershot, UK and Brookfield, VT, USA: Edward Elgar.

Storm, S. (2019), 'Summers and the road to Damascus', Institute for New Economic Thinking, New York, 3 September, accessed 23 March 2022 at https://www.ineteconomics.org/perspectives/blog/summers-and-the-road-to-damascus.

Summers, L.H. and A. Stansbury (2019), 'Whither central banking?', Project Syndicate, 23 August, accessed 23 March 2022 at https://www.project-syndicate.org/commentary/central-bankers-in-jackson-hole-should-admit-impotence-by-lawrence-h-summers-and-anna-stansbury-2-2019-08.

Taylor, J.B. (1993), 'Discretion versus policy rules in practice', Carnegie-Rochester Conference Series on Public Policy, Stanford University, CA, **39**, 195–214.

Taylor, J.B. (2000), 'Teaching modern macroeconomics at the principles level', *American Economic Review*, **90** (2), 90–94.

The Economist (2021), 'Does anyone actually understand inflation?', *The Economist*, 9 October, accessed 23 March 2022 at https://www.economist.com/finance-and-economics/2021/10/09/does-anyone-actually-understand-inflation.

Woodford, M. (2003), *Interest and Prices: Foundations of a Theory of Monetary Policy*, Princeton, NJ: Princeton University Press.

1. Will central bank independence withstand political pressure?

Charles Goodhart and Manoj Pradhan

1. AN UNEXPECTEDLY EASY START

Central bank independence (CBI) was introduced at the end of the 1980s in New Zealand,[1] followed by other countries, like Canada, at the beginning of the 1990s, with the intention of preventing politicians from adopting their preferred policies. There was widespread agreement that there was a political business cycle (Nordhaus, 1975), whereby politicians suffering from time inconsistency (Kydland and Prescott, 1977) would delay making the necessary changes, primarily in the form of tightening monetary policy, especially in the run up to new elections.[2] Such delays would allow inflation to become more entrenched in expectations, thereby requiring even stronger disinflationary measures to combat it, which could easily trigger recessions, and cause politicians to then backtrack and/or turn to direct controls on wages/prices, which generally only worked temporarily and to a limited degree.

The purpose of CBI was, therefore, to take both the timing and quantification of monetary policy decisions out of the hands of politicians. Such CBI decisions should be based not on a political calculus, but on the need for central banks (CBs) to achieve an inflation target (IT). There have been, of course, many important details relating to questions about how such a target should be set and interpreted, which are not germane to the subject of this chapter. The key point is that the idea was that the combination of CBI and ITs might lead CBs to raise interest rates on occasions when this would be inconvenient and disliked by politicians[3] (or to lower them more slowly than politicians would have wished). Thus an important element of CBI (plus ITs) lay in the expectation that this would often place them at odds with the government of the day. The purpose was to prevent ministers of finance (e.g., the UK Chancellor of the Exchequer) from conducting their preferred policies on political grounds, and to create constructive dissension between the ministry of finance (treasury) and the central bank.

But this has not turned out to be the case thus far. Instead, throughout the 30 or so years of CBI, plus ITs, CBs have remained, with very few exceptions, the best friends of finance ministers. Moreover, this has been largely true whether such CBI was in place in autocratic regimes, such as China and Russia, or in democratic countries, such as the USA, the UK and Japan. The few exceptions have mostly related to those countries whose policies have led to a collapse of their exchange rate and a danger of accelerating inflation; e.g., both Argentina and Turkey, where the ruling government has often been unwilling to stomach the policy-tightening necessary to achieve an IT. In such cases CBI has usually been overthrown, even if events, and external forces, often did eventually bring about (temporary) monetary tightening.

Why has there been such harmony, when the purpose of CBI (plus ITs) was to cause constructive discordance? The basic answer to this is that, over the last 30 years, there have been strong disinflationary forces in operation. This has allowed CBs to lower interest rates continuously while at the same time achieving their IT.[4]

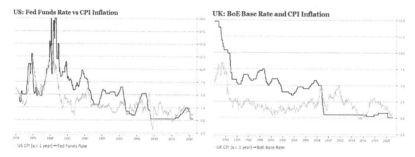

Note: BOE – Bank of England.
Source: Macrobond.

Figure 1.1   *Policy rates in the Advanced Economies are near zero while inflation has fallen, and remained, below target*

Indeed, since the onset of the Great Financial Crisis (GFC) in 2008–2009, and particularly with the Covid pandemic, bringing interest rates down to their effective lower bound (ELB) and introducing extra unconventional monetary policies (UMP), especially quantitative easing (QE), has not sufficed to raise extremely low inflation rates back to target.

Such disinflationary forces, and other longer-term structural factors, like the ageing of populations and growing inequality in the Advanced Economies (AEs), have also led governments there to run continuous deficits, with the result that public sector debt ratios have been rising, especially since the GFC, faster than ever before in peacetime. Of course, deficits and debt ratios rose faster and further in prior times of war, but war was, and was widely expected to be, temporary. While Covid should also be temporary, the structural tendency towards rising deficits and debt ratios was evident, for example in the forecasts for the UK and USA, before Covid struck. The pandemic has just given a large step up to what already looked like an almost exponential increase in such debt ratios.

Baseline projections of the primary balance and PSND

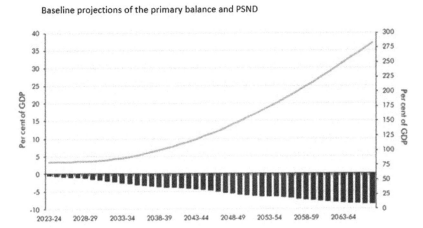

Notes: PSND – Public Sector Net Debt. Left-hand side axis – Primary Balance; right-hand side axis – PSND.
Source: OBR, 2018.

Figure 1.2   *UK: The Office for Budget Responsibility's (OBR's) 2019 (pre-Covid) projections already had debt rising sharply, primarily due to ageing related spending*

So far, such a continuing rise in public sector debt ratios has been accepted with equanimity, even complacency, because their effect on debt service ratios – the amount that the debtor, here the public sector, has to pay out in interest and net redemptions each year – has been almost exactly offset, or more than offset, by the trend decline in interest rates. Figure 1.4 shows this for a selection of countries. Falling interest rates also encouraged both lower mortgage rates and hence increases in home ownership and asset price inflation, including rising property prices and thus greater household wealth, all politically desirable.

No wonder that central bankers have become the best friends of ministers of finance! They have allowed such ministers to continue down the primrose path of deficits and debt accumulation with hardly any adverse side effects.

Debt and Deficits Federal debt held by the public is projected to equal 195 percent of gross domestic product (GDP) in 2050, and the deficit is projected to equal 13 percent of GDP.

Percentage of Gross Domestic Product

In CBO's projections, federal debt held by the public surpasses its historical high of 106 percent of GDP in 2023 and continues to climb in most years thereafter. In 2050, debt as a percentage of GDP is nearly 2.5 times what it was at the end of last year.

Source: Congressional Budget Office, November 2020.

Figure 1.3   US: The Congressional Budget Office's debt projections have shown a one-time jump for the pandemic, followed by a persistent rise due to ageing

In our book, *The Great Demographic Reversal* (2020), we attribute the greater part of such disinflationary forces to a combination of globalisation and demography, bringing about the greatest positive labour shock ever seen. Globalisation has been deflationary because adding huge low-wage regions, notably China and Eastern Europe, with relatively efficient centralised governments and well-educated work forces, into the world's trading system shifted production of moveable items to low-wage areas, gave employers in AEs a credible threat (of moving) for holding down wages locally and shifted production from manufacturing to services in AEs, where workers were less well organised, with less bargaining power. As a result, trade union strength declined. Similarly, demographic trends raised the proportion of the population of working age (18–64 years old), and greatly increased the participation rate within that age group of women. Contraceptives led to a lower birth rate while the introduction of better consumer durables freed women from mundane tasks that were automated.

Workers are disinflationary almost by definition, since their production must be greater in value than their wage to make it worthwhile to employ them. Out of their wages, workers have to save for their retirement, and so consume considerably less than they produce, and so are disinflationary. Dependents do not work, and hence consume without producing anything; i.e., they are inflationary. So an increase in the proportion of workers in a population is strictly disinflationary.

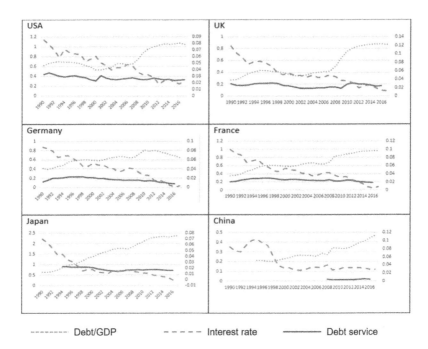

------- Debt/GDP   ----- Interest rate   ——— Debt service

Source: National sources, Macrobond.

*Figure 1.4   Rising debt has been perfectly offset by falling interest rates
to keep debt service costs low*

Globalisation and demography were not, however, the only disinflationary
forces. Technical progress has been commonly labour-saving; secretaries are
a vanishing breed, and robots have taken over on the manufacturing conveyor
belt. Business may have become more monopolistic and more hard-nosed, able
and prepared to drive a harder bargain with workers, whose bargaining power
has ebbed away (Philipon, 2019; Stansbury and Summers, 2020).

In terms of understanding the relationship between CBs and ministers of
finance over the last 30 years, the relative weighting that may be given to the
various causes of structural disinflation does not matter much. But it does
matter for the future of such relationships, because the various past trends in
disinflation are likely to change in future. As a result, the relationship between
CBs and ministers of finance will change too.

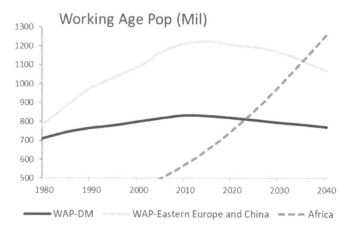

Note: WAP-DM – Working Age Population – Developed Market economies.
Source: UN Population Statistics.

Figure 1.5a   *Globalisation meant the rapid integration of the workforces
                  of China and Eastern Europe ...*

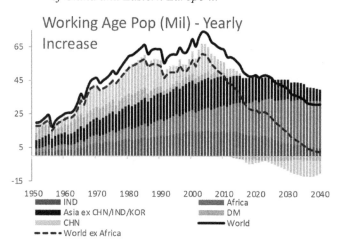

Note: IND – India, CHN – China, KOR – Korea.
Source: UN Population Statistics.

Figure 1.5b   *... while demography led to a global increase in the working
                  age population until about 2010*

2.   PEERING INTO AN UNCERTAIN FUTURE

One key lesson that the Covid pandemic that began in 2020 has taught or reminded us is that the future is not ours to see, or at least not clearly. That said, one advantage of demography is that, absent man-made catastrophes (such as nuclear war) and even worse plagues than Covid, the numbers of those aged over 18 in the world between now and 2050 are fairly well set and determinate. Given the political unpopularity of mass migration in recipient countries, that is also true for most individual countries. Although demographers have failed in the past to predict birth trends accurately, any such unforeseen changes are likely to be so slow-moving and starting from such a low base that we can regard the demographic structure of our countries as relatively predictable over the next three decades, until 2050 at least.

What such predictable demographic trends show is a major adverse (from an economic viewpoint) shift in age structures in most countries (apart from almost all of Africa and India), with the serried and sere ranks of the aged, over 65, rising relative to a proportionately declining share in the population of workers. Indeed, in those countries which have recently grown fastest – e.g., China and Germany – the actual number of workers will now shrink. Since growth arises from a combination of an increase in the number of workers interacting with improving worker productivity, that means that overall growth

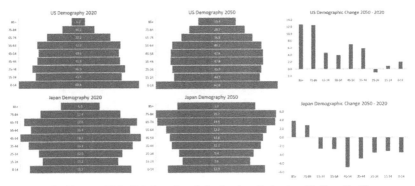

Source: United States – United Nations, Population by Age, Projection, Medium-Fertility Variant; Japan – United Nations, Population by Age, Projection, Medium-Fertility Variant.

Figure 1.6   Age structures are due for rapid change in the AEs and Emerging Market Economies (EMEs): demographic change in the United States and Japan from 2020 to 2050 (in millions, by age cohorts)

rates will decline, unless matched by an offsetting sharp rise in worker productivity; possible but unlikely.

If one combines this demographic story with a contemporary decline in globalisation – the systemic rivalry between the USA and China, Brexit, etc. – then the previous extraordinary positive labour supply shock of the last three decades seems likely to be replaced by a broadly negative labour supply shock. Off-shoring will be replaced by on-shoring. But there will not be enough workers to meet demand, especially in economically low-value jobs, such as seasonal agriculture, hospitality and caring.

In so far as the prior positive labour supply shock led to strong disinflationary forces, so its reversal will, we believe, lead to equally strong inflationary forces.[5] Of course, there will be mitigating factors, which we assess in Chapter 10 of our book. Briefly, these involve:

1. Africa and India: They will do well compared to their past economic performance, but problems of governance will keep them from becoming the next China(s).
2. Greater participation of the elderly; e.g., by raising the retirement age and reducing state pensions. Raising the retirement age is less likely due to its political unpopularity, while labour participation rates among the elderly have already been rising for the last 20 years now.
3. Automation: There are strongly differing views on the likely future of technical progress. Not having expertise in this field ourselves, we abstain from taking a position, just noting that innovation would have to be much faster and more labour-saving than in the past to offset the worsening demographic picture.

Moreover, there may be other forces tending to raise inflation further. Thus, climate change, which we do not discuss in our book, may have an adverse effect on agricultural supply in those areas where rainfall declines, while raising the need for flood protection and sea defences elsewhere. Similarly, climate change counteraction could lead to an earlier scrapping of much fossil-fuel-related capital, and the need for its replacement by eco-friendlier capital equipment: electric cars, new central heating, etc.

3. LOOKING FORWARD, WHEN CAN WE EXPECT INFLATION TO TURN?

Rather like the process of turning a supertanker, the changing trends in demographic and globalisation, which only really started to happen from about 2010 onwards, could take quite a long time to impinge on wage dynamics and inflation. The bargaining power of labour in the private sector of AEs, and the strength of private sector trade unions, has been crushed by the adverse (to them) trends of the previous three decades, so it might take some serious labour shortages to bring about wage reflation. To put it another way, these structural trends may have significantly lowered the Natural (or Non-inflationary) Rate of Unemployment, at least for the time being. Thus, even many of those who accepted the basic validity of our thesis have thought the adverse inflationary effects of this might not come through until the next decade (2030 and beyond), or even later. In the meantime, it was argued, it would still be 'lower for longer'; and any predicted event as far ahead as 5–10 years is beyond the effective horizon not only of almost all politicians, but also of almost all macro-economists.

But the Covid pandemic is primed to change that. The short-run effect of the pandemic has been to depress prices, but in rather an odd way. Where lockdown has reduced supply – e.g., of air travel and hotels – the response of those with empty seats, beds, etc., has generally been to lower prices, not to raise them. Meanwhile, the decline in supply has led to extraordinary increases in savings ratios and related declines in the velocity of money. CBs have monetised a massive increase in fiscal deficits, aimed (correctly) at keeping firms and employees afloat. Without such a policy mix, the global economy would otherwise have led to massive insolvencies, unemployment, poverty and general misery.

Even if there is only a partial return to normality in savings behaviour and velocity, our expectation is now for quite a response from inflation, once vaccination has overcome the winter surge in infection (in 2021). So, around a year after the vulnerable in our societies have all been vaccinated, we expect inflation to be well in excess of the 2 per cent IT. Initially, and up to a point, CBs will even welcome this, as an offset to the prior undershooting of ITs, congratulating themselves for the success of their new average inflation targeting (AIT) regime.

Such a prospective blip in inflation is not (yet) built into most macro-forecasts (as of the end of 2020), and, even if it should occur, CBs will claim that it will be a temporary affair. Mainstream analysts believe that the scarring caused by the pandemic, the resultant continuing higher uncertainty and unemployment, will result in a subsequent return to low inflation. But the continuing effects of expansionary policies, the extraordinary flowering of the magic money tree, and the need of the private sector to raise margins and prices in order to generate profits with which to pay down debts, will have the opposite effect. And in the particular case of the United States the Democrats now control Congress and the White House, and are keen to use their power to push for bigger fiscal expenditures.

Never before has there been such a contrast and conflict between the two main theories of the cause of inflation; i.e., the Phillips curve analysis that sees inflation as arising from excess demand in goods and labour markets, and the monetary analysis that sees inflation as arising from too much money chasing too few goods. The former analysis suggests continuing low inflation (after a possible blip), while the latter would indicate continuing higher inflation (and a post-pandemic blip would shake inflationary expectations, however much CBs claim that it would be a temporary one-off effect).

4.   A MORE DIFFICULT FUTURE FOR CBI?

Thus, the mainstream of macro-economists and central bankers sees inflation as remaining 'lower for longer', at least as far ahead as the policy horizon (three years, perhaps). If that turns out to be true, CBs would remain the best friends of ministers of finance in particular, and politicians in general. The magic money tree will continue to flourish, and harmonious cooperation between fiscal and monetary policies will remain the order of the day.

There is sometimes an added rider to such a comforting, even compla-cent, prediction, which is that 'Even if inflation should re-appear, we [i.e., macro-economists and central bankers] know how to deal with it.' In any case, premature policy-tightening, whether fiscal or monetary, is seen by the main-stream as a far greater danger.

But that is to forget both how difficult, and politically and economically dangerous, it was to break the inflationary spiral in 1979–82. It took great courage from Reagan, Fed Chair Paul Volcker and Thatcher, for example; short rates spiked up to 25 per cent in the United States; it led to the Mexican, Argentinian and Brazilian crisis and a lost decade for Latin America; most of the city centre banks in New York and some European-headquartered interna-tional banks were technically bankrupt; it was the most financially dangerous episode between 1914 and 2008.[6]

Moreover, it was in some crucial respects a great deal easier to crush inflation by monetary policy in 1979–82 than it would be to pull off the same trick in, say, 2023. The reason is that debt ratios, both in the public sector and among non-financial corporates, are now much higher. Figure 1.7 provides the evolution of general government debt from 1980 to 2022, for several AEs.

The point of this is that the immediate adverse effect on public sector finances, and on the debt service ratio, will be far greater now than in 1980. This is particularly so because QE and the payment of interest on excess reserves (IOER) has been effectively lowering the duration of public sector debt in the hands of the public, rendering the condition of the debt more vul-nerable to inflationary shocks.[7]

The same considerations are also largely true for the private non-financial corporate sector in AEs. A prior decade of (partially unforeseen) inflation in the 1970s had left corporates with a relatively low leverage ratio by the end

General Government Gross Debt

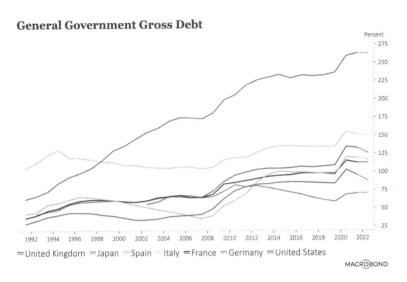

Source: Macrobond.

Figure 1.7   Government debt has risen steadily over the last few decades

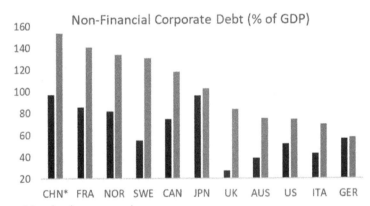

Source: Macrobond.

Figure 1.8   Corporate debt has increased markedly too

of the 1970s. In contrast, three decades of falling inflation and interest rates, reaching historically and extraordinarily low levels, combined with managerial incentives to raise leverage, in order to enhance the return on equity, had led this sector to historically high debt ratios, as shown in Figure 1.8.

Then came the Covid pandemic, with its lockdowns and the temporary closure of certain sectors. The most affected sectors are, and will remain for quite a number of years, in a fragile state. They are in no condition to weather any sizeable and/or sudden increase in interest rates.

The tightening of policies in the UK (1980/81), especially the sharp rise in the sterling exchange rate, led to the demise of much of the UK's manufacturing capability. Given present fragilities, what would a monetary tightening now do to a wider swathe of business?

In 1979–82 many of the large international banks were technically insolvent, and saved by a combination of forbearance and officially encouraged ever-greening (i.e., lending to Mexico, Argentina and Brazil, so they could continue to service their existing bank debts). Could, would, such policies be countenanced now? Admittedly post-GFC regulatory reforms have led to significantly higher capital ratios, but the economic fallout from the Covid

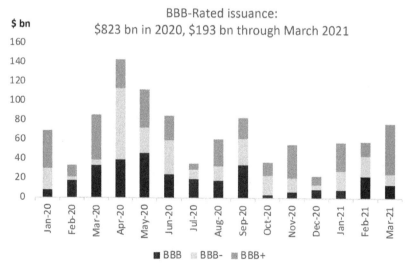

Source: Refinitiv.

Figure 1.9   *BBB-rated companies have borrowed aggressively during the pandemic*

pandemic could well be considerably more severe from 2021 onwards – e.g., in the guise of much higher non-performing loans – than in 1979–82.

Now that Covid has been largely overcome by vaccination, there may be a recovery relief surge in consumer expenditure and demand, leading very likely to a blip in inflation. If that does not exceed 5 per cent (or even possibly more), CBs may initially welcome this as a counter-balance to the previous undershoot, as consistent with AIT. In any case, they will claim that it will be purely temporary, and that (permanently enhanced) uncertainty, the scarring aftermath of the pandemic, and higher unemployment will soon serve to drive inflation back to prior low levels, back to the IT or below again.

But what if that prediction is wrong, as we believe, and inflation remains significantly higher than the target, say through 2022 and 2023? How will CBs, and politicians, react?

Let us suggest three alternative scenarios.

We shall call the first the Strict scenario, the second the Accommodative and the third the Conflictual scenario.

In the Strict scenario, the CB sticks quite rigidly to its IT and, protected by treaty or some other reason, cannot be prevented by politicians from tightening monetary policy in order to achieve its target. The result would be sufficient recession to hold back inflation to target, but also probably increased disaffection with the institutional and constitutional structure that has allowed such conditions to be established. Weaker countries and companies with high debt ratios would succumb in large numbers, and the doom loop, if this was to be applied in the European Union, would re-emerge.

In the Accommodative scenario, both the CB and the politicians agree that the prevention of recession and the maintenance of high employment are more important than the near-term achievement of the IT. Inflation not only remains above target, but also begins to accelerate, as expectations gradually become unanchored (as the CB consistently finds inflation exceeding its target). As (partially unforeseen) inflation rises, it both becomes more politically unpopular and also erodes debt ratios, the more so since official short-term (and even perhaps long-term) interest rates are held down by policy measures, well below inflation rates; i.e., real interest rates become very negative. At some future date, when inflation has become unbearable but debt ratios much less troubling, there would have to be a sharp U-turn to policy. Probably the CB would prefer such a U-turn to occur before the politicians come to the same view, in which case the scenario shifts to the third version. How quickly the U-turn might be reached depends on a set of imponderables, such as the strength of the economic recovery or the generalised dislike of inflation.

In the Conflictual scenario, the CB would like to take stronger steps to curb inflation than the politicians are happy to endorse. The general expectation is that politicians would place more weight on output/employment and less on price stability than CBs, especially in advance of elections. This was, as noted at the outset, the condition that was originally expected to become the norm, but has not, for the reasons already explained, actually transpired. So it actually remains to be seen how such a conflict situation will play out. There are a number of stages in such a conflict scenario. If the conflict is minor, any appearance of political meddling with CBI carries a cost, so initially the CB might appear able to impose its desired policies. But if the conflict intensifies, the politicians will respond by trying to ensure that appointees, those that they continue to control, have the same ideological weightings as themselves. Indeed, beyond some point, the politicians could take steps aimed at forcing the existing governor/chairs out of office. This has happened, often enough, in less developed countries (India being a prominent recent example); indeed Cukierman et al. (1992) use the rate of turnover of governors/chairs in less developed countries as a measure of their independence. Under sufficiently severe pressure, that could also happen in AEs. Finally, and at the limit, CBI was introduced as a legislative Act. What one legislative body has done, its successor can undo.

Effectively, most CBs realise that their independence is quite limited. CBI gives them some leeway to set policy in a way that differs from political preferences. That leeway is greater, the more that the public understands the rationale for such policies and trusts the CB (more than the politicians). But the room for such policy independence is, in most cases, quite strictly limited. Ultimately the political authorities have the whip hand, whether in authoritarian or democratic countries. Central banks usually take into account these political constraints when they act, and their actions may well be such that no political red lines are crossed. They may know how to deal with an economic scenario which crosses these lines, but it is not clear that they will always be allowed to do so.

NOTES

1.   One of us was present at the outset of this new institutional policy when the Reserve Bank of New Zealand asked Goodhart to act as an external advisor at the end of the 1980s.
2.   The general rule over the last few decades had been for fiscal policy to be a redistributive/structural tool while monetary policy has been the countercyclical measure. That has clearly had to change in the current, 2021–22, expansion, which means that fiscal dominance has become a far greater threat.
3.   Even from the outset of this exercise, however, there were limits to the extent that CBs would be prepared to infuriate politicians. Thus, if a general election was known to be set for a particular date, it would be extremely rare for a CB to raise rates immediately beforehand.

4.   With the inestimable benefit of hindsight, and had we appreciated the existence of such strong disinflationary forces, it would have been better to have set the inflation target to zero, rather than the standard 2 per cent generally applied.

5.   Sceptics of our view always point to Japan as an example of a major country where ageing has not led to more inflation; indeed, inflation has been particularly low there. But in a world that saw globalisation surging, why would Japan inflate when its near neighbours in North-East Asia were offering low-wage opportunities for moveable production? Japanese companies took advantage of this opportunity to move jobs from high-wage manufacturers to low-wage, often part-time, services. Moreover, Japan reacted to falling demand by cutting hours, rather than jobs. All this is set out in Chapter 9 of our book.

6.   It may also be worth remarking that, probably in any year before the GFC, an overwhelming majority of economists would have believed that a CB can *always* create more inflation by expansionary policies. Now we know the limitations of CB powers in this respect. The same should lead to greater caution about CBs' abilities to constrain inflation.

7.   Thus Section 1.11, p. 8, of the UK's OBR report (November, 2020) reads: '1.11 The increase in borrowing does, however, render the public finances more vulnerable to changes in financing conditions and other future shocks. This heightened vulnerability is compounded by the shortening of the effective maturity of that debt as a result of both a greater focus on short-term debt issuance by the Treasury and further Bank of England purchases of longer-dated gilts financed through the creation of floating rate reserves. Taken together, these leave debt interest spending twice as sensitive to changes in short-term interest rates than prior to the pandemic. Arresting the continued rise in public debt is likely to require some fiscal adjustment once the virus has run its course. Only in our upside scenario, in which the pandemic is swiftly ended and there is little lasting damage to activity, does borrowing fall below the level required to stabilise the debt-to-GDP ratio by the forecast horizon. In our central forecast and downside scenario, tax rises or spending cuts of between £21 billion and £46 billion (between 0.8 and 1.8 per cent of GDP) would be required merely to stop debt rising relative [to GDP].'

REFERENCES

Cukierman, A., Webb, S.B., and B. Neyapti (1992), 'Measuring the independence of central banks and its effect on policy outcomes.' *World Bank Economic Review*, 6 (3), 353–398.

Goodhart, C., and M. Pradhan (2020), *The Great Demographic Reversal: Ageing Societies, Waning Inequality, and an Inflation Revival.* London: Palgrave Macmillan.

Kydland, F.E., and E.C. Prescott (1977), 'Rules rather than discretion: the inconsistency of optimal plans.' *Journal of Political Economy*, 85 (3), 473–492.

Nordhaus, W.D. (1975), 'The political business cycle.' *Review of Economic Studies*, 42 (2), 169–190.

OBR (Office for Budget Responsibility) (2018), *Fiscal Sustainability Report.* https://obr.uk/fsr/fiscal-sustainability-report-july-2018/.

Philippon, T. (2019), *The Great Reversal: How America Gave Up on Free Markets.* Cambridge, MA and London: Belknap Press of Harvard University Press.

Stansbury, A., and L.H. Summers (2020), 'The declining worker power hypothesis: an explanation for the recent evolution of the American economy.' *National Bureau of Economic Research Working Paper*, 27193, May.

2. Some of the effects of monetary structures, politics, and memories on central banking[1]

John H. Wood

1. INTRODUCTION

The Federal Reserve Act of 1913 was designed by and for the big banks. It provided for the discounting of bank loans by the newly created Federal Reserve System, which also took on the expense of holding the US gold reserve and made a market for the newly legalized bankers' acceptances, without offering competition with privately owned commercial banks. Among the Federal Reserve's first actions was the seasonal stabilization of interest rates and assistance in the cartelization of deposit rates. The principal officials – Federal Reserve Board members in Washington and the heads of the twelve district Federal Reserve Banks – were mainly bankers and the rest businessmen and a few academics. The 1913 Act provided for a Federal Advisory Council of twelve bankers to meet regularly with and advise the Federal Reserve Board. It would be surprising if Federal Reserve decisions did not take bank interests into account (Griffin, 1994; Wood, 2005, pp. 158–166; Warburg, 1930; Miron, 1986; Havrilesky, 1992, pp. 251–273; Kirshner, 2007).

The Bank of England was chartered in 1694 by a financially strapped government at war in exchange for a below-market-rate loan. The Bank was privately owned but had special legal privileges and governance regulated by law. Its sixteen directors were primarily merchant bankers (family/partnership trading and finance firms) who took turns as deputy-governors and governors, usually for two years at each post, and its prosperity depended on the community's.

Monetary policies and central banking in general must of course be political. Interests with superior political powers/influences ought to be those most likely to secure their desired monetary and other government policies, which in turn depend on the compositions/structures/sensitivities of policymaking bodies such as central banks. This chapter reviews examples of these relations during eight crises or other stressful situations involving the British pound or American dollar. We find distinctions between the reactions of the politically remote Federal Reserve during the Great Depression and the publicly more sensitive monetary authority (the US Treasury) monitored by Congress during the post-Civil War resumption of the gold standard; and between the early private and market-sensitive Bank of England and the effectively public institution after 1914. There has been substantial theoretical development of optimal monetary policies, but we have found that the democratic (effective) political accountability of monetary institutions also matters, which may affect their lessons from experience.

2.   THE BANK OF ENGLAND

2.1   The Post-French Wars Resumption

The Bank had been weakened by government loans during the war with France, and in 1797 a run forced suspension of the gold convertibility of its notes. Prices nearly doubled by 1813. An Act of 1803 required the resumption of convertibility at the 1797 rate of exchange within six months of the end of the war, which in 1814 was moved back to July 5, 1815, then to July 5, 1816, then to July 5, 1818. The authorities "were, generally speaking, in favour of a return to cash payments on the old basis – sometime," but they hesitated to force deflation on the economy. Finally, in 1818, tired of waiting, the government secured committees of inquiry into resumption in both Houses of Parliament, and in May 1819 the Resumption Act, called Peel's Act after the chairman of the Commons committee, prescribed a strict schedule of resumption. It is interesting that the first Sir Robert Peel, textile manufacturer, opposed his son's bill and urged the House, "before a measure so destructive of the commercial interests of the country was passed," to consider the recent Petition of the Merchants of London in Favour of the Restriction of Cash Payments (Feavearyear, 1931, p. 204; Sraffa, 1952, p. 365). The Bank also protested:

> [W]hen the Directors are now to be called upon, in the new situation in which they are placed by the Restriction Act, to [support] the whole National Currency, either in Bullion or in Coin, and when it is proposed that they should effect this measure within a given period, by regulating the market price of Gold by a limitation of the Issue of Bank Notes, with whatever distress such limitation may be attended to individuals, or the community at large, they feel it their duty to state their sentiments ... to His Majesty's Ministers on this subject that a tacit ... concurrence at this juncture may not, at some future period, be construed into a previous implied sanction on

their part of a System which they cannot but consider fraught with great uncertainty and risk.

It is impossible for them to decide beforehand what shall be the course of events for the next two, much less for the next four years; they have no right to hazard a flattering conjecture, for which they have not real grounds, in which they may be disappointed, and for which they may be considered responsible. They cannot venture to advise an unrelenting continuance of pecuniary pressures upon the Commercial world of which it is impossible for them either to foresee or estimate the consequences. (Representation by the Directors of the Bank of England to the Chancellor of the Exchequer, May 20, 1819)

The prime minister, Lord Liverpool, defended the plan by stressing its gradual and therefore "less injurious" operation. In any case, it was time to join the general, at least conservative, desire to return to normality, to a fixed standard of value. Those who opposed the plan in reality objected "to returning to cash payments at all." Unrestricted paper money had never been adopted "by any civilized country from the beginning of the world." In fact, resumption was achieved in half the time planned, and David Ricardo, whose plan was the basis of the Act, was blamed for the accompanying depression. It was rumored that he recanted on his death bed (Yonge, 1868, pp. 386–387; Sayers, 1953).

The left portion of Figure 2.1 shows the British price level during the 1797–1822 suspension and resumption, along with the similar American episode during and after the War of 1812. The middle and right side of the

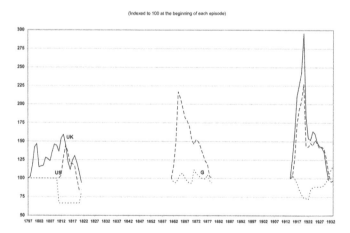

Note: Solid lines for the UK, dashed lines for the US, dotted lines for gold production.
Source: Jastram 1976, pp. 32–33, p. 217, pp. 223–255.

Figure 2.1　　*US and UK wholesale prices and world gold production during suspensions and resumptions*

figure show the American Civil War experience and then both countries for World War I.

The distinction here is between the eagerness of the government to return to normality compared with the Bank's hesitation to embark on a risky and possibly dangerous course for the economy and itself.

2.2   The Commercial Crisis of 1847

There was a good deal of dissatisfaction with the Bank after the resumption, especially in the variability of prices resulting from its alternating expansions and contractions. It was more inclined to join than to moderate booms. It contributed to the Latin American boom of the 1820s and the railway boom of the 1830s, and in 1839 had to turn to the Bank of France for a credit to offset the loss of gold. An index of prices rose from 84 to 113 between 1835 and 1839, and back to 84 in 1843.

Nevertheless, the Bank's notes were made legal tender in 1833, and together with gold constituted the monetary base, or high-power money. An outstanding monetary issue concerned the regulation of these notes. The Bank Charter Act of 1844 stipulated that the Bank's notes be tied to its gold, so that, Samuel Jones Loyd argued, the monetary base would perform as in a pure gold standard, and rid the country of the troublesome fluctuations of the currency arising from the Bank's urge to "support the public credit" (Gregory, 1929; Committee of 1840, Q2654 and Q2784).

Because the Bank's two primary functions were its contribution to economic growth through bank loans and to stability by means of the link of its notes to gold, the 1844 Act separated it into corresponding departments, Banking and Issue, shown in Table 2.1. The Issue Department's assets consisted of a constant fiduciary issue of £14 million and its precious metals (mainly gold), financed by its note issues. The Banking Department's reserve consisted largely of its note holdings (£8,175,025 on September 7, 1844).

The bill received significant opposition. Birmingham industrialist George Muntz asked: "What would happen in consequence of there being such an export of gold as would render it impossible for the Bank to pay its liabilities in gold and thereby affect the circulation of the country?" (Hansard, May 6, 1844). Bankers expressed similar views in correspondence with Peel, who was now prime minister (Parker, 1899, iii, pp. 140–141). His response to these misgivings was contained in a letter to the Bank's governor, who had requested provisions allowing suspension of the Act:

> My confidence is unshaken that we are taking all the precautions which legislation can prudently take against the recurrence of a monetary crisis. It may occur in spite of our precautions, and if it does, and *if it be necessary* to assume a grave responsi-

Table 2.1   Bank of England return, September 7, 1844

Issue department		
Government securities	£11,015,100	£28,351,295 Notes
Other securities	£2,984,900	
Gold coin and bullion	£12,657,208	
Silver bullion	£1,694,087	
Assets	£28,351,295	£28,351,295 *Liabilities*

Banking department		
Government securities	£14,554,834	£3,630,809 Government deposits
Other securities	£7,835,616	£8,644,348 Other deposits
Notes	£8,175,025	£19,148,083 Other liabilities and capital
Gold and silver coin	£857,765	
Assets	£31,423,240	£31,423,240 *Liabilities and capital*

Note: The Bank's return was required to be published weekly in the *London Gazette*, and was also published elsewhere, including *The Economist*. The items have been rearranged and some have been renamed in conformity with modern usage.
Source: The author, from the Bank of England.

bility for the purpose of meeting it, I dare say men will be found willing to assume such a responsibility. I would rather trust to this than impair the efficiency and probable success of those measures by which one hopes to control evil tendencies in their beginning, and to diminish the risk that extraordinary measures may be necessary. (Parker, 1899, pp. 140–141; emphasis in original)

Loyd (1844, p. 439) maintained that there should be no contingency plan for the rule's suspension under pressure. Unless it is "strictly adhered to, it becomes a nullity."

In the event, the Banking Department took advantage of its abundant reserves at the end of 1844 – £9 million in notes and coin compared with deposit liabilities of £12.3 million – by joining the railroad mania. It cut its lending rate from 4 to 2.5 percent, an historic low, and by summer 1846, loans had increased 60 percent. Added to this were increased imports following the poor harvests of 1845 and 1846, and a reduction in the Issue Department's gold to £2.6 million in April 1847. The rise of grain prices had

produced a wave of speculation and an inordinate number of corn bills which the banks were called upon to discount ... The Bank of England, having supplied the market with from 7–10 millions ... was in a bad position both for curbing speculation and for checking the drain. As soon as it attempted to do so there was bound to be a shrinkage of credit and a risk of panic. (Feavearyear, 1931, p. 261)

The Bank raised its rate from 3 to 4 percent in January 1847, and to 5 percent in April, and informed its customers that their discounts would be cut in half, but relaxed in the face of weakness among the debtors. A good harvest brought the price of wheat down from 14 to 8 shillings a bushel, and in August grain merchants began to fail. By mid-September, the crisis had spread to the bill brokers, and panic spread through trades and industries. The note reserve fell, the bank rate was raised to 5.5 percent, and the Bank announced the end of public securities as collateral for loans, which led to frantic sales and a panic on the Stock Exchange.

Country banks also felt the pressure of the Bank's tight money, and asked for assistance. People turned to the government, and for "a fortnight the Chancellor of the Exchequer [Sir Charles Wood] was occupied continuously in meeting the arguments and pleadings of those who wanted the Act suspended. Again and again he refused" (Feavearyear, 1931, p. 263). Wood told the House (November 30):

> Parties of every description made applications to us for assistance [saying] 'We do not want notes, but give us confidence.' They said: 'We have notes enough, but we have not confidence to use them; say you will stand by us, and we shall have all that we want; do anything, in short, that will give us confidence. If we think that we can get bank notes, we shall not want them. Charge any rate of interest you please, ask what you like'. (Feavearyear, 1931, p. 263)

Finally, after several large banks failed, the chancellor told the Bank to lend as freely as it wished, although at a high interest rate (see the letter below), and if this involved an increase in the fiduciary issue beyond the legal maximum, Parliament would be asked for an act of indemnity.

> To the Governor and Deputy Governor of the Bank of England. From Downing Street, 25 October 1847. Her Majesty's Government have seen with the deepest Regret the Pressure which has existed for some Weeks upon the commercial Interests of the Country, and that this Pressure has been aggravated by a Want of that confidence which is necessary for carrying on the ordinary Dealings of Trade. [The] Government have come to the Conclusion that the Time has arrived when they ought to attempt by some extraordinary and temporary Measure to restore Confidence to the mercantile and manufacturing community.
>
> For this Purpose, they recommend to the Directors of the Bank of England in the present Emergency, to enlarge the Amount of their Discounts and Advances upon approved Security; but that in order to retain this Operation within reasonable Limits, a high Rate of Interest should be charged ...
>
> If this Course should lead to any Infringement of the Existing Law, [the] Government will be prepared to propose to Parliament ... a Bill of Indemnity ...
>
> Her Majesty's Government are not insensible of the Evil of any Departure from the Law which has placed the Currency of the Country upon a sound Basis; but they feel confident that in the present Circumstances, the Measure which they have proposed may be safely adopted and at the same Time the main provisions of that

Law, and the vital Principle of preserving the convertibility of the Bank Note, may be firmly maintained.

Your obedient humble servants, J. Russell and C. Wood (Prime Minister and Chancellor of the Exchequer). (Gregory, 1929, ii, pp. 7–8)

News of renewed Bank lending restored confidence immediately, and formerly hoarded gold and notes became plentiful once they were no longer wanted. The new notes hurriedly printed by the Bank were not taken, and the fiduciary issue was not exceeded (House of Commons, 1848).

The Act's alleged primary object – the convertibility of the note – had been violated, but the authorities had behaved in accordance with John Stuart Mill's interpretation of the Act. He wrote for the 1857 edition of *Principles of Political Economy* (p. 657) that "I think myself justified in affirming that the mitigation of commercial revulsions [rather than the convertibility of the issue] is the real, and only serious, purpose of the Act of 1844. No Government would hesitate a moment" to stop convertibility in order to assure the continuity of the Bank of England's support of the financial system "if suspension of the Act of 1844 proved insufficient."

The purpose of the rule was admirable, but a responsible Bank and government would not allow its strict application to impoverish the country by obstructing the currency. Breaking the law in desperate circumstances was thought good policy.

2.3   The Post-World War I Resumption

The order of concerns described by Mill was reversed after the Bank of England had effectively become a public institution during the war. The Bank was not officially nationalized until after the coming of the Labour government in 1945, but after disagreements about the financing of World War I, it was made clear that the Bank had to yield to government policies (Sayers, 1976, pp. 99–107). Still, as we will see, the Bank could by force of argument and/or circumstances have considerable influence on monetary policies.

The war was financed to a large extent by borrowing, the gold convertibility of the pound was suspended, and, as in many other countries, British prices more than doubled between 1914 and 1919. The value of the pound had fallen to $3.38 in March 1920, compared with the prewar par of $4.86. There was a general desire to return to prewar conditions, and in the UK the Cunliffe Commission, chaired by a former governor of the Bank, declared it

> imperative that ... the conditions necessary to the maintenance of an effective gold standard should be restored without delay. Unless the machinery which long experience has shown to be the only effective remedy for an adverse balance of trade and an undue growth of credit is once more brought into play, there will be a grave

danger of a progressive credit expansion which will result in a foreign drain of gold menacing the convertibility of our note issue and so jeopardizing the international trade position of the country. (Gregory, 1929, ii, p. 361)

The permanent Secretary of the Treasury wrote that "we ought to make it perfectly clear that we regard a return to a free gold market at the pre-war parity without long delay as of vital importance." By 1924, he was willing "to wait for a short time" for American prices to rise (which they did not in spite of its large gold accumulations during the war), but "we do not propose to wait indefinitely" (Moggridge, 1972, p. 49).

Economists and businessmen tended to oppose an early return. The necessary dear money and deflation, including wage adjustments, the FBI (Federation of British Industry) petitioned, "would ... seriously increase the difficulty of maintaining industrial peace, [and result in] turmoil, unrest and strikes." Those who preferred to wait for a more propitious time, however, were dismissed as inflationist, with "flabby" arguments. The cry of "cheap money," "more for psychological than for fundamental reasons ... is the Industrialists' big stick and should be treated accordingly," Bank governor Montagu Norman advised. "In connection with a golden 1925, the merchant, manufacturer, workman, etc. should be considered, but not consulted any more than about battleships." The revolving two-year terms of merchant-banker governors had been replaced by long terms, the longest being Montagu Norman (1920–1944). Later governors, serving for five to ten years, were mainly from the Bank's permanent staff (Moggridge, 1972, p. 46; Krooss, 1969, p. 49).

The Bank was a different institution, run by different kinds of people with priorities of their own, after the war. Its management ceased to be experienced directors of the Bank on short-term loan from financial firms, imbued with City traditions and values, but rather politically acceptable members of the Bank's staff. Norman's merchant-banking career, in the family firm, had been brief and unsatisfactory, although he became a Bank director in 1907. He was an advisor to various government departments after 1914, became a full-time deputy governor of the Bank in 1917, and governor in 1920. His information came from a full-time technical staff which he assembled (Boyle, 1967). The next in line, Cameron Cobbold, joined the Bank in 1933 at age 29, became deputy governor in 1945, and governor from 1949–1961. The Earl of Cromer (George Baring), former managing director of Barings, became governor for one contentious term, 1961–1966. He took the fixed-exchange-rate assignment more seriously than the prime minister. He was replaced by Leslie O'Brien, who had joined the Bank out of grammar school in 1927, and rose through the ranks to become chief cashier, deputy governor, and governor from 1966–1973. He was present during the 1967 devaluation, the Heath–Barber[2] inflation, coal strikes, and the adoption of a floating pound, and resigned halfway through his second term.

The Bank and government policy had been on the way to success when the pound was returned to convertibility at $4.86 in April 1925. However, prices fell for the next six years, unemployment rose, and a general strike came in 1926, as the Bank borrowed from abroad in its attempts to maintain the exchange rate. The Macmillan Committee on Finance and Industry was appointed "to inquire into banking, finance and credit, ... and to make recommendations calculated to enable those agencies to promote ... trade and commerce and the employment of labour" (1931, p. 1). When Norman told the committee that the bank rate was "effective" in "preserving the stock of gold," the chairman wondered whether the effectiveness of tight money on the international front "may not [have] unfortunate repercussions internally by restricting credit and enterprise?"

> Norman: Well I should think that its internal effect was as a rule greatly exaggerated ... – much more psychological than real.
>
> Chairman: But ... they may be depressing consequences, and may be serious?
>
> Norman: Yes, but not so serious as they are usually made out to be, and I think that the benefit on the whole of the maintenance of the international standard is [a] great advantage at home for industry [and] commerce ...
>
> Chairman: What is the benefit to industry of the maintenance of the international position?
>
> Norman: This is a very technical question which is not easy to explain, but the whole international position has preserved for us in this country the wonderful position which we have inherited, which was for a while thought perhaps to be in jeopardy, which to a large extent, though not to the full extent, has been re-established. We are still to a large extent international bankers. We have great international trade and commerce, out of which I believe considerable profit accrues to the country; a free gold market ... and all of those things, and the confidence which go with them are in the long run greatly to the interest of finance and commerce.

Winston Churchill, the beleaguered Chancellor of the Exchequer (1924–1929), officially responsible for the Bank's restrictive policy, had memoed a pro-resumption advisor: "I would rather see Finance less proud and Industry more content" (Moggridge, 1972, pp. 42–43). The Conservatives were replaced by Labour in 1929, and the leaders of the new government continued the existing policy despite the cost of balancing the budget by cutting unemployment benefits. This was opposed by most Labour Members of Parliament, but they were circumvented by the formation of a coalition government in August 1931, only to see a run on the pound in September and another suspension – which meant the effective end of the gold standard, in spite of the Bank and government, because of the short-term effects valued by the electorate.

2.4   After World War II

The Great Depression, Keynes's *General Theory*, and perceived policy fail-ures of the interwar period changed the attitudes of policymakers, including the Bank's. The Treasury view of government spending as a diversion of resources from other uses had shifted to Keynesian demand management. "There is probably no country in the world that has made a fuller use than the United Kingdom of budgetary policy as a means of stabilizing the economy," a former Treasury official wrote. "Since 1941, almost all adjustments to the total level of taxation have been made with the object of reducing an excess in total demand or of repairing a deficiency" (Dow, 1964, p. 178).

The Bank was obliged to subject its policies to the rigidity of a fixed-rate monetary system derived from America's optimistic haste to restore the pre-1914 international order. One of its pre-versus-post-World War II differ-ences, however, resembled the Treasury's in its new emphasis on the short run. It did not think the country was ready to jump into a convertible fixed-rate currency, either immediately or as a long-term plan. It wanted small move-ments as the country showed itself ready for them. The Bank and Keynes had exchanged views of fixed plans.

Keynes and Harry Dexter White had represented the UK and US Treasuries, respectively, during negotiations leading to the creation of the International Monetary Fund (IMF) in 1944, although its rules were dominated by the Americans, who wanted monetary reformations (usually tighter money) by those countries having difficulties maintaining their exchange rates, and were less forgiving than Keynes and his proposed subsidies that would probably come at the expense of the United States (Gardner, 1956).

The Bank distrusted these "grandiose" schemes, which it feared would

> be regarded as painless cures, diverting national attention from fundamental prob-lems. [It was] haunted by its own bitter experience of 1925–1931 and fearful lest the British authorities should again undertake external monetary commitments, in particular the early resumption of external convertibility at a fixed rate of exchange, which they would find that they were unable to honour. (Fforde, 1992, p. 33)

The IMF was a system of fixed exchange rates that could only be changed by consent of the members when they agreed that the existing rate was in "funda-mental disequilibrium," and subject to conditions that would enable or force the troubled country to maintain its rate. The IMF never operated as intended because of its fundamental inconsistencies, first of all the full-employment goal valued by most countries at the expense of their so-called fixed exchange rates. World inflation was significant between 1947 and 1970, and variable between countries, averaging about 2.5 percent per annum for developed countries (76 percent for the period, much greater than before 1914), a little more in the UK – not a world conducive to fixed exchange rates.

There was also a gold shortage in two senses: low production because of the rise in costs compared with the fixed price of $35 per ounce, and the dominance of American holdings. The United States held 24 of 34 billion dollars of the world's gold reserves in 1948. The system was called the dollar standard because international transactions were conducted primarily in dollars, backed by gold, although conversions were discouraged.

International trade grew in spite of exchange controls but in line with expanding economies, and by 1970 had reached their 1929 percentage of the world economy. Because of a stagnant gold stock, the required growth in international (gold and dollar) reserves depended on American trade deficits, which it dutifully supplied, although this necessary development was an increasing concern for the country's policymakers.　Finally, in 1971, with rising inflation, falling US gold reserves, a threatened run on the dollar, and a looming election, President Nixon suspended convertibility and the new world of flexible-exchange rates between fiat currencies began. The nations whose representatives had formulated the liberal trading policies underlying the Fund "were unable to accept the disciplines necessary to permit those policies to work" (Mikesell, 1954, p. 29).

The government, which had assumed control of the bank rate in 1932, continued the policy of "cheap money" into the postwar. We "must be on the side of the borrowers of money as against the money lenders, on the side of the active producer as against the passive *rentier*," Chancellor Hugh Dalton said. So the contradictory policies included commitments to a fixed exchange rate, expanding government spending, and low interest rates, which required the suppression of private consumption and investment, to be administered by the Bank. The Bank was a reluctant agent. It nagged chancellors for increases in the bank rate and fewer controls. It was called disloyal and obstructionist, but after all, although nationalized, it was still in the City, immersed in private interests (Brittan, 1971, p. 79; Sampson, 1961, pp. 356–357).

When the Treasury asked the Bank to look into ways of limiting bank loans (without raising their cost), the latter responded that qualitative guidelines would not prevent loans from increasing in line with prices. "As long as the price-weapon, i.e. the rate of interest, is forsworn, there is no other criterion" (Fforde, 1992, p. 362).

Was the Bank trying hard enough? Chancellor Hugh Gaitskell (1950–1951) thought it would "be simpler merely to give [banks] direct instructions about the level of advances, with perhaps some guidance as to the particular borrowers who should be cut," always subject to the condition "that there should be no increase in the rate at which the Government borrows short-term." Governor Cobbold replied:

> The main thought in our mind is that having gone a long distance, with consider-able success, in keeping down advances by co-operation with the banking system, what is needed is something which will also influence the attitude of the potential borrower. [N]o action will bite [like] a rise of a point or two in interest rates [which] would well justify the increased charge on the Exchequer. Governor to Chancellor, June 21, 1951. (Fforde, 1992, p. 392)

The head of the Economic Section and chief economic advisor to the government from 1947–1961 was dissatisfied with the Bank's cooperation. After an angry meeting, Robert Hall (1989) wrote: "It is hard not to get the impression that the Bank, and the banks generally, do not think at all about credit control as economists do, and indeed that they don't quite understand what it is all about." He later complained to his diary that "all we are asking is that the Bank should be neutral and not act against us in our struggle, as they must have been doing." Sometimes he thought that although the Bank had declared that nothing could be accomplished without raising interest rates, "they have told the offending banks all the same to go easy on their advances" (September 11 and November 18, 1948; January 18 and February 2, 1949).

Hall's research at Oxford had included a questionnaire circulated in the mid-1930s – when interest rates were virtually constant and inflation was sig-nificant – to which businesses responded that (a) interest rates played no role in their investment decisions and (b) they did not set prices to clear markets or maximize profits, but rather charged "fair" mark-ups over costs (Hall and Hitch, 1939).

The cost-push formula was convenient for those who envisioned cheap money without inflation, and the policy that followed from this reasoning required the demonization of labor and a policy straitjacket that was to bring down governments of both parties. Those chancellors who looked on wage and price controls as impolitic and impractical had been encouraged, Hall thought, by Treasury officials who were "market men" at heart.

The postwar decades of alternate fiscal expansions and monetary stringen-cies have been called "stop–go," and saw frequent crises that led governments to seek more rather than fewer controls. The Treasury suggested that the Bank ask banks to provide monthly instead of quarterly data; "not worth the extra work," the Bank responded. Cobbold wanted to hold back advances to mollify the chancellor, but disliked strong-arm tactics. He "was not keen to write letters," and avoided directives, preferring oblique signals in polite conversa-tion. The bankers were less polite, complaining "that it was difficult to select the victims of restriction and they grumbled about the lack of restraint by nationalised industries." They seemed unconcerned over their customers' and bank managers' lack of cooperation (Fforde, 1992, pp. 632–633).

Tensions between the Bank and the government increased with the coming of Harold Wilson's Labour government in 1963, after twelve years of Tory rule. The pound was under attack after Tory chancellor Reginald Maudling's "reflation," but Wilson feared that a devaluation would be an admission of Labour's inability to govern. So he chose monetary stringency, which conflicted with his government's ambitious social program.

Dissatisfied with the Bank lifer, Cobbold, the government had turned to someone outside the Bank as his successor. George Baring, the Earl of Cromer, had not been a director, nor had he held any other position in the Bank, and was one of the few governors who had not been deputy governor. At 43, he was the youngest governor in two hundred years, and a new kind. On the other hand, he was a throwback to the pre-Norman governors who had not (before their deputy governor service) been full-time in the Bank. Cromer was a merchant banker who would soon return to his firm (Barings). Although governors of the "old Bank" had been long-serving directors, they were, like Cromer, typically brought up as merchant bankers in family firms to which they devoted their lives. Cromer had not been softened by the bureaucratic relationship between the Bank and government that had grown up since 1914, and did not see why he had to get along.

Conflict was inevitable regardless of personalities when the government wanted an accommodative governor who would at the same time instill confidence in the currency, and Cromer's style was confrontational and public. For one reporter, he "emerged as the keeper of his country's financial conscience … when he sounded solemn warnings against 'indulging ourselves' by 'an enlargement of governmental spending'" (Wechsberg, 1966, p. 163).

> [I]n January, 1965, at a private lunch at No. 10, … I told [Cromer] that Government expenditure was committed far ahead; schools which were being built, roads which were part-way to completion, had been programmed by our Conservative predecessors in 1962–63. Was it in his view, I asked him, that we should cut them off half-finished – roads left as an eyesore on the countryside, schools left without a roof, in order to satisfy foreign financial fetishism? This question was difficult for him, but he answered, 'Yes.' (Wilson, 1971, as quoted by Wood, 2005, p. 322)

A Wilson biographer observed that Cromer "found Wilson slippery and unsound and made little attempt to hide the low opinion he held of the prime minister; Wilson for his part found Cromer hectoring and bigoted, a wolf from the capitalist pack determined to thwart socialist policy if not actually destroy the administration" (Ziegler, 1995, p. 194). These conflicts were moderated by the collapse of the IMF fixed-exchange-rate system in 1971, although inflation (over 12 percent per annum for the next dozen years) and industrial strife increased.

3.   THE UNITED STATES

3.1   The Resumption of 1818–1821

The second Bank of the United States (BUS) was chartered in 1816 primarily to force the resumption of convertibility following the War of 1812, and served as a political buffer for the Treasury's contractionary policy. The war was unpopular, especially in maritime New England, still smarting from Jefferson's embargo by which he had hoped to avoid war with Britain and France. President Madison's June 1812 call for a declaration of war with the UK passed the House 79–49 and the Senate 19–13, and the Democratic administration continued its opposition to internal taxes so that the war had to be sustained on public credit at high interest rates.

Between 1811 and 1816, the number of banks rose from 88 to 246, and their circulations from $23 million to $68 million, while their metallic-reserve ratio fell from 42 percent to 28 percent (Gallatin, 1831, iii, pp. 286–296; Bureau of the Census, 1975, p. 1018; Comptroller, *Annual Reports*, 1876, xl, and 1920, ii, p. 846). Prices rose 40 percent. The war debt had been financed by debt purchased with state bank notes. Federal revenues actually fell between 1811 and 1814, which was not surprising since they were mainly customs duties. The national debt, which had been reduced from $83 million to $45 million between 1800 and 1811, reached its pre-Civil War peak of $127 million in 1815. The British invasion and burning of Washington in August 1814 occasioned a general suspension of convertibility (except in New England).

Congress decreed that effective February 1817, the government would accept payment only in coin or redeemable bank notes, and would keep no deposits in "any bank which shall not pay its notes, when demanded, in the lawful money of the United States" (*Annals of Congress*, April 30, 1816, pp. 1440, 1919). This resumption proved "neither universal nor genuine," however, and the new BUS, which was supposed to help enforce the restriction, in fact joined the credit boom by failing to control its branches, which were not held individually responsible for their issues (Smith, 1953, p. 104; Hammond, 1957, pp. 248–250, pp. 260–262).

The Treasury was also tolerant of the irredeemable state bank notes under the pressure of an electorate that did not wish their banks closed. By 1818, however, Secretary William Crawford began to accept only convertible notes, and to insist on the same by the BUS. The change in policy was especially hard on the South and West, where the land boom had been greatest.

> The Bank was forced in self-preservation to do exactly the opposite of what a central bank should do: it should check expansion and ease contraction. As lender of last resort and keeper of ultimate reserves it should have those reserves in readiness before trouble comes ... Instead, [it] had stimulated the expansion and now must intensify the contraction [the panic of 1819 and first American depression].

"A popular hatred of it based on the grim efforts made to collect or secure what was receivable ... was never extinguished." (Hammond, 1957, pp. 249, 258–259). "The Bank was saved," wrote the Jacksonian advisor, William Gouge, "and the people were ruined". Although the BUS got most of the blame, the "resumption ... was the Secretary's own. The Bank supplied the machinery, the secretary supplied the brains" (Gouge, 1833, ii, p. 110).

> The sufferings which have been produced by the efforts that have been made to resume, and to continue specie payments, have been great. They are not terminated, and must continue until the value of property and the price of labor shall assume that relation to the precious metals which our wealth and industry compared with those of other states, shall enable us to retain. Until this shall be effected, an abortive attempt, by the substitution of a paper currency, to arrest the evils we are suffering, will produce the most distressing consequences. The sufferings that are past will, in such an event, recur with additional violence, and the nation will again find itself in the situation which it held at the moment when specie payments were resumed. (Crawford, 1820, p. 39)

3.2   The Post-Civil War Resumption

Fort Sumter fell on April 13, 1861, the dollar's gold convertibility was suspended at the end of the year, prices had more than doubled by 1864, and a House resolution by a vote of 144–6 directed the Secretary of the Treasury to contract "the currency with a view to as early a resumption of specie payment [at the old rate] as the business interests of the country would permit." The Secretary took his assignment seriously, but the "resolution soon proved not to reflect the real sentiment of the people" (Congressional Globe, 39th Cong., 1st sess., p. 75; Dewey, 1922, p. 335). He and the Congress were deluged with complaints from citizens suffering from the resulting deflation. "[A]lthough it might be admitted that the entire nation would be benefited by the ultimate result [of contraction]," Republican leader James G. Blaine (1886, p. 328) wrote, "the people knew that the process would bring embarrassment to vast numbers and would reduce not a few to bankruptcy and ruin."

Between the termination of the second BUS in 1836, and the inception of the Federal Reserve in 1913, the principal monetary authority and holder of the nation's gold reserve was the US Treasury, which often acted to moderate financial fluctuations through reserve supplies by early redemptions of securities. It acted principally under the watchful eye of the House of Representatives. During a discussion of the Treasury's cash management, Kentucky senator James Beck reminded his colleagues that whereas the laws creating the other executive departments enjoined their secretaries to advise and act under the direction of the president, the Secretary of the Treasury was required to "report and give information to either branch of the Legislature [and] to perform all such services relative to the finances as he shall be directed to perform ... We with the Secretary of the Treasury manage the purse; the president and the other secretaries control the sword" (Congressional Record, 49th Cong., 1st sess., p. 7565).

Resumption was not achieved until 1879, and was the outcome of political positions ranging from sound money to the Greenback Party, and succeeded through increases in income rather than decreases in money. Prices fell to their 1860 level as the country grew into its money stock. Output was strong. The reason for the long, controversial, and relatively painless resumption may have been the structure of the monetary authority: the Treasury, monitored by a Congress sensitive to the electorate.

3.3   The Great Depression

During hearings on the *Stabilization of Commodity Prices* in April 1932, Mississippi Congressman Thomas Jefferson Busby urged the Fed to "launch out and shake off some of its fears about what might happen" if it addressed the fall in prices.

> I do not know whether you know it or not, but about one-fourth of the homes in my state have been sold for taxes during the present month ... Sixty thousand homes, 7,000,000 acres of land, one-fourth of all the property, because the people can not pay taxes, and when people get in that kind of condition, they can not ... listen to fine-spun theories of fears that might arise in the event you took some step forward.

The New York Fed's George Harrison replied:

> But you have got to remember ... Mr. Congressman, there is always difficulty about the mechanics and speed with which we operate. [Y]ou run the risk, if you go too fast, of flooding the market or the banks with excess reserves faster than they can use them, or faster than it is wise for them to use them. The proper and orderly operation of the open market, I think, is to create a volume of excess reserves gradually ... and not have periods when you have got excess reserves one week and none another week.

The Fed's desire for orderly money markets (meaning primarily New York) at the expense of national money, credit, and prices (not to mention income and employment) was reinforced by the independence written into the Federal Reserve Act and respected by Congress and the president. The Fed was intended to provide an elastic currency but was most concerned about meeting its legal (especially gold) restrictions and a money-market policy rule that had begun to give false signals, although it was free of the pains inflicted on the economy.

The national money stock and price level fell 38 percent and 27 percent, respectively, between October 1929 and April 1933. The Fed more than doubled its holdings of government securities between April and June 1932, while Congress was in session, in order to forestall pressure for more vigorous action, and then virtually stopped. Nearly all the increases in high-powered money during the 1930s resulted from the increase in the price of gold in 1933 (Friedman and Schwartz, 1963, pp. 384–385; Wood, 2005, p. 205).

Claims that the Fed failed to perform its function of lender of last resort are incorrect if its interests were limited to the central money markets. The New York Reserve Bank responded vigorously to the 1929 crash. After a 3 a.m. meeting with his directors, Governor Harrison (Reserve Bank heads were called governors until the 1935 Banking Act made them presidents) informed the Stock Exchange Clearing Committee before it met that the New York Fed was prepared to buy $100 million of government securities. "The situation was greatly eased [by these] timely and effective actions," according to Friedman and Schwartz (1963, p. 335, p. 339). "[T]here were no panic increases in money-market rates such as those in past market crises." After the close of the Dow Jones Industrial Index of 299 on Saturday, October 26, it collapsed on the following Monday and early Tuesday to 212, before rallying to 230 at Tuesday's close and 274 on Thursday.

Harrison argued for continued open market purchases until the next September, when he joined the majority of Reserve Banks in favor of the status quo, seeking purchases only to offset gold exports – after the money markets had settled down. New York City deposits were as high in June 1930 as the previous December, after which they fell with the economy (Federal Reserve Board, 1943, p. 81).

3.4   The Great Recession

We heard from the chairman of the Federal Reserve that unless we act the financial system of this country and perhaps the world will melt down ... There was complete silence for twenty seconds. The oxygen left the room. Chairman Bernanke said, 'If we don't do this tomorrow, there won't be an economy on Monday.' (Senate Banking Committee Chairman Christopher Dodd on a meeting of legislative leaders with Bernanke and Secretary Paulson on September 17, 2008 [interview with Charlie Rose, November 26, 2008])

The Great Recession is known for the housing boom and bust, followed by the collapse and government bailouts of large financial institutions. After doubling during the previous decade, house prices stabilized in spring 2006, and broke a year later, falling 30 percent over the next two years. Speculation on rising house prices had been facilitated by easy terms given to credit-challenged borrowers by financial institutions able to pass on the risk of subprime mortgages through securitization. Government-sponsored enterprises (Fannie Mae and Freddy Mac) bought risky securities under the pressure of Congresses and administrations dedicated to increased homeownership. Regulators failed to restrain leverage or loan risk, understandable in a period of high bank earnings and few problem banks. Risky behavior was also encouraged by the conflicted rating agencies' practice of awarding high grades to securitized subprime mortgages.

The boom was fueled by easy Fed credit. Real interest rates were negative early in the decade, and there was a feeling that the Fed would not let asset prices fall: the so-called "Greenspan put" (*Financial Times*, 2000, December 8). "[T]he extraordinary risks taken by managers of large financial firms ... were the result, not of 'random mass insanity' but of moral hazard resulting in large part from the Fed's willingness – implicit in previous practice – ... to rescue creditors of failed firms" (Calomiris, 2009; Selgin et al., 2012). Many of these hopes were disappointed when the Fed responded belatedly to the recession.

After easing for several months following the 2000–2001 recession, the Fed finally reacted to inflationary fears, and maintained tight money until late 2008, even through the mid-year crises. "[S]hocks to energy prices and the housing sector started a moderate recession in December 2007, [which a] contractionary monetary policy ... intensified ... in summer 2008." The recession's "severity derived from the combined contractionary monetary policy of all the world's central banks," who worried about inflation (Hetzel, 2012, p. 208, p. 220). Instead of the ease called for by the recession, the Fed decided to reallocate credit in ways that disrupted the markets it hoped to save. Throughout the period the Fed departed from its traditional policy of "leaning against the wind," and accentuated economic fluctuations.

Authorities came to the assistance of large financial firms, undercutting the capital markets because potential purchasers were unwilling to bid against the infinitely deep pockets. The Fed's $180 billion loan to AIG allowed it to pay $53.5 billion to Credit Default Swap (CDS) counterparties, the largest being Société Générale, Deutsche Bank, and Goldman Sachs. (A CDS is a derivative contract involving a buyer who makes periodic payments to a seller, and receives a payoff if an underlying security defaults.) The largest of the government bailouts was TARP, the Troubled Asset Relief Program, for which Congress allocated $700 billion to buy banks' bad loans. The bill was loosely written and Congress was led to believe that distressed borrowers would be relieved.

It should have known better. The bulk of the funds used went into corporate coffers. It should not have been expected that lenders would throw more money into the failing housing market. Few surveyed banks cited lending as a priority. Most saw the program as a no-strings-attached windfall that could be used to pay down debt, acquire other businesses, or invest for the future. John C. Hope III, chairman of the Whitney National Bank in New Orleans, said: "They didn't tell me I had to do anything particular with it ... Make more loans? We're not going to change our business model or our credit policies to accommodate the needs of the public sector."[3]

These were not the only transfers of wealth from taxpayers to finance. The quasi-fiscal subsidies handed out by the Fed (and other central banks) were huge. Central banks are able to engage in quasi-fiscal actions; i.e., actions equivalent to taxes, subsidies, and redistributions of income and wealth, such as reserve requirements, loans to the private sector at interest rates that do not at least cover risk, accepting overvalued collateral, or purchases of securities at prices above fair value. The Fed did all these in enormous amounts. When the crisis began in August 2007, the Fed's balance sheet was just under $1 trillion – about 7 percent of annual US GDP. By the end of 2008, it had doubled.

There is no provision in American government for a quasi-fiscal role for the Fed other than that inherent in the pursuit of its legitimate macro and financial stability objectives, Buiter (2010) argues. It should fund liquidity operations aimed at solvent counterparties. If it is its policy to deal (as agent of the Treasury) with potentially insolvent counterparties, the risks should be assumed by the Treasury, which is not the practice of any of the leading central banks. It is a political decision reserved under the US Constitution to the "Power [of Congress] To lay and collect Taxes, Duties, Imposts and Excises, to pay the Debts and provide for the common Defense and general Welfare of the United States."

4.   CONCLUSION

In the episodes presented here, at least, the compositions and experiences of central banks appear to have influenced their policies. The dependence of the private, profit-seeking, Bank of England on the economy was revealed in its reluctance to force a deflation after 1815, and also its willingness to abandon restrictions on credit later in the century – which differed from the post-1914 government agency's determination to resume convertibility virtually regardless of domestic considerations. Even so, it remained sensitive to finance, and its depression experiences increased its caution.

The American post-Civil War resumption, conducted almost directly by Congress, was the most politically sensitive, and least damaging, of those considered here – unlike the Great Depression and the Treasury's use of the BUS as a buffer after the War of 1812. More recent bailouts by the Fed have shown its continued consideration for bank over general economic interests.

NOTES

1. I am grateful to Bob Hetzel for helpful comments.
2. Edward Heath and Anthony Barber, Prime Minister and Chancellor of the Exchequer, respectively, 1970–1974.
3. In a speech at the Palm Beach Ritz-Carlton, MetaFilter, January 18, 2009.

REFERENCES

Barofsky, N.M. (2012), *Bailout*. New York, NY: Free Press.
Blaine, J.G. (1886), *Twenty Years in Congress*. Norwich, CT: Henry Bill.
Boyle, A. (1967), *Montagu Norman*. London: Cassell.
Brittan, S. (1971), *Steering the Economy*. New York, NY: Penguin.
Buiter, W.H. (2010), "Reversing unconventional macro policy: technical and political considerations." In M. Balling, J.M. Berk and M.O. Strauss-Kahn (eds), *The Quest for Stability*. Vienna: SUERF, pp. 23–43.
Bureau of the Census (1975), *Historical Statistics of the U.S., Colonial Times to 1970*. Washington, DC: US Government Printing Office.
Calomiris, C.W. (2009), "Banking crises and the rules of the game." *NBER Working Paper 15403*, September.
Capie, F.H. (1993), *History of Banking*. London: Pickering.
Committee (Macmillan) on Finance and Industry (1931), *Report*, Cmd. 3897. London: HMSO.
Comptroller of the Currency (1876 and 1920). *Annual Reports*. Washington, DC: Office of the Comptroller of the Currency.
Crawford, W.H. (1820), "Banks and the currency." *American State Papers, 1789–1838, Finance*, 3, 24 February, House of Representatives, 16th Cong., 1st sess.
Dewey, D.R. (1922), *Financial History of the United States*, 8th ed. New York, NY: Longmans, Green and Co.
Dow, J.C.R. (1964), *The Management of the British Economy, 1945–60*. Cambridge: Cambridge University Press.
Feavearyear, A.E. (1931), *The Pound Sterling*. Oxford: Clarendon Press.
Federal Reserve Board (1943), *Banking and Monetary Statistics, 1914–41*. Washington, DC: Federal Reserve Board.
Fforde, J.S. (1992), *The Bank of England and Public Policy, 1941–58*. Cambridge: Cambridge University Press.
Friedman, M., and A.J. Schwartz (1963), *A Monetary History of the United States, 1863–1960*. Princeton, NJ: Princeton University Press.

Gallatin, A. (1831), *Considerations on the Currency and Banking System of the United States*. Philadelphia, PA: Carey & Lea.

Gardner, R.N. (1956), *Sterling-Dollar Diplomacy*. Oxford: Oxford University Press.

Gouge, W.M. (1833), *A Short History of Money and Banking in the United States*. Philadelphia, PA: Grigg & Elliott (reprinted A.M. Kelley, 1968).

Gregory, T.E. (1929), *Select Statutes, Documents & Reports Relating to British Banking, 1832–1928*. Oxford: Oxford University Press.

Griffin, G.E. (1994), *The Creature from Jekyll Island*. New York, NY: American Media.

Hall, R.L. (1989), *Diaries, 1947–53*, edited by A. Cairncross. London: Routledge.

Hall, R.L., and C.J. Hitch (1939), "Price theory and business behavior." *Oxford Economic Papers*, 2 (1), 12–45.

Hammond, W.B. (1957), *Banks and Politics in America from the Revolution to the Civil War*. Princeton, NJ: Princeton University Press.

Havrilesky, T. (1992), *The Pressures on American Monetary Policy*. New York, NY: Springer.

Hetzel, R.L. (2012), *The Monetary Policy of the Federal Reserve*. Cambridge, MA: Cambridge University Press.

House of Commons (1848), "Reports from the Secret Committee," *British Parliamentary Papers, Monetary Policy, Commercial Distress*, 1, 2, June and August 2.

Jastram, R.W. (1976), *The Golden Constant*. Hoboken, NJ: Wiley.

Kirshner, J. (2007), *Appeasing Bankers*. Princeton, NJ: Princeton University Press.

Krooss, H.E. (1969), *Documentary History of Banking and Currency in the United States*. New York, NY: Chelsea House.

Loyd, S.J. (1844), *Thoughts on the Separation of the Departments of the Bank of England*. London: Pelham Richardson (reprinted Capie, 1993).

Mikesell, R.F. (1954), *Foreign Exchange in the Postwar World*. New York, NY: Twentieth Century Fund.

Mill, J.S. (1857 [1909]), *Principles of Political Economy with Some of their Applications to Social Philosophy*, edited by W.J. Ashley. London: Longmans, Green and Co.

Miron, J.A. (1986), "Financial panics, the seasonality of the nominal interest rate, and the founding of the Fed." *American Economic Review*, 76 (1), 125–140.

Moggridge, D.E. (1972), *British Monetary Policy, 1924–31: The Norman Conquest of $4.86*. Cambridge: Cambridge University Press.

Parker, C.S. (1899), *Sir Robert Peel from His Private Correspondence*. London: John Murray.

Sampson, A. (1961), *Anatomy of Britain*. London: Hodder & Stoughton.

Sayers, R.S. (1953), "Ricardo's views on monetary questions." *Quarterly Journal of Economics*, 67 (1), 30–49.

Sayers, R.S. (1976), *The Bank of England, 1891–1944*. Cambridge: Cambridge University Press.

Selgin, G.A., Lastrapes, W.D., and L.H. White (2012), "Has the Fed been a failure?" *Journal of Macroeconomics*, 34 (3), 631–636.

Smith, W.B. (1953), *Economic Aspects of the Second Bank of the United States*. Cambridge, MA: Harvard University Press.

Sraffa, P. (1952), "Notes on the evidence of the resumption of cash payments." In D. Ricardo (ed.), *Works, Vol. 5*. Cambridge: Cambridge University Press.

Warburg, P. (1930), *The Federal Reserve System: Its Origin and Growth*. London: Macmillan.

Wechsberg, J. (1966), *The Merchant Bankers*. New York, NY: Pocket Books.

Wood, J.H. (2005), *A History of Central Banking in Great Britain and the United States*. Cambridge, MA: Cambridge University Press.
Yonge, C.D. (1868), *The Life and Administration of Robert Banks Jenkinson, Second Earl of Liverpool*. London: Macmillan.
Ziegler, P. (1995), *Wilson: The Authorized Life*. New York, NY: HarperCollins.

3. The whys and how of central bank independence: from legal principles to operational accountability[1]

Maqsood Aslam, Etienne Farvaque and Piotr Stanek

1.   INTRODUCTION

Central bank governance at the end of the 20th century has led to more and more independence of these institutions. The movement towards independence generalized in the 1980s, after the burst of inflation known in the aftermath of the oil price shocks and the induced stagflation of the 1970s. Governments across the world have introduced different reforms and restructured central bank governance to revamp existing situations (Crowe and Meade, 2007). This matters, because the management and governance of central banks influence a wide range of important economic variables (inflation dynamics, short-run economic growth, and development in the long run), via the tools of monetary policy.

However, political influence and state interventions in central banks' affairs still exist, in both developing and developed countries. The degree of central bank independence is considered a landmark against which one can appreciate the commitment of governments towards price and financial stability, as well as sustainable growth. Notwithstanding, the autonomy conferred to a central bank can sometimes contradict government's objectives, and such a conflicting situation would lead to a trade-off for society.

Political processes and institutions can thus either act as barriers or as complements to central bank independence. For politicians, it is difficult to be unbiased towards benefits arising from expansionary monetary policy in the short term. According to the time-inconsistency argument (Kydland and Prescott, 1977), politicians seeking re-election and having short-term goals may not be interested in long-term benefits. The repercussions arising from time inconsistency can be avoided by delegating power and authority to institutions like central banks. For instance, recently the government of Pakistan proposed a bill to make the State Bank of Pakistan (SBP) more autonomous, which would help to make effective and transparent monetary policy and minimize political influence over monetary policy. The detractors of independent central banks build their thesis on the argument that too much power can set free the central bank from accountability, while the other side narrates the advantages of central bank independence (e.g., price stability, transparency and getting closer to the prevailing international standards and practices). Nevertheless, there have been substantial increments in central bank independence in emerging countries – e.g., Poland and Bosnia and Herzegovina – over time, and there has been no significant amendment in the American Fed's law for a long time, although there are regular threats over this institution's independence (think of the 'Ban the Fed' campaign, for example). So, in search of an ideal setting from legal and economic aspects, economists, political scientists and lawyers still debate the benefits of increasing central bank independence.

The basic tenet of central bank independence is a legal one. Legal aspects can reveal the willingness of public representatives to grant a certain degree of independence to the central bank. Essentially, legal texts surrounding independence entail features like the governors' modalities of appointment and of removal, the office term, the ways of conflict resolutions amd the limitations related to the formulation of monetary policy – i.e., restrictions on lending and interest rates (Cukierman et al., 1992). Similarly, central bank independence is generally measured through legal features collected from their statutes. A higher degree of central bank independence is generally characterized by the independent appointment of the governor, the definition of lending limits to the government, the degree of potential political influence on decisions and clearly defined objectives (Crowe and Meade, 2007).

However, legal independence is just one of the many key factors responsible for the actual independence. This can vary from the actual (so-called de facto) degree of independence. For example, the personal characteristics of central bankers also affect the policy decision making and thus the actual degree of independence (Farvaque et al., 2020; Aslam and Farvaque, 2021; Aslam et al., 2021).

Given the importance of central bank independence, delegating monetary policy should entail a high level of responsibility and accountability, because too much of a good thing may backfire. A famous instance of protection provided by his country's central bank's law is the case of Antonio Fazio, Governor of the Bank of Italy, who was protected from resignation, with ensuing political debates and difficulties. To avoid this kind of problem, countries have attempted to ensure accountability of independent central banks by two mechanisms. First, by narrowing the mandate, which is aimed at achieving some specific goal. Second, by ensuring public accountability; i.e., central banks have to regularly report to legislators for their actions (Crowe and Meade, 2007).

Communication of goals, and of the successes achieved in reaching the goals, to the general public by central banks is inevitable, and it ensures transparency and effectiveness of monetary policy, if only because imparting information tends to decrease public uncertainty regarding inflation expectations. Transparency and inflation targeting regimes are also closely associated (Bernanke et al., 1999). Announcements of meetings' conclusions, press releases and language shifts also improve the transparency through delivery of information. Recent advances in communication means, such as the internet and the related means of communication and social networks, offer better ways of opening the technical decisions to the analysis by a broader audience.

This chapter is thus divided into two parts. The first one reviews the (economic and legal) principles that gave support to, and induced the move towards, independent central banks. The second looks at the way central banks deal with the accountability, transparency and communication requests that emerge from the very principle of independence.

2.   WHY CENTRAL BANK INDEPENDENCE?

The independence of central banks from political power is an institutional mode of management of monetary affairs whose predominance is relatively recent in Europe, both Western or Central and Eastern. Since the literature on time consistency of decisions has turned to politicians' choices (Kydland and Prescott, 1977), the relation between the 'conservatism'[2] of central bankers and central bank independence has been considered as implying a large degree of independence between politicians (elected or autocrats) and the monetary institutions (Rogoff, 1985). The majority discourse within the community of economists makes the choice of this type of management of monetary affairs a signal of the price attached by a society to monetary stability. In other words, with independence, the central banker becomes the guarantor of the maintenance of the monetary order and, beyond that, of the social order (Aglietta and Orléan, 1982).

The justification for the independence of central banks is originally a legal one, and it is based on the American political philosophy. This political philosophy is the one that animated the drafters of the American Constitution, gathered at the Convention of 1787. The legitimacy of independence is perceived, according to this tradition, essentially as a reaction to two types of fears. First, the capacity of the executive power to cause harm leads to the need for strict control and supervision of the executive. To this is added a second fear, expressed by those who are now called the Founding Fathers, of losing a freedom – dearly acquired – as a result of demagogic manipulations, leading to sudden movements of opinion.

Distrust of the executive and fear of instability thus laid the foundations of the American Constitution and, beyond that, provided the keys to the legitimization of delegated powers, foremost among which was monetary power. The rationale for independence is provided, in particular, in Article 78 of the *Federalist Papers*. It is probably the first theorization of the recourse to independence, according to a reasoning that is both rigorous and pragmatic (for a review, see Farvaque, 2007). Independence in this argumentation appears as a necessity, being instrumental and efficient in countering the instability induced by potential changes and reversals in a polity's preferences.

However, the principle of independence is only compatible with democracy if people can assert their preferences. Independence aims to make the voters confirm the variation of their preferences, after a period of information and reflection through, for example, a political campaign leading to a national election or a referendum. This process provides a period of reflection for voters, which may result (or not) in a constitutional amendment. It will therefore require a solemn, legal act for the founding text to be amended. The solemnity required of the necessary act is intended, of course, to moderate the ardor of passions and to ascertain the temporary or permanent nature of the shift in public preferences. Independence comes at the end of the reasoning as the means of guaranteeing the 'courage' of judges (which will be achieved in the United States, for example, by the unlimited duration of the term of office of Supreme Court judges). They must indeed provide a counterweight to the instability of passions by reminding voters what their own (or the previous generations') choices were, and why they were made. Of course, this belief in the virtues of independence can only be understood if one considers that the independence of judges can only be the basis of the people's confidence. In turn, this requires that people can be confident in their institutions if their office-holders are virtuous, which is what their appointment procedure should aim to guarantee.

In this line of reasoning, independence does not offend democratic culture because its adoption is itself the result of a political process, of a rational choice by the electorate: in a nutshell, 'removing monetary policy, foreign policy or broadcasting from the sphere of politics is in itself a political act' (Elster, 1983, 1993).

The real foundation of central bank independence therefore originates as a reflection of a given political philosophy, which has been echoed at the constitutional level since the conception of the American Constitution, about two centuries ago. The underlying political mechanism goes as follows: (1) a strong executive is likely to pervert democracy, so it is necessary to control it; (2) it is primarily up to the representatives of the people to perform this role, but they, like the people themselves, are susceptible to passions that may challenge the institutional edifice; (3) in order to reduce the risk of institutional upheaval, it is necessary to institute a constitutional review which, to be impartial, will have to be independent.

The principle of independence does not therefore pervert democracy. On the contrary, in this reasoning, it guarantees its durability. Far from the conflagration of the political scene, from temporary reversals, from partisan confrontations, from the whims of passions (Hirschman, 1977), the authority to which a parcel of power has been delegated will be able to carry out the mission entrusted to it by the legislator, without risk of a break in continuity.

However, for this argumentation to be valid, independent central banks cannot emerge in a vacuum. An independent central bank can only exist and function in a coherent, incentive-compatible, set of political institutions. In other words, central bank governance has gone towards larger degrees of independence granted to those institutions (Crowe and Meade, 2007), but without always considering that an independent central bank needs institutional counterparts.

Some authors have tried to look at this question, starting with Hayo (1998), who exhibited the link between the degree of independence and the evidence he could gather about what he dubbed 'inflation culture'. That is, some societies/polities are more inflation-averse than others, and this aversion is apparent in the degree of independence the society gives to its central bank. Maxfield (1997), Bagheri and Habibi (1998), Banaian and Luksetich (2001) or more recently Masciandaro and Romelli (2019) have also considered that the degree of central bank independence should be treated as an endogenous variable determined by political variables such as political freedom, political instability or economic freedom. Moser (1999) confirmed that view by considering how political structures are related to central bank independence: he notably showed that the higher the degree of checks and balances inside the political institutions, the higher the degree of central bank independence. His results have been confirmed and extended by Farvaque (2002), who showed that the presence of a higher chamber in a parliament played an important role in the results, and that federal countries relied more on independence than centralized ones.

Overall, thus, political and monetary institutions have to be incentive-compatible. This may sound surprising as, and the literature on time consistency has shown it clearly, even though independence can be welfare-improving, it is costly for politicians to delegate. The fact that this cost has been confronted by some polities to different degrees is revelatory of the equilibrium a society has struck between (present and future) politicians in power and their (present and future) opposition. Clearly, the structure of checks and balances in a political system is a feature of this equilibrium, as

Montesquieu (1748) famously showed in his *Spirit of the Laws* piece. It can be claimed that central bank independence is another important feature of this equilibrium.

McCallum (1995) has criticized the literature on time consistency that was considered as supporting independent and conservative central bankers (in the line of Rogoff, 1985). He has brought a different argument, that delegating monetary policy cannot be considered as a solution to the time-consistency problem of elected policy-makers. According to his view, any central bank receives independence from politicians, who always retain the possibility of giving away this independence. If the central bank pursues a policy that is too far from the society's preferences, the institution takes the risk of being overridden by the government. Recent episodes, from the United States under Trump, Turkey under Erdoğan, or India under Modi, have revealed such pressures from governments, and thus the merits of McCallum's argument. In McCallum's (1995) words, central bank independence is only 'relocating' the source of the commitment problem. While, in the first step, rooted in the monetary policy area, independence just sends it further, to the political arena, where the terms of the delegation contract have to be enforced.

Giordani and Spagnolo (2001) have looked at this important critique, and have shown that, even though it may not be the solution to a commitment problem, independence increases the cost of a return to discretion. If the cost is high enough, it could be enough to deter any politician from confronting the independent institution. In the words of McNamara (2002, p. 55), what can be said is that 'delegation does not occur in a political vacuum', even though politicians have given the central bank 'an intentionally high degree of agency slack'.

As a consequence, one can even propose the following (apparent) paradox: by delegating monetary policy, a society can consolidate its degree of democracy, and build institutions that are all the more likely to be sustainable. In other words, the argument is that, by making the denial of independence more transparent (as politicians are generally more closely scrutinized by the public than central bankers), delegation is more than the answer to a purely functional problem. There may even be a democratic appeal in central bank independence.

Though seemingly provocative, this proposition can be supported when one considers how conflicts between a society's choice and the monetary authority are solved. The German example of the beginning of the 1990s, the Australian case reviewed in Coleman (2001) or the scrutinization of the European Central Bank (ECB) by the German Supreme Court (Feld and Wieland, 2020) make clear that, far from being contained in ministries' offices, the discussion had to take place in the fresher atmosphere of a political debate; i.e., under the scrutiny of mass media and the general public. Public debating would be enough to root out an institution whose foundations would not be deep enough, given the surrounding political context and institutions.

Moreover, empirical studies have shown that even the most independent central bank cannot stay indefinitely deaf to changes in a society's needs and preferences. Given the uncertainties about the real effects of monetary policy, central banks cannot act in complete isolation from the political sphere (Quaglia, 2008). Central bankers complain enough about the bashing they have to bear while doing their job for one to raise any doubt. This bashing has been proved theoretically to influence a bank's policy (Waller, 1991), and most empirical studies support the argument: when testing central banks' reaction functions, results tend to show that, whatever they may say, central banks also consider 'real' (i.e., output or unemployment) variables in their policy decisions. This point has notably been made by an academic insider for the Fed (Blinder, 1998), but also for the ECB (Drometer et al., 2018, even exhibit that the ECB may have followed a policy oriented towards the most afflicted countries during the Global Financial Crisis of 2007–2008). Of course, there also exists a Public Choice-inspired literature exhibiting the influence of political 'advice' to the central bank (see, among others, Havrilesky, 1991). In any case, the recent crises (the 2007–2008 crisis, the euro crises of the 2010s and the COVID-19 pandemic-induced crisis) have shown that central banks have been reactive (see, for example, Aslam and Farvaque, 2021).

Hence, degrees of central bank independence depend on the costs a society wants to face; i.e., on how much polities want to restrain the power of the executive. A testable implication is then that the more polities want to curb the executive power, the higher the degree of independence. This consistency between monetary and political institutions has not attracted a lot of attention from observers, but the results from Moser (1999) and Farvaque (2002) are consistent with such a view.

In other words, whereas McNamara (2002, p. 67) considers as flawed the economic foundations of delegation, and points to the illegitimacy of independent central banks, it can be argued that independent central banks can be fully compatible with democracy. The real question, in our view, thus becomes: how to sustain such an equilibrium? Our view is that it can be sustainable if the central bank is accountable to politicians, but also, and maybe even more so, to the markets and to the general public. Communication and scrutinization are thus the keys to make independent central banks accountable, responsible and, in the end, legitimate institutions.

3.   HOW SHOULD AN INDEPENDENT CENTRAL BANK COMMUNICATE?

3.1   Accountability: A Framed Communication with the Principal

Although Issing (2005, p. 66) traces the discussions about independence, accountability and transparency in monetary policy led by the Bank of England back to 1931 (within a debate between Keynes and Harvey inside a Committee on Finance and Industry), the general perception of central banks as mysterious or even mystical institutions still prevailed in the 1980s (Brunner, 1981; Goodfriend, 1986).

Briault et al. (1996) note that accountability implies some form of explanations in a principal–agent relationship (assuming that the central bank is the agent of the government conducting monetary policy). They differentiate between more or less stringent forms of accountability (*de jure* vs. informal) on the one hand, depending on the type of addressees of explanations (the government vs. the general public), and on the other hand, accountability measures influenced by the scale and type of central bank independence (instrument vs. goal independence). In the subsequent literature, accountability seems to be directed mainly to the democratically elected institutions (notably parliaments, but also governments as their emanations), whereas transparency of monetary policy is addressed to the general public and financial markets and can thus be mainly associated with central bank communication (Masciandaro and Romelli, 2016). Goodhart and Lastra (2018) additionally suggest that accountability goes beyond mere information (transparency) and necessarily includes an element of 'defending the action, policy, or decision for which the accountable is being held to account' (note 36, p. 61). However, Best (2016) noted that, at least until the financial crises of 2008–2010, central bank accountability was limited to transparency-based measures. This argues in favor of extending accountability towards more 'robust' modes; i.e., deliberation-based ones. As one can see, transparency and accountability are clearly related, if not even interwoven, but here we stick to the view that accountability is directed towards the (direct) principal and includes elements of solid argumentation explaining the agent's actions and achievements.

Accountability may take a plethora of forms, and many tools can be used to ensure it. These have been summarized in several central bank accountability indices. Indeed, most of them start with the simple fact of providing information, go through requiring precise explanations and end with measures undermining independence, such as overriding the decision or firing the central banker. Briault et al. (1996) consider publishing monetary policy reports – other than central bank bulletins – or the minutes of meetings, going on to stricter tools such as monitoring by the parliament or indeed the possibility of the central bank being overridden in case of shocks. De Haan et al. (1998) cover a mixture of objective-related (which we would rather consider in independence), transparency-related and final-responsibility assessments (which could be seen as accountability in the narrow sense, going from monitoring by the parliament to a possibility of dismissal of the chair of the institution based on bad performance). Bini-Smaghi and Gros (2000) consider *ex ante* (announcement and explanation of objectives), *ex post* (information and explanation of decisions, deviations from targets, public reports or hearings) and procedural accountability (possible presence of observers from the government during meetings, and publication of minutes and votes of the decision-making body). A useful survey of the issue is provided by Dumiter (2014).

Even if, as was already noted by Briault et al. (1996), some elements of accountability can be present in non-independent central banks or in non-democratic institutional contexts, there is a general agreement among scholars in the field that more central bank autonomy (which started to expand from late 1980s) translates into more accountability and transparency (Jeanneau, 2009; Bernanke, 2013; Masciandaro and Romelli, 2016), and that this is socially beneficial. Revealingly, Blinder (2004) qualifies transparency as one of the dimensions of the 'quiet revolution' in central banking – noteworthy together with collective decision making and changing attitudes towards financial markets.[3]

3.2 Transparency and Communication: For the Market or for the People?

Central bank transparency has been defined as 'the extent to which central banks disclose information that is related to the policymaking process' (Eijffinger and Geraats, 2006, p. 3). These authors have subdivided the area of transparency into the following five categories: political, economic, procedural, policy and operational transparency. Each of these fields were furthermore characterized by three elements,[4] and assessing each of those on a 0–1 scale (sometimes allowing for a fractional realization) yielded their first comprehensive transparency index, producing a numerical assessment with a 0–15 final score. This initial index, compiled for nine major central banks, was later extended by Dincer and Eichengreen (2014) to cover 120 central banks from 1998 to 2010.

In principle, a higher degree of transparency should facilitate a better understanding of the policy-making process and decisions by the financial markets and general public. That, in turn, should improve the functioning of the transmission channels of monetary policy by reducing policy risk, and ultimately allow for inflation expectations being firmly anchored. However, this relationship is in practice more complex.

For example, excessive transparency might enable political pressure on the central bank and the members of its decision-making bodies (Cukierman, 2009). This might be especially the case in the Governing Council of the ECB (or other federal central banks), where the interests of national central bank governors of individual euro area countries are not necessarily perfectly aligned. Additionally, publication of unconditional forecasts or interest rate paths (inherently subject to some stochastic volatility, model uncertainty, unknown shocks, etc.) may be understood as a commitment of the central bank and, in case of any significant deviations, could undermine its credibility (e.g., Giavazzi and Mishkin, 2006; Morris and Shin, 2005). Goodhart (2013) also pointed out that, in practice, decisions on forward guidance by a committee would be complicated at best. An interesting theoretical argument against full transparency at all times was advanced by Gosselin et al. (2008). They notably argue that opacity may be creative and welfare increasing, but transparency is preferable if a central bank's information is of relatively higher precision or available earlier than the private sector's and if current inflation adjusts quickly to expectations. Similarly, Kool et al. (2011) warn that increased central bank transparency could crowd out investment in private information by market participants, which results in poorer-quality forecasts.

All in all, many scholars – and especially those with practical experience in monetary policy decision making – have argued against unlimited transparency (e.g., Issing, 2005; Mishkin, 2007; Baeriswyl, 2011). On the other hand, Svensson (2009) argues that if appropriately communicated with the disclaimer that this is only a forecast and not a commitment, the pros of the forward guidance exceed the cons (if any). Additionally, Qvigstad (2006), while presenting the criteria for a 'good-looking' interest rate path, describes the modus operandi of preparing and communicating this element of transparency at the Norges Bank (in place since November 2005).

Importantly, he notes that 'what is "good" for the monetary policy committee (MPC) of Norges Bank is not necessarily "good" for other MPCs' (p. 14), agreeing with Blinder (2007) that the institutional setup of the monetary policy committee determines its communication. Blinder (2007) focuses on differences in communication between an individual decision-maker (as in New Zealand), 'autocratically-collegial committee' (presumably the Fed under Alan Greenspan), 'genuinely-collegial committee' (e.g., the ECB Governing Council) and an 'individualistic committee' (such as the Bank of England MPC), concluding that 'When it comes to transparency, one size does not fit all' (p. 122). Recently, the International Monetary Fund, in its Central Bank Transparency Code, also stated that transparency needs 'to strike a balance between transparency and the legitimate needs for confidentiality' (IMF, 2020,

p. 4). We would go along by repeating that such a balance may differ from one institutional context to another.

Given the key role in monetary transmission played by the financial markets and institutions, central banks traditionally focused on how communication and transparency measures would be perceived by the financial sector. Among empirically investigated consequences of higher transparency, positive outcomes certainly prevail. For example, Tomljanovic (2007) argues that a higher degree of transparency helps the financial markets to become more efficient in the sense of decreasing the forecast error of interest rates; Van der Cruijsen and Demertzis (2007) find that more transparent monetary policies are associated with a weaker link between current and expected inflation, which can be interpreted as a result of higher central bank credibility; Hayo and Mazhar (2014) show that more transparency helps to contain inflation variability and inflation expectations; Papadamou et al. (2014) infer that higher transparency leads to smaller stock market volatility; while Eichler and Littke (2018) demonstrate its ability to limit exchange rate fluctuations, a feature which can be particularly important for emerging economies.

More informed voters make in general better choices in democracies (Glaeser et al., 2007; Pande, 2011; Cruz et al., 2021). Thus, even if central banks and monetary policy do not enter into the core of electoral campaigns,[5] education directed to the general (non-economic) public seems vital to ensure understanding of the measures taken by the central bank and, ultimately, defines the public support from which the institution will benefit. However, this has been investigated relatively recently. For example, Haldane and McMahon (2018) explored the consequences of central banks' communication with the general public. As could be expected, a greater knowledge and greater satisfaction with monetary policy are correlated with a smaller gap between inflation expectations and the inflation target of the Bank of England. Interestingly, this institution is also shown as an exemplary promoter of current macro-monetary theories refuting 'folk-theory' in which the central bank has control over the quantity of money in circulation (Braun, 2016).

Central bank communication addressed to the general public differs from that dedicated to financial markets and may be seen mainly as intended to incite (or maintain) trust (Braun, 2016). The fact that trust is important for the functioning of such institutions as central banks has not been disputed since at least the seminal contribution by La Porta et al. (1997). However, the trust in central banks, notably the ECB, has undergone some important fluctuations since the Global Financial Crisis (Bursian and Fürth, 2015), and is determined by such factors as education or the quality of information acquired (Hayo and Neuenkirch, 2014) as well as by socio-demographical features of respondents together with macroeconomic factors (Farvaque et al., 2017). Importantly, a higher degree of trust not only translates into support and thus democratic legitimacy, but also to such a crucial (from the macroeconomic perspective) variable as inflation expectations (Christelis et al., 2020). These goals could be attained with well-designed and clear communication. However, if it is executed with excessive intensity, at least some addressees (business executives) might perceive it in a negative way (Hwang et al., 2021). Similarly, too much transparency might harm trust, as shown in the Eurobarometer data by Horvath and Katuscakova (2016).

As Cecchetti (1999, p. 512) noted, transparency allows central banks to reconcile their independence with their general accountability. This seems still valid after more than two decades of the vigorous debate on the independence and accountability of monetary institutions. However, we would augment such a statement by saying that a well-designed accountability framework ('robust' communication with the elected bodies) ensures legitimacy vis-à-vis the (direct) principal, while appropriate communication with the financial markets leads to smoother and more predictable monetary policy transmission, and education of the general public contributes to increased trust and ultimately support of the central bank as a key institution of the economic system.

4.   CONCLUSION

The main conclusions from our survey of the literature go along the following lines:

1.   Central bank independence is fully compatible with democracy even if central bank officials are not elected, but requires the catalytic presence of appropriate accountability measures, transparency and clear communication with both financial markets and the general public.
2.   Accountability, understood as the way of communicating and explaining policy and actions by the central bank to the 'principal' (represented by democratically elected institutions – such as parliaments), necessarily needs to be rooted in the polity and legal framework of individual countries.
3.   One size does not fit all, either in optimal transparency actions that depend, inter alia, on the structure of the monetary decision-making body, a nation's culture (e.g., preference for uncertainty avoidance), or the way the markets or general public would react to significant central bank forecast or policy errors.
4.   Transparency and good communication with the financial sector may indeed smooth monetary transmission, lead to better private forecasts, and lower stock market and exchange rate volatility.

5. Clear communication with the general public helps to generate trust in the central bank and ultimately anchors inflation expectations around inflation targets.
6. In their communications, central banks should stick to the state of academic research and explain to the general public (and possibly also to financial markets) how monetary policy is made and decided, while avoiding confusion with the easier-to-understand but no longer valid 'folk-theory' of money (Braun, 2016).
7. Central banks should be aware that too much communication or its implementation in an unclear or incoherent way could undermine their credibility. Therefore, moderation might be recommended to avoid the impression that central banks' communication becomes 'cheap talk' or propaganda.

NOTES

1. The authors would like to thank Guillaume Vallet for his support and trust. The research has been funded by the National Science Centre Poland, Harmonia program, under the reference number 2018/30/M/HS4/00896. The usual disclaimer applies.
2. 'Conservatism' in the monetary context means aiming at low inflation or to stabilize the price level.
3. The discussion here focuses on the 'top-down' view of accountability, relating to the politician(s) as a 'principal' monitoring the 'agent' (the central bank). A complementary view is that voters have to consent to the delegation, and that the power they confer to the central bank must be controlled, and not only by their delegates (elected politicians). Monitoring in this sense can come from the press or social medias, for example. This aspect, of a 'bottom-up' logic of delegation, is certainly related to the constitutional stage (when the central bank receives its independence), reviewed in the previous section, and its day-to-day monitoring aspect is also to be considered.
4. Economic transparency covers disclosure of data, models and forecasts; political transparency requires information on objectives, numerical targets and institutions (such as central bank independence or inflation contracts); procedural transparency covers publications of strategy, minutes and voting; policy transparency relies on presentation of monetary policy decisions, their explanations and the inclination or path for the subsequent steps; and finally operational transparency necessitates information on control errors, transmission mechanisms and affecting shocks (Eijffinger and Geraats, 2006, pp. 3–4).
5. Exceptions to such a rule are analyzed by Dwyer (2004) or Taylor (2009).

REFERENCES

Aglietta, M., and A. Orléan (1982), *La violence de la monnaie*. Paris: Presses Universitaires de France.

Aslam, M., and E. Farvaque (2021), 'Once bitten, twice bold? Early life tragedy and central bankers' reactions to COVID-19.' *Finance Research Letters*. https://doi.org/10.1016/j.frl.2021.102060.

Aslam, M., Farvaque, E., and F. Malan (2021), 'A disaster always rings twice: early life experiences and central bankers' reactions to natural disasters.' *Kyklos*, 74(3), 1–20. https://doi.org/10.1111/kykl.12267.

Baeriswyl, R. (2011), 'Endogenous central bank information and the optimal degree of transparency.' *International Journal of Central Banking*, 7(2), 85–111.

Bagheri, F.M., and N. Habibi (1998), 'Political institutions and central bank independence: a cross-country analysis.' *Public Choice*, 96(1–2), 187–204.

Banaian, K., and W.A. Luksetich (2001), 'Central bank independence, economic freedom, and inflation rates.' *Economic Inquiry*, 39(1), 149–161.

Bernanke, B.S. (2013), 'A century of US central banking: goals, frameworks, accountability.' *Journal of Economic Perspectives*, 27(4), 3–16.

Bernanke, B.S., Laubach, T., Mishkin, F.S., and A.S. Posen (1999), *Inflation Targeting: Lessons from the International Experience*. Princeton, NJ: Princeton University Press.

Best, J. (2016), 'Rethinking central bank accountability in uncertain times.' *Ethics & International Affairs*, 30(2), 215–232.

Bini-Smaghi, L., and D. Gros (2000), *Open Issues in European Central Banking*. Basingstoke: Macmillan.

Blinder, A.S. (1998), *Central Banking in Theory and Practice*. Cambridge, MA: MIT Press, Lionel Robbins Lectures.

Blinder, A.S. (2004), *The Quiet Revolution. Central Banking Goes Modern*. New Haven, CT: Yale University Press.

Blinder, A.S. (2007), 'Monetary policy by committee: Why and how?' *European Journal of Political Economy*, 23(1), 106–123.

Braun, B. (2016), 'Speaking to the people? Money, trust, and central bank legitimacy in the age of quantitative easing.' *Review of International Political Economy*, 23(6), 1064–1092.

Briault, C., Haldane, A., and M. King (1996), 'Independence and accountability.' *Bank of England Working Paper*, 49.

Brunner, K. (1981), 'The art of central banking.' In H. Göppl and R. Henn (eds), *Geld, Banken und Versicherungen*, Volume 1. Karlsruhe: VVW.

Bursian, D., and S. Fürth (2015), 'Trust me! I am a European central banker.' *Journal of Money, Credit and Banking*, 47(8), 1503–1530.

Cecchetti, S. (1999), 'Accountability of the central bank for monetary policy.' In International Monetary Fund (ed.), *Current Developments in Monetary and Financial Law*, Volume 1. N.p.: International Monetary Fund.

Christelis, D., Georgarakos, D., Jappelli, T., and M. van Rooij (2020), 'Trust in the central bank and inflation expectations.' *International Journal of Central Banking*, 16(6), 1–37.

Coleman, W. (2001), 'Is it possible that an independent central bank is impossible? The case of the Australian notes issue board, 1920–1924.' *Journal of Money, Credit and Banking*, 33(3), 729–748.

Crowe, C., and E. Meade (2007), 'The evolution of central bank governance around the world.' *Journal of Economic Perspectives*, 21(4), 69–90.

Cruz, C., Keefer, P., and J. Labonne (2021), 'Buying informed voters: new effects of information on voters and candidates.' *Economic Journal*, 131(635), 1105–1134.

Cukierman, A. (2009), 'The limits of transparency.' *Economic Notes*, 38(1–2), 1–37.

Cukierman, A., Webb, S.B., and B. Neyapti (1992), 'Measuring the independence of central banks and its effect on policy outcomes.' *World Bank Economic Review*, 6(3), 353–398.

Dincer, N.N., and B. Eichengreen (2014), 'Central bank transparency and independence: updates and new measures,' *International Journal of Central Banking*, 10(1), 189–259.

Drometer, M., Siemsen, T., and S. Watzka (2018), 'The monetary policy of the ECB: caring for the weakest links.' *Kyklos*, 71(4), 537–556.

Dumiter, F.C. (2014), 'Central bank independence, transparency and accountability indexes: a survey.' *Timisoara Journal of Economics and Business*, 7(1), 35–54.

Dwyer, J.H. (2004), 'Explaining central bank reform in Japan.' *Social Science Japan Journal*, 7(2), 245–262.

Eichler, S., and H.C.N. Littke (2018), 'Central bank transparency and the volatility of exchange rates.' *Journal of International Money and Finance*, 89(C), 23–49.

Eijffinger, S.C.W., and P.M. Geraats (2006), 'How transparent are central banks?' *European Journal of Political Economy*, 22(1), 1–21.

Elster, J. (1983), *Sour Grapes*. Cambridge: Cambridge University Press.

Elster, J. (1993), *Political Psychology*. Cambridge: Cambridge University Press.

Farvaque, E. (2002), 'Political determinants of central bank independence.' *Economics Letters*, 77, 131–135.

Farvaque, E. (2007), 'Fondements constitutionnels de l'indépendance des banques centrales: des Pères fondateurs de la nation américaine à la Banque Centrale Européenne.' *Revue d'économie financière*, 87, 225–239.

Farvaque, E., Hayat, M.A., and A. Mihailov (2017), 'Who supports the ECB? Evidence from Eurobarometer Survey Data.' *World Economy*, 40(4), 654–677.

Farvaque, E., Malan, F., and P. Stanek (2020), 'Misplaced childhood: when recession children grow up as central bankers.' *Journal of Economic Dynamics and Control*, 110, 103697.

Feld, L.P., and V. Wieland (2020), 'The German Federal Constitutional Court ruling and the European Central Bank's strategy.' *Freiburger Diskussionspapiere zur Ordnungsökonomik*, 20/05.

Giavazzi, F., and F.S. Mishkin (2006), *An Evaluation of Swedish Monetary Policy between 1995 and 2005*, Sveriges Riksdag, The Committee on Finance. www .riksdagen.se/globalassets/10.-sprak/engelska/reports-from-the-riksdag/an -evaluation-of-swedish-monetary-policy-between-1995-and-2005.pdf.

Giordani, P., and G. Spagnolo (2001), 'Constitutions and central-bank independence: an objection to "McCallum's second fallacy".' *Working Paper*, 426, Stockholm School of Economics.

Glaeser, E.L., Ponzetto, G.A.M., and A. Shleifer (2007), 'Why does democracy need education?' *Journal of Economic Growth*, 12(2), 77–99.

Goodfriend, M. (1986), 'Monetary mystique: Secrecy and central banking.' *Journal of Monetary Economics*, 17(1), 63–92.

Goodhart, C. (2013), 'Debating the merits of forward guidance.' In W. den Haan (ed.), *Forward Guidance: Perspectives from Central Bankers, Scholars and Market Participants*. London: CEPR, VoxEU eBook, pp. 151–156.

Goodhart, C., and R. Lastra (2018), 'Populism and central bank independence.' *Open Economies Review*, 29(1), 49–68.

Gosselin, P., Lotz, A., and C. Wyplosz (2008), 'The expected interest rate path: alignment of expectations vs. creative opacity.' *International Journal of Central Banking*, 4(3), 145–185.

De Haan, J., Amtenbrink, F., and S.C.W. Eijffinger (1998), 'Accountability of central banks: aspects and quantification.' *CentER Discussion Paper*, 1998-54, Macroeconomics.

Haldane, A., and M. McMahon (2018), 'Central bank communications and the general public.' *AEA Papers and Proceedings*, 108, 578–583.

Havrilesky, T. (1991), 'The frequency of monetary policy signaling from the administration to the Federal Reserve.' *Journal of Money, Credit and Banking*, 23(3), 423–428.

Hayo, B. (1998), 'Inflation culture, central bank independence and price stability.' *European Journal of Political Economy*, 14(2), 241–263.

Hayo, B., and U. Mazhar (2014), 'Monetary policy committee transparency: measurement, determinants, and economic effects.' *Open Economies Review*, 25(4), 739–770.

Hayo, B., and E. Neuenkirch (2014), 'The German public and its trust in the ECB: the role of knowledge and information search.' *Journal of International Money and Finance*, 47(C), 286–303.

Hirschman, A.O. (1977), *The Passions and the Interests: Political Arguments for Capitalism Before its Triumph*. Princeton, NJ: Princeton University Press.

Horvath, R., and D. Katuscakova (2016), 'Transparency and trust: the case of the European Central Bank.' *Applied Economics*, 48(57), 5625–5638.

Hwang, I.D., Lustenberger, T., and E. Rossi (2021), 'Does communication influence executives' opinion of central bank policy?' *Journal of International Money and Finance*, 115, 102393.

International Monetary Fund (2020), *The Central Bank Transparency Code*. www.imf.org/-/media/Files/Publications/PP/2020/English/PPEA2020038.ashx.

Issing, O. (2005), 'Communication, transparency, accountability: monetary policy in the twenty-first century.' *Federal Reserve Bank of St. Louis Review*, 87(2), pp. 65–83.

Jeanneau, S. (2009), 'Communication of monetary policy decisions by central banks: what is revealed and why.' *BIS Papers*, 47. Basel: Bank for International Settlements.

Kool, C., Middeldorp, M., and S. Rosenkranz (2011), 'Central bank transparency and the crowding out of private information in financial markets.' *Journal of Money, Credit and Banking*, 43(4), 765–774.

Kydland F., and E. Prescott (1977), 'Rules rather than discretion: the inconsistency of optimal plans.' *Journal of Political Economy*, 85(3), 473–491.

La Porta, R., Lopez-de-Silanes, F., Shleifer, A., and R.W. Vishny (1997), 'Trust in large organizations.' *American Economic Review*, 87(2), 333–338.

Masciandaro, D., and D. Romelli (2016), 'From silence to voice: monetary policy, central bank governance and communication.' In D. Masciandaro and E. Gnan (eds), *Central Banking and Monetary Policy: What Will Be the Post-Crisis New Normal?* Vienna: Larcier, pp. 71–88.

Masciandaro, D., and D. Romelli (2019), 'Peaks and troughs: economics and political economy of central bank independence cycles.' In D.G. Mayes, P.L. Siklos and J.-E. Sturm (eds), *The Oxford Handbook of the Economics of Central Banking*. Oxford: Oxford University Press, pp. 58–98.

Maxfield, S. (1997), *Gatekeepers of Growth: The International Political Economy of Central Banking in Developing Countries*. Princeton, NJ: Princeton University Press.

McCallum, B. (1995), 'Two fallacies concerning central-bank independence.' *American Economic Review*, 85(2), 207–211.

McNamara, K.R. (2002), 'Rational fictions: central bank independence and the social logic of delegation.' *West European Politics*, 25(1), 47–76.

Meade, E. (2012), 'Institutional governance and monetary arrangements.' *International Finance*, 15(1), 137–151.

Mishkin, F.S. (2007), 'Can central bank transparency go too far?' In F.S. Mishkin (ed.), *Monetary Policy Strategy*. Cambridge, MA: MIT Press, pp. 48–65.

Montesquieu, C.L. de (1748), *De l'esprit des lois*. Geneva: Barillot et Fils.

Morris, S., and H.S. Shin (2005), 'Central bank transparency and the signal value of prices.' *Brookings Papers on Economic Activity*, 36(2), 1–66.

Moser, P. (1999), 'Checks and balances, and the supply of central bank independence.' *European Economic Review*, 43(8), 1569–1593.

Pande, R. (2011), 'Can informed voters enforce better governance? Experiments in low-income democracies.' *Annual Review of Economics*, 3(1), 215–237.

Papadamou, S., Sidiropoulos, M., and E. Spyromitros (2014), 'Does central bank transparency affect stock market volatility?' *Journal of International Financial Markets, Institutions and Money*, 31(C), 362–377.

Quaglia, L. (2008), *Central Banking Governance in the European Union: A Comparative Analysis*. London: Routledge/UACES.

Qvigstad, J.F. (2006), 'When does an interest rate path "look good"? Criteria for an appropriate future interest rate path.' *Norges Bank Monetary Policy Working Paper*, 5, 24.

Rogoff, K. (1985), 'The optimal degree of commitment to an intermediate monetary target.' *Quarterly Journal of Economics*, 100(4), 1169–1189.

Svensson, L.E.O. (2009), 'Transparency under flexible inflation targeting: experiences and challenges.' *Sveriges Riksbank Economic Review*, 1, 5–44.

Taylor, M.M. (2009), 'Institutional development through policy-making: a case study of the Brazilian central bank.' *World Politics*, 61(3), 487–515.

Tomljanovich, M. (2007), 'Does central bank transparency impact financial markets? A cross-country econometric analysis.' *Southern Economic Journal*, 73(3), 791–813.

Van der Cruijsen, C., and M. Demertzis (2007), 'The impact of central bank transparency on inflation expectations.' *European Journal of Political Economy*, 23(1), 51–66.

Waller, C. (1991), 'Bashing and coercion in monetary policy.' *Economic Inquiry*, 29(1), 1–13.

4. Bankocracy, or a new age of the European Central Bank

Marie Cuillerai

1.　INTRODUCTION

In *The Class Struggles in France*, while analyzing the period from February to June 1848, Marx evokes the indebtedness of the state as a means to enrich itself for the "finance aristocracy":

> A faction of the *bourgeoisie*, to which the state deficit was really the main object of its speculation; every new loan offering new opportunities for defrauding the state, which was kept artificially on the verge of bankruptcy ... In this way the February Revolution directly strengthened and enlarged the bankocracy which it should have overthrown. (Marx, 1972, p. 8)

Where Marx speaks of the *finance aristocracy* and *bankocracy*, we now speak of the financial economy. In this new age of capitalism, central banks play a central role.

My approach concerns only the European Central Bank (ECB) and in particular its role in the indebtedness of European countries which are currently facing a health crisis, which is also an economic and social crisis. For most observers, the ECB is at a crossroads. Either it verifies the logic of the debt denounced by Marx, or the opportunity could be seized to review the priorities of the ECB, and for it to assume a service of the *common* good of the people. This would relate not only to the common goods of the inhabitants of the countries of the eurozone, but beyond them, to the inhabitants of the planet, financing the objectives of a climate transition that draws, like it or not, a *common* future.

Today, the ECB's institutional transformations, which actually date back to the 2008 crisis, are consolidating and relate to the tools for pooling public debts. The slogan of these ongoing changes is "Whatever it takes". This slogan sheds light on the particular power of the central bank system, in an economy grappling with problems that are no longer only federal, nor regional, but also broadly global such as those that the pandemic forces us to face.

To analyze the political scope of the ECB's unconventional action strategies, we will first shed light on the context in which the debt problem, both private and public, unfolds. This environment becomes clear when we realize that the ECB's institutional transformations are being carried out piecemeal, following the rhythm of the shocks that the eurozone has experienced since 2008, from the dramatic turn of events that set the stage for the Greek people's referendum in July 2015 on the debt adjustment proposals of the Troika (formed by the ECB, International Monetary Fund and European Commission), right up to the current situation. Secondly, we will present how the bankocracy has exercised its hegemony in the settlement of the Greek crisis at the expense of democratic values. We will then look at the issue of the ECB's sovereignty through the policies it has pursued over the past two decades and new issues related to the pandemic. The last part of this article is devoted to debt and monetary creation. We see at work the power of bankocracy, but also the opening of an alternative horizon linked to the democratization of money.

2. BANKOCRACY: THE SYSTEMIC DEBT ENVIRONMENT

Capitalism today is no longer Marx's, and there is not a question of placing his analysis on a completely different reality, nor denying that the very concept of "crisis" remains extremely ambiguous. In any case, we should insist that there is no single crisis, that it is not a matter of *the* crisis. What will concern us here is the transformation of the loans of central banking into an announced public deficit "crisis", with a single currency shared between different states.

It is difficult indeed to think of the central bank institution without situating it in the environment that constitutes it, in this case without putting it in relation to the reality of public and private debt. According to some authors (Lazzarato, 2011; Avgouleas, 2020) there is a debt market whose structural scale characterizes contemporary debt-driven capitalism. This focuses on what Crouch calls "private Keynesianism" where access to credit for the middle class and poor (Crouch, 2009; Streeck, 2014; Gago, 2017), has become necessary to ensure social reproduction and to finance consumption and access to education, health or business investment. The establishment of this environment was formed through legal and institutional mechanisms, which can be summed up by the formula of the "3 Ds" (Bourguinat, 1987) (disclosure, disintermediation, deregulation). These "3 Ds" have made it possible to reorient the international financial system in which central banks operate.

Banking deregulation has thus guaranteed wider access to credit and increased household debt by developing mortgages and consumer credit. And as shown by the subprime crisis in the United States real estate market triggered in 2008, these changes have prepared the neoliberal transformation of the welfare state into a debtfare state (Marazzi, 2013). Such a debtfare state, characterized by the transfer of financial responsibilities for risk management to the state, preserves the profits of the private banking sector under the principle that certain entities are "too big to fail". Moreover, the counterpart of this increased government responsibility for the bankruptcies of the banking system is an increasing individualization of the liability of small debtors, students, landlords and households. At this individual level, taking out credit is considered to be part of a freely chosen contract according to the contractor's interest.

The possibility of being unable to repay is analyzed as a miscalculation of the risk, the cause of which is either a lack of information or the psychological flaw of a consumerist pathology. In both cases, infantilization leads to increased control and discipline over bad payers. However, this disciplinary individualization of private debt, cut off from its systemic environment, has also developed beyond the scope of micro-economic analyses of private debt. Indeed, this disciplinary view has shifted against the sovereign debts of some countries infamously known by the stigmatizing acronym of "PIGS" (Portugal, Ireland, Greece, Spain).

Behind these anathemas and accusations of budgetary mismanagement, whether that of households or that of spending states, lies in reality the mechanism stigmatized by Marx as bankocracy. The historical context has changed, but the environment that characterizes the link between private and public debt today is based on similar mechanisms. Following the 2008 financial crisis, the need for European states to borrow at rising debt-to-GDP (gross domestic product) ratios has increased public government indebtedness to the ECB, due to its spending on the rescue of the banking system. There was talk of an amount of aid paid between 2008 and 2012 in the order of 13 per cent of European GDP.[1] This aid has weighed on the budgetary efforts of the states, which have been ordered to discipline their spending, leading to unprecedented austerity measures in Europe.

3.   GREEK TRAGEDY

As Greece's recent history reminds us, it is the effort to save the international financial system that has contributed greatly to the sovereign debt crisis in Europe. For example, many economists have since estimated that the collapse of Greece during 2008–2012 could be compared to the Great American Depression of the 1930s. Greek GDP had fallen by 25 per cent, unemployment reached 27 per cent, pensions fell by 40 per cent. The role of the ECB in Greece from 2015 was recounted in Yanis Varoufakis's book *Adults in the Room* (2017).

Varoufakis, the finance minister of Alexis Tsipras' government, elected in January 2015, secretly registered Eurogroup meetings where he was trying to negotiate new terms for the repayment of sovereign debt, to get the country out of five years of austerity imposed by the Troika. He recounts the months of negotiations over the Greek crisis around the memorandum of understanding concluded by previous governments under two bailouts.

The country had just elected in January 2015 the left-wing Syriza party, whose campaign promise was to end the Troika, which continued to demand a budgetary excess of 4.5 per cent. The ECB under Mario Draghi had already begun a policy of quantitative easing, of buying back sovereign debt, but in February it decided not to accept Greek securities deposited by banks. European Commission President Jean-Claude Junker warned Europeans that treaties trump elections. This episode re-opened a political crisis in Europe, giving the impression that within the Eurogroup there was in fact a clash between the eurozone states, some states considering themselves creditors, and a Greek government considered not as a government winner of a legitimate election, but as a bad debtor.

One of the lessons of this historical episode, regardless of the partiality of the person who reports it, is that in this play the ECB takes on the clothes of the title role of the sovereign, since its strategy made possible the protection of a part of the member countries of the euro area, while excluding one of them from its protection. Historian Adam Tooze (2018) agrees, recalling how the subprime mortgage holders' crisis spread throughout the world economy and led to the episode that put Greece under the tutelage of the Troika. After Lehman Brothers went bankrupt, European banks, which were widely exposed to the United States, no longer found the dollar funds needed for the day-to-day financing of their commitments. The Fed, in December 2008, reached an agreement with the ECB for a swap exchange to provide it with dollar funding. Again, central bankers thus, in fact if not in law, have been holding themselves in the title role, by acting as guarantors of international monetary stability, and giving the ECB a role of quasi-sovereign not only of the European monetary system, but of the institutional existence of Europe. As if it were ultimately reduced to a single currency market.

Tooze does not question the economic relevance of these decisions, which have effectively anticipated the social consequences of a systemic and global financial crisis. But we also know that the rescue of European and American banks must have been accompanied by the commitment of public finances in all the countries of the euro area. And on this scale, the decisions adopted have never been the subject of discussion or democratic debate in national parliaments. The ECB thus reveals the reality of the structure of monetary union, which cannot be reduced to the federal support of democratic representation in the European Parliament and Commission. In view of the ECB's actions in the context of the previous crisis, the EU looks less like a set of countries united in solidarity around a democratically framed market space than it is an unbalanced set of creditors and debtors.

As in the case of Greece, a bankocracy is being set up, well beyond the national perimeter mentioned by Marx and which ultimately rests on the part that is played out between creditors and debtors. The memoirs of Varoufakis, like the book of Tooze, update Marx's terms. If 21st-century capitalism has changed, it is mainly because of the financialization that has placed private and public debt at the heart of wealth production. But the debt mechanism has also changed. As Marx clearly understood, it is not really a question of repaying these public debts, but of continuing to exchange them and doubly benefiting from them.

On the one hand, this can be seen as a gain in terms of strengthening a cultural hegemony. A reminder that Gramsci's influential concept of hegemony defines the ability of those in power to make the world match how they want it to look. The hegemonic narrative of triumphant neoliberalism is the famous "TINA" ("there is no alternative"), to which alternative narratives would be characterized as untruth, coming from "special interests", or simply fake. With regard to Greece, it is the dogma of a repayment "whatever it costs *socially*" that has established itself as the only rationality of the common system of public debt with the ECB. This dogma of the virtue of the working "ants" (parsimonious people who know the virtues of austerity) sheds light on the reality of the policy that is played out between creditors and debtors. The tragedy recounted by Varoufakis took place in the unelected Eurogroup, and as such, the gain in terms of intellectual hegemony is immediately correlated with a loss of democratic confidence.

But on the other hand, this loss of confidence in European democracy is also proportional to a budgetary gain capable of strengthening hegemony in one country, in this case Germany; and credited to Germany's finance minister, Wolfgang Schauble. He demanded in the discussions reported by Varoufakis that the gains made on Greek debt be returned not to Greece as proposed by the Greek minister, but to Germany, as stipulated in the memorandum. Of course, the amount collected, in the order of EUR 2.9 billion, may seem light given the sums involved. However, it is symbolic of the victory of a dogma over all economic pragmatism.

4.   A QUASI-SOVEREIGN IN THE TITLE ROLE

In ancient tragedies, the choir plays a special role. It is made up of costumed citizens, who sometimes speak to the public, comment on events and guide the public's understanding. One can imagine a completely different perspective on these conversations between adults. One might say, for example, that it is

Europe that must feel indebted to Greece for forcing the ECB to develop an unconventional monetary policy, "softened" by quantitative easing and low rates; a policy that has benefited all European countries, except for Greece itself. Another might point out how the power of the rulers is not a function of their democratic legitimacy but of their ability to adapt to dogma, to take the directives and apply them.

The financial system's rescue prerogative is comparable to the prerogative over money that characterizes the sovereign's power. The Fed and the ECB were the only institutions capable of maintaining a payment system and therefore the only ones able to re-arm domestic economies, because they functioned as lenders of last resort (LLRs). But this role of LLR, which is not intended to convert central bankers into insurance services for states, has not redirected this debt towards democratically decided objectives. The ECB, through its monetary policy, delegates measures to support the economy to the banks without requiring more specific targets in terms of lending. They have not been directed, for example, towards reducing inequalities between the living standards of national populations within the euro area; and even less towards the rescue of social insurance systems or public health services, research, education or justice.

In any case, the bailout will have made it possible to save the private banks. Thus, the ECB, located at the articulation of the public finances of states and the international financial market, has played a role that can be described as a quasi-sovereign role. The term "quasi-sovereign" describes loans whereby issuers are supported by an "*implicit* guarantee" from the state. The ECB is quasi-sovereign, since it operates in the field of international relations: the field of the *imperium*, traditionally devolved to the states. For it is indeed the guarantor of an international balance, ensuring the sustainability and stability of interdependent, financial and economic relations. And it does so while continuing to assert its independence *explicitly* from the member states in the decisions it takes as an LLR, but it does so with the *implicit* consent of the governments of the nation states, which are sure to reaffirm the logic of its functioning. Quasi-sovereign also on the grounds of what could be termed as the *dominium*, the area of the common market, the regional economy of Europe, where it maintains the hegemony of dogma through its statutory independence. The German philosopher Carl Schmitt ([1938] 1992) advanced this partition of the world between *imperium* and *dominium* to criticize the extension of market domination over the grip of national sovereignty. The ECB and the Fed have shattered such a separation of sovereign prerogatives.

On this dual level of *dominium* and *imperium*, the ECB operates in the absence of any recourse to politics. But it has in fact squandered its political and symbolic credit, the confidence that citizens had in an institution. The system of public debt has placed the old mechanisms of feeding national budgets – in France, the Trésor – under the dependence of an independent bank. For a large part of the middle and working classes of Europe, the ECB is now in a state of confidence insolvency. In any case, this is the diagnosis made by Streeck (2014), which pits a "market people" against the "people of states", like two opposite peoples, and leads Streeck to talk about a divorce between democracy and capitalism.

5.   "THERE IS NO SUCH THING AS A FREE LUNCH"

The hegemony of budgetary rigor and the duty to repay has continued to grow since the Greek crisis, without questioning the neoliberal principles of deregulation, and deregulation of public and private financing systems that led to the first crisis and its effects in Greece. On the contrary, the great bankocratic narrative has gradually been built on the oblivion of the real origin of the crisis. The books of Tooze and Varoufakis can be understood in this respect not only as an alternative narrative, but above all as a counter-narrative of a confiscated story, bringing testimonies of what is happening behind the curtains of power. A counter-history, as Michel Foucault would say, in which the archives of meetings, held in private, have committed the citizens of the euro area to a particular version of the future.

Instead of the genealogy of the Greek crisis as a consequence of the 2008 crisis documented by these two books, the narrative of neoliberal orthodoxy presents the debt of the state as systematically derived from unproductive public expenditure, such as health, education, transport or unemployment insurance, all responsible for budgetary excesses according to this neoliberal dogma. And it is indeed the heart of this dogma that reappears here, in the purest tradition of the normative narrative of economic science as rationality, without alternative for the allocation of resources in a situation of scarcity. What was once financed by the treasury is now suspended from debt to the ECB (Lemoine, 2016). Thus, health, education, infrastructure and social security against the vagaries of life are never conceived as wealth or productive expenditure. On the contrary, fiscal austerity, spending cuts and repayment of public debt without tax increases are among the watchwords of economic health, morality and reliability of debtors.

This narrative borrows from the tradition of fabulists such as Jean de La Fontaine. Thus, the fable of working ants and lazy, spendthrift cicadas was revived in April 2020. After some six years of discussions, the constitutional judges in Karlsruhe rejected the complaints of German Eurosceptics against the ECB's unconventional policy of buying up sovereign securities initiated in 2015. A decision that was intended then to prevent the interest rates of the member countries from diverging excessively, which would have threatened the single currency. The ants of this fable consider that they have maintained the cicadas of the South, forgetting that they could only release surplus value because these cicadas of Europe absorb a good part of the exports of the ants of the North.

The lessons of these fables and counter-narratives are many, but they all highlight a contradiction in the relationship between the ECB and private banks. For the shareholder value of private banks, in the name of which they justify their risk-taking, is in fact guaranteed and supported by the subsidies received by the ECB, which allows them to finance themselves at negative rates, and which gives them total freedom over the use of monetary creation, without forcing them to a real self-assurance of the risks it incurs. When it is the national banks that are challenging the ECB's unconventional measures, such a contradiction proves even more glaring. We saw this in Europe at the beginning of the Covid pandemic, regarding the proposal of "coronabonds" designed to pool the debt of the bailouts contracted to respond to the economic and social consequences of the health crisis. Coronabonds would have added to the ECB's support plan for the European economy, mainly consisting of the public and private debt buyback program launched as early as March 2020 (the Pandemic Emergency Purchase Program, which had enabled states to cope with the health crisis "at whatever the cost"); the quantitative easing program and cheap loans to banks were suspended in March 2022.

The Karlsruhe ruling re-staged the protests of the national bank, the Bundesbank, but also recently the Bank of France. Both in a different way warn of, if not threaten, a necessary return to fiscal austerity, to the imperative to repay the colossal debts granted today by the ECB under the health crisis. Also, the role of the ECB is revealed in its ambivalence. Either the ECB is considered to be indirectly financing the public deficits of member countries through its policy of buying back securities, or it can force states to austerity through a policy of raising rates.

The sight of governments bailing out not only banks but also consumers and mortgage holders has the strange virtue of making the unconventional not only necessary, but strangely normal. From the beginning it has led governments, such as the United Kingdom or Denmark, to cover 75 per cent of the wages of workers who would otherwise be laid off. From crisis to crisis, a new normal is emerging, repudiating the ancient dominant positions' ethical abnormality. The pandemic can therefore be seen as highlighting the crisis management strategies of the global financial crisis. By pushing the reasoning to the limit, it can be said that the economic rationality that supported collective immunization strategies for a time is a matter of a necro-political rationality.

Foucault, and after him Mbembe (2019), used this terminology in the context of neocolonialism and unequal exchange. This vocabulary can be used to consider that structural adjustment programs have long been applied to the

Global South in defense of a crass social Darwinism. This is the other side of the same currency of neoliberal biopolitical rationality. World public opinion will have traveled to the hell of Manaus, in the Amazon, and been able to see what is happening there as in other cities of Brazil due to Covid. Studies from the Centre for Research and Studies of Health Law at the Faculty of Public Health in São Paulo, in collaboration with the non-governmental organization Conectas Direitos Humanos, as well as a study published in the *Lancet*, document precisely the loss of life caused by the refusal to follow the World Health Organization's health management guidelines regarding Covid.[2] It cannot be ignored that these losses affect the poorest, the most insecure and the vulnerable in the first place; can such a reality be better described than by this term of necropolitics? Even if this Foucaultian vocabulary deserves a longer analysis than the space of an article can contain, there is no denying that the pandemic forces us to rethink the very meaning of the economy. And our ancient choir could still consider that Covid has made a radical change in the logic that prevailed until then to the extent that it reversed the priority of economic rationality, since the Global North's countries have shut down economies in the name of public health.

6.   "ONE MORE STEP"

More than the mega-fires that devastated Australia for eight months, more than previous pandemics or heat waves, the Covid pandemic has revealed to the greatest number of people the "unsustainable" nature of industrial development, the ineffectiveness of neo-management applied to public policies in public services (police, justice, health, education) and the widening of inequalities hardly compatible with the dogma of trickle-down economics. To what extent can the neoliberal bankocracy compete with another assessment of the issue of the public debt held by the ECB?

As the Greek tragedy has highlighted, the failure of a state that cannot meet its financial obligations mainly raises the question of the use of the debt granted. The debt of a state can indeed be considered in theory as a solution, since it allows private banks to have the means, through credit, to create access to the liquidity necessary for investments that will free up the growth levers allowing its repayment. Thus, it is the strict ability to repay and how this repayment will take place that is the real issue, more than the debt itself. Therefore, current plans to protect employment and fill consumers with "helicopter money" (a term coined by Milton Friedman in 1969) in order to revive "activity" mark a certain return of the sovereign, but a return proves to be fully compatible with neoliberal dogma. State interventionism can, when necessary, seize the function of LLR (or that of correcting the deviations of pure and perfect competition) as soon as it comes to starting the recovery with a policy of supply and subsidizing financial capital and banks.

It is all about the public debt threshold. The existence of the threshold represents the instrument from which the proponents of budgetary orthodoxy can convince themselves that the solution is on the way to becoming the problem again. Its amount ultimately does not matter. It is enough to brandish it, not to demand reimbursement but to bring back into force the dogma of growth driven by supply. *Exit* the threat that past austerity poses to the financing of the welfare state. *Incipit* the structural reforms of future austerity. Support for the private sector can be equally adorned with green growth appeal or political agreements between environmentalists and neoconservatives, as in Austria.

The billions poured out by the central banks in support of the economy of advanced countries have shown, since the 2008 crisis, that monetary leverage alone is not enough, and that it must be accompanied by budget deficit and public debt policies, indirectly financed by central banks. The mechanism of the European bankocracy is well trodden. Debt-issuing states are indebted to investors in financial markets, and central banks buy back these debt securities, as any investor would. But in reality they keep them, roll them and therefore monetize them, until the states can hypothetically buy them back, which they never do. This support, which currently maintains very low rates, makes it clear that public debt is not the problem as stocks rise without the cost of debt rising. One could recall that the mechanism of infinite debt is precisely what Marx identified as the structure of domination. In the context opened by institutional changes since 2008, infinite debt determines as current common knowledge the actual functioning of the ECB; condemned to pursue unconventional behavior that has become consensual for both heterodox and orthodox economists.

But this consensus is based on the fact that central banks act as normal investors, which they are not. Central banks are not just any investors of any kind, and it is precisely because they are not that their quasi-sovereign power holds yet another characteristic. This feature comes from the structural debt environment. As we have seen, its quasi-sovereign power is exercised diachronically in the environment generated by crises that have made unconventional a new norm. However, the pandemic situation reveals, more than the past crises, how their quasi-sovereignty is exercised on another dimension of debt in its relation to the future. It is in this sense that the situation of the pandemic sheds new light on the relationship between the institution of the Central Bank of Debt and Credit.

The disciplinary dimension of debt, which as we have seen was based on a psychology of fault, has given way to a governmentality through debt, now granted as a valuable bargain. This transformation is not a real novelty. Nietzsche had pointed out in *On the Genealogy of Morality* ([1887] 1994) how the common noun *Schuld* means both "fault" and "debt", and *schuldig* means both "the culprit" and "the debtor". Benveniste ([1969] 1973) also recalls the root of the word "credit" in the Indo-European *Kred* ("belief" and "faith") and Latin *fides*, as in the logic of finance. In this brief etymological overview, the metaphysical dimensions of finance, faith, belief and fault are interwoven. Credit and debt are the two opposite sides of the same link to the future. Memory digs into those who have given their word, and they cannot fail to keep their word without fault. Their story knots their existence between two moments, the past of a promise and the future of its fulfilment. The time determined by the commitment of the given word is opposed to the time of credit opened by the trust received. On the one hand the promise to be fulfilled, on the other the confidence gained via the bet on an expected return. The time of debt anchors the future to the past. It is retroactive, time in arrears to reimbursement. The time of credit is proactive; it directs the indeterminate future towards the open future of investment. In the case of debt, time is productive, since there must be an equivalent and/or higher rendering of the receipt. In the time of credit, indeterminacy represents the risk of the unproductive. In this sense, as Derrida points out, the *Kred* of credit can only open a future of events that are not determined by the past, because it is a gift, without counterpart (Derrida, 1991).

This detour through etymology leads us to a better understanding of the current economic situation. Central banks face an alternative. On the one hand, debt with its positive virtues can only be temporary and a reduction in the stocks of debt issued must be implemented by a pro-growth policy, and therefore for the orthodox people/institutions in favor of a supply-and-trade policy. The use of debt should not be directed towards the unproductive, as this cannot generate profits for the reduction of the debt held by the ECB. The ECB's accommodative securities buyback policy since 2013 defines only by default the fiscal policies of member states. Hypocritically, one might say, since it leaves no choice but to reduce the expenditure, as the Greek tragedy reminded us.

7.   THE PRICE OF MONEY CREATION

On the other hand, there is a challenge on the use of debt by the states and by the ECB, a use that may not converge towards the same objectives; to put it briefly, the "whatever it takes" does not necessarily converge with "quantitative easing for the people". Behind this discrepancy looms the fact that we may not find one single interpretation of what could be a "quantitative easing for the people", the question raised no longer by the use of debt, but by what allows the creation of the debt; that is, money. The ECB can create the currency it needs to buy back sovereign securities. But these securities were first bought and then resold to the ECB. So the money from their purchase seems to exist somewhere. Even so, it is somehow doubled by the operation of monetary creation intended for the purchase. Hence the ECB has the opportunity to cancel this debt (Couppey-Soubeyran, 2020; Scialom, 2020), since the money it creates is not the counterpart of anything due. The monetization of the debt thus represents a gentle way of reducing debt that it would be necessary to push up a notch in order to achieve a complete cancellation. Such an option would remove the threat of a return to the "abnormal" of fiscal austerity and its orientation towards market growth, since the sum of this fiat currency is not borrowed from anyone.

However, as we have seen, monetary creation is also supposed to be a debt, which commits the debtor to the initial gift. Could the ECB be a donor of a gift without counterpart? If it is the credits that make future deposits, it is because they are geared towards productivity meeting a pending economic demand, allowing the re-injecting of remuneration activity and honoring the promise of the original credit: to repay. The ECB's money would thus become a kind of helicopter money, but one can presume it would not be one of the kind that Friedman had in mind in the seventies, since it would transform the link between money, finance and the productive system, as it is the case with social currencies in a Local Exchange Trading System (LETS) (Blanc, 2018) or "ecological money" (Grandjean and Dufrêne, 2020). A currency designed to meet needs that are not those of the accumulative economy, but those of another economy ensuring the needs of the inhabitants of the planet, according to their vital links with their environment. A debt, but a "debt of life" (Théret, 2009), escaping the circulation of capital money by non-market monies.

By pushing the reasoning to the limit, beyond the neo-chartalism perspective of monetary creation, we can assume that these theoretical debates re-examine the place of sovereignty. Heterodox assumptions (of a cancellation of sovereign debt held by the ECB, or that of the helicopter money) have thus fueled other narratives that enlarge the very notion of economy. These measures do not speak for themselves to the neophyte eager to ask why the ECB's pragmatic cancellation of the debts of its state debtors does not lead to the cancellation of the proper functioning of the ECB itself. The alternative that pandemic pressure imposes on the use of debt by the ECB and by the states reveals another dimension of the sovereignty of this quasi-sovereign. The question of the use of debts, which refers as much to the environment of the actors of the bankocracy as to the conjecture of a pandemic capable of bringing the system to a standstill, actually reveals that sovereignty is situated at a different level than that of the institution of the central bank.

The chartalist prospect of cancelling the debts held by the ECB, if not settling the question of the relationship of sovereignty with the ECB, highlights the political power of money, what Aglietta and Orléan call "money as sovereignty", to distinguish it from a sovereignty over money through debt (Aglietta and Orléan, 2002). Sovereignty that is not *over* money, since money does not exist as a treasure, a savings that should be hoarded, manipulated, obstructing the future with no alternative other than this unlivable reproduction of the market order. But money as sovereignty because, far more than a tool, money is a political mediation based on collective intergeneration valuation.

Money can be democratized, as the LETS demonstrates. Pre-capitalist societies also remind us that there is non-capitalist money. Thus, the monetary question is perhaps not an issue to be left to economists alone, because by it we can finally glimpse the horizon that would be a market-debt-free economy. Getting out of the bankocracy is probably today a civilization issue, and the paradox would be to get away with money itself.

NOTES

1. These figures, and these rates, have been widely debated and contested. They contribute to the dramatization of indebtedness in order to discipline debtors. See *L'Express*, "Les Etats européens ont versé 1600 milliards d'euros d'aides aux banques depuis la crise", 2012, https://lexpansion.lexpress.fr/actualite -economique/les-etats-europeens-ont-verse-1600-milliards-d-euros-d-aides-aux -banques-depuis-la-crise_1324825.html.
2. See the website www.conectas.org/quem-somos.

REFERENCES

Aglietta, M., and A. Orléan (1998), *La Monnaie Souveraine*. Paris: Odile Jacob.
Aglietta, M., and A. Orléan (2002), *La Monnaie entre violence et confiance*. Paris: Odile Jacob.
Aglietta, M., Ould Ahmed, P., and J.F. Ponsot (2018), *Money: 5000 Years of Debt and Power*. London: Verso.
Avgouleas, E. (2020). "COVID-19 exposes the limits of debt-driven capitalism, writes Emilios Avgouleas". University of Edinburgh. https://blogs.ed.ac.uk/ covid19perspectives/2020/05/26/covid-19-exposes-the-limits-of-debt-driven -capitalism-writes-emilios-avgouleas/.
Balibar, E. (2020), Lecture, London Critical Theory Summer School 2020 Virtual Programme, Institute for the Humanities, Birkbeck College, London.
Benveniste, E. (1969) 1973, *Indo-European Language and Society*, trans. E. Palmer. Coral Gables, FL: University of Miami Press.
Blanc, J. (2018), "Making sense of the plurality of money: a Polanyian attempt". In G.M. Gomez (ed.), *Monetary Plurality in Local, Regional and Global Economies*. London: Routledge, pp. 48–66.
Blanc, J., Alary, P., Desmedt, L., and B. Théret (2020), *Institutionalist Theories of Money: An Anthology of the French School*. Cham: Palgrave Macmillan (ebook), Springer Nature.
Bourguinat, H. (1987), *Les Vertiges de la Finance Internationale*. Paris: Economica.

Couppey-Soubeyran, J. (2020). "L'annulation de la dette publique détenue par la BCE libérerait les acteurs économiques de la crainte d'une future augmentation d'impôts". http://jezabel-couppey-soubeyran.fr/img/book/Le_Monde_dette.pdf.

Crouch, C. (2009), "Privatised Keynesianism: an unacknowledged policy regime". *British Journal of Politics and International Relations*, 11 (3), 382–399.

Cuillerai, M. (2018), "Peuples endettés". In J. Christ and S. Gilads (eds), *La dette souveraine. Economie politique et Etat*. Paris: Éditions de l'EHESS, pp. 231–249.

Derrida, J. (1991), *Donner le temps I. La Fausse Monnaie*. Paris: Galilée.

Gago, V. (2017), *Neoliberalism from Below: Popular Pragmatics and Baroque Economies*. Durham, NC: Duke University Press.

Gramsci, A. (1929–1935), *Selections from the Prison Notebooks of Antonio Gramsci*. Translated by Q. Hoare and G. Nowell Smith. London: Lawrence and Wishart.

Grandjean, A., and N. Dufrêne (2020), *Une Monnaie Ecologique pour Sauver la Planète*. Paris: Odile Jacob.

Lazzarato, M. (2011), La Fabrique de l'Homme Endetté: Essai sur la Condition Néolibérale. Paris: Éditions Amsterdam.

Lemoine, B. (2016), *L'Ordre de la Dette. Enquête sur les Infortunes de l'Etat et la Prospérité du Marché*. Paris: La Découverte.

Marazzi, C. (2013), *The Violence of Financial Capitalism*. Cambridge, MA: MIT Press.

Marx, K. (1972), *The Class Struggles in France 1848 to 1850*. Moscow: Progress Publishers.

Mbembe, A. (2019), *Necropolotics*. Durham, NC: Duke University Press.

Nietzsche, F. (1887) 1994, *On the Genealogy of Morality: A Polemic*, trans. C. Diethe, ed. Keith Ansell-Pearson. Cambridge: Cambridge University Press.

Schmitt, C. (1938) 1992, "Du rapport entre les concepts de guerre et d'ennemi", in *La notion de politique*, trans. M.-L. Steinhauser. Paris: Flammarion.

Scialom, L. (2020), "Nous avons collectivement perdu la main sur la politique monétaire". *Alternatives économiques*, 143 (7).

Sterdyniak, H. (2015), "La dette publique comme produit du capitalism". *Regards croisés sur l'économie*, 2 (17), 173–186.

Streeck, W. (2014), Du temps sans cesse ajournée du capitalisme démocratique. Paris: Gallimard.

Théret, B. (2009), "Monnaie et dette de vie". *L'Homme*, 2 (190), 153–179.

Tooze, A. (2018), *Crashed: How a Decade of Financial Crises Changed the World*. New York, NY: Viking.

Varoufakis, Y. (2017), *Adults in the Room: My Battle with Europe's Deep Establishment*. London: Bodley Head.

5. Central banking and inequalities: old tropes and new practices

François Claveau, Clément Fontan, Peter Dietsch and Jérémie Dion

1. INTRODUCTION

In the years following the financial crisis of 2007, central banks earned the reputation of being "the only game in town" in macroeconomic policy (El-Erian, 2017). Faced with the risk of financial market collapse, they turned to unconventional monetary policies such as quantitative easing (QE) to weather the storm. They justified their actions by stating that extraordinary times required extraordinary measures.

When the COVID-19 crisis became a pandemic in March 2020, central banks quickly reverted to their 2007 playbook and even doubled down on it. They launched large stimulus programmes to keep the economy afloat during extended lockdowns and periods of both suppressed demand and breakdowns of international supply chains. Their balance sheets swelled once again, as shown in Figure 5.1 for the Bank of Canada (BoC) and the US Federal Reserve (Fed). Looking back over the last 15 years, the extraordinary has become the norm (Best, 2018).

The unconventional monetary policy instruments used over this period have unintended side-effects. In particular, they affect the distribution of income and wealth in society through a variety of channels. Since unelected officials such as central bankers are not supposed to make deeply political decisions (Tucker, 2018), they have come under increasing public pressure to justify their policies in light of these distributive consequences.

This chapter presents a critical analysis of the stance taken on inequality by two central banks since 2015: the BoC and the Fed.[1] The analysis is informed by a computer-assisted discourse analysis of how central bankers from the two institutions position themselves when it comes to issues of inequality. Can the stances taken by BoC and Fed officials be justified from a normative perspective? In other words, do they stand up to scrutiny when evaluated not just within the narrow confines of central bank mandates, but from a broader

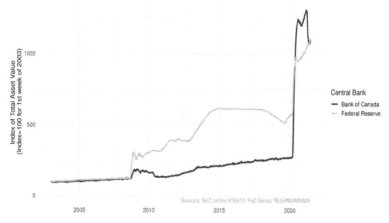

Source: The authors.

Figure 5.1   *Total asset value of two central banks indexed at their early-2003 levels*

perspective that sees central banks as one cog in the institutional wheels of societies that pursue a number of sometimes conflicting objectives?

We use this analysis to make one observation and present one argument. We observe that the position on inequality of the two central banks has changed in recent years and continues to do so. We argue that the stance on inequality taken by the BoC and the Fed suffers from a number of both inconsistencies and shortcomings. Most importantly, their unprecedented actions during the COVID-19 crisis belie the old trope that they cannot contribute to fight inequality because their tools are too blunt.

The methodological details of our computer-assisted discourse analysis are in a web appendix on Zenodo,[2] where we describe, justify, and share our code and our corpus (1,494 documents from the Fed and 646 from the BoC). The chapter thus focuses on the substance of our analysis. In the next section we provide a short primer on central banks and inequality to situate the argument of the chapter in the conceptual landscape. The two main sections of the chapter focus on the inter-crisis period (2015–2020) and the COVID-19 response respectively. The former is structured around three questions: Why care about inequality? Do central bank actions impact inequality? Should central banks fight inequality? In the section covering the COVID-19 crisis, we highlight a stark tension. On the one hand, the BoC and the Fed claim that monetary policy instruments are too blunt to target specific sectors of the economy. On the other hand, with their response to COVID-19, they have demonstrated that such targeting is possible after all.

2.   CENTRAL BANKS AND INEQUALITIES: A CONCEPTUAL PRIMER

Central bank actions and socio-economic inequalities connect in several different ways. To avoid confusion, it is key to distinguish some of these connections up front. The distinctions drawn here will underpin the structure of our analysis throughout the chapter.

First, it is surprisingly untrivial to point out that central bank actions and socio-economic inequalities *do* in fact connect. One of the most persistent myths in scholarship on money has been the idea that money constitutes a mere veil, and that it does not affect the real economy – including inequality – in the long run (e.g., Ingham, 2020). Among the more recent defenders of this position were the monetarists of the late 20th century led by Milton Friedman. Let us call the debate about the neutrality of money the "old" debate concerning the link between central bank actions and inequality.

Even though the idea that money is neutral is intellectually dead and not borne out by the facts (Tobin, 1972; Blanchard and Summers, 1992; Minsky, 1993; Ingham, 2004), it still has a surprising grip on some scholars and policy makers.[3] Incidentally, if money was in fact neutral, it would be hard to find proper justifications for the radical interventions of other central banks in the economy since the Global Financial Crisis (GFC) over the last 15 years (Rochon and Yinka Olawoye, 2012). This acts as a distraction and obscures from view what one might call the "new" debate on the link between central bank actions and inequality. It is this new debate that lies at the heart of this chapter.

We distinguish three facets of this debate that will structure our discussion below.[4]

First, why do we or should we care about socio-economic inequality? Anyone, including central bankers, might care about inequality for two reasons. On the one hand, the reason can be instrumental. To the extent that inequality undermines the attainment of an objective one has, one should care about the reduction of inequality as a means to this end. For instance, central bankers should care about inequality to the extent it undermines their mandate (typically, price stability and financial stability). On the other hand, inequality matters not only for instrumental reasons, but in its own right. As we shall see, the position of central bankers on inequality as an intrinsic bad has evolved since the financial crisis and continues to do so.

The second facet of the debate is whether central bank actions themselves exacerbate inequality. As we shall see, the unconventional monetary policies employed by central banks since 2008 have been criticized for their unintended negative side-effects on inequality. Is this criticism justified?

Finally, independently of whether or not monetary policy has distributive effects, the third facet focuses on the question whether central banks should play a role in fighting inequality. Once we recognize the potential of money as a "social technology" (e.g., Ingham, 2020, p. 7; Hockett and James, 2020), then how can central banks justify not tapping into this potential more actively? The three facets just sketched overlap both in theory and in practice. However, they still prove useful in exploring different levels of engagement by central banks when it comes to the issue of inequality.

3.   THE INTER-CRISIS PERIOD (2015–2020)

Between the two crises, the Fed and the BoC intensified their analysis of income and wealth distribution. On the one hand, the two central banks engaged with a wide range of economic actors to have a better understanding of the distributive dynamics during the economic recovery. On the other hand, they augmented their research activities on the distributive consequences of conventional and unconventional monetary policies. Some of their analysis was performed in the context of reviews of the banks' respective policy frameworks. Since 2001, the BoC has completed a review of its inflation-targeting framework every five years, culminating in a renewal of its mandate with the Government of Canada. Following the completion of one of its reviews in 2016, the BoC launched its "Toward 2021" initiative in 2017, laying the groundwork for the 2021 renewal of its mandate.[5] The BoC's latest review included research activities as well as numerous outreach activities in the form of workshops, surveys, and focus groups. Similarly, the Fed engaged in 2019 in the first-ever public review of its monetary policy framework. Dubbed "Fed Listens," it included 19 dedicated meetings with a wide range of stakeholders, a related research agenda, and a discussion of the outcome of the review among policymakers. These activities were conducive to move the issue of inequality up the agenda at both central banks. In this section, we study whether and how the discourse on inequality from representatives of our two central banks changed prior to the onset of the COVID-19 crisis. We show that, despite a richer engagement with distributive considerations than in the previous years, central bankers still used questionable tropes.

4.   WHY CARE ABOUT INEQUALITY?

As we have shown in previous work (Fontan et al., 2016), central bankers have generally recognized the *instrumental* importance of taking inequality seriously, and at least some of them signal that some forms of inequality – e.g., inequality of opportunity for the Fed – are intrinsically bad. Back in 2007, Ben Bernanke from the Fed summarized these two kinds of reasons: "Equality of economic opportunity appeals to our sense of fairness [intrinsic reason], certainly, but it also strengthens our economy [instrumental reason]."[6]

At the BoC, Carolyn Wilkins elaborated in 2017 on the idea that inequality should be a concern of central bankers for *instrumental* reasons. According to her, more income inequality could lead to more "financial instability" and "alter the channels through which monetary policy actions affect the economy."[7] It follows from these considerations that, even in the confines of their current mandates, central banks should instrumentally care about inequality. Indeed, if inequality threatens one of their mandated goals – e.g., financial stability – or if it weakens their capacity to accomplish their mandate by disrupting the channels through which they affect the economy, it will be relevant for monetary policy decisions.

Another indicator that central banks care about inequality is the extent to which they monitor and discuss distributive dynamics. From Figure 5.2 we can see that the Fed signals this kind of concern with inequality more frequently than the BoC. Indeed, since 2008 the proportion of paragraphs in speeches with at least one of our keywords is systematically higher for Fed than for BoC

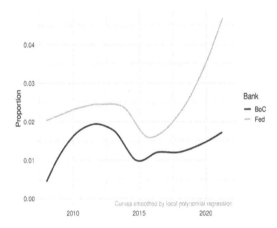

Source: The authors.

Figure 5.2   *Proportion of paragraphs on inequality or poverty in speeches since 2008. Paragraphs are identified as discussing these themes based on the presence of one of our terms related to inequality and poverty (see the technical appendix on Zenodo for the list of terms; endnote 2)*

officials. Furthermore, we see that, after a trough in 2015–2016, Fed officials have spoken more frequently about the topic in the late inter-crisis period while BoC officials have been slightly more outspoken only since the onset of the COVID-19 crisis.

During this period, central bankers sometimes continue to frame inequality in terms typical of the 20th century: "You know, the stagnation of middle-class incomes, the relatively low mobility that we have, the disappointing level of wages over a long period of time, it is all of a piece."[8] The implicit representation of how society is structured here is between levels of income (middle-class and upper-class, with a limited mobility from one to the other) and sources of income (wage earners versus employers or investors).

Yet, another frame has gained prominence in the period, foremost in the United States: inequality as concerning the relationship of some social or ethnic groups and communities with the rest of society. As Figure 5.3 shows, central bankers at the Fed and to a lesser extent at the BoC have been increasingly outspoken about concerns for women, for poor neighborhoods, and especially for minority communities (African Americans, Native Americans, Hispanics). One way to characterize this shift is to say that the emphasis in concern with socio-economic inequalities has shifted from a primary concern

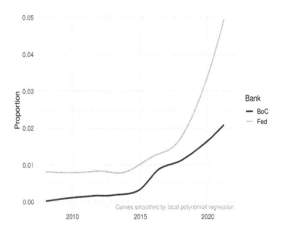

Source: The authors.

Figure 5.3   *Proportion of paragraphs mentioning women, minorities, or inclusion in speeches since 2008. Paragraphs are identified as discussing these themes based on the presence of at least one keyword (see the technical appendix on Zenodo for the regular expression used; endnote 2)*

with the *economic* dimension and the distribution of resources to various aspects of the *social* dimension that structure the economic dimension, such as race or gender.[9]

This increasing importance of "inclusive growth" in the discourse of central bankers is partly due to them being pressed by elected officials and activists on the issue. For instance, Janet Yellen of the Fed replies in 2016 to Congress members that "there are subgroups of the population who experience lower income and more distress in the labor market" and "there remains so much distress among African Americans."[10] On the activist front, the Fed Up campaign,[11] started in 2014, questioned the Fed on issues of inequality, diversity, and inclusion and led to a meeting at Jackson Hole on 25 August 2016 between activists and Fed officials.[12] During the Jackson Hole meeting, Fed officials endorsed the campaigners' concerns in strong terms. Regarding the US economy, Neil Kashkari from the Minneapolis Fed maintained: "[W]e want this economy to work for every single American, every single one."[13] And Loretta Mester from the Cleveland Fed added: "[W]e're Federal Reserve people, but we're citizens of the United States, and we want the United States to be – right? – the best it can be for all its people."[14]

During the same Jackson Hole meeting in 2016, Fed officials promised to ramp up research on economically marginalized communities and to have more regular meetings with organizations serving these communities. They have followed up on these promises. In March 2017, at the National Community Reinvestment Coalition, which aims to direct credit towards "low- and moderate-income neighborhoods," Yellen recognized that "while the job market for the United States as a whole has improved markedly since the depths of the financial crisis, (there is a) persistently higher unemployment rate in lower-income and minority communities."[15] Most significantly, the Fed Listens initiative in 2019 involved many meetings discussing concerns relating to inequality, diversity, and inclusion. Richard Clarida recounts some of the encounters: "In Dallas, we heard from local leaders about the challenges facing lower-income communities. In Minneapolis, we listened to researchers discuss the distributional consequences of the economic cycle and of monetary policy."[16]

In sum, from 2015 to 2020, central bankers have recycled some usual tropes about why inequality should be a concern, but their discourse has also shifted on this issue, especially so at the Fed. First, Fed officials have discussed the topic more frequently since 2016. Second, the Fed has significantly ramped up research on how marginalized groups and communities are affected by inequality. One potential explanation of the difference in discourse and research emphasis on this issue compared to the BoC lies in the dual mandate of the Fed. As Wilkins of the BoC puts it (2018), "Canada's framework is less definitive about the importance of employment and labour market conditions in determining the appropriate path for interest rates." Another potential explanation is the centrality of race to US politics. Yet, we will see that the BoC has been in catch-up mode on this issue during the COVID-19 crisis.

5. DO CENTRAL BANK ACTIONS IMPACT INEQUALITY?

For central bankers, it is one thing to say that they care about inequality, but quite another to say that their actions have impacted inequality in the past or could deliberately impact it in the future. We will see in this section and the next how their discourse on these two dimensions has evolved in conflicting directions during the inter-crisis period.

Although QE and other tools have been in the central bank toolbox for more than a decade now, the distinction between conventional and "extraordinary" measures is still used in the context of discussing the distributive impact of monetary policy. We will thus use it to structure this section.

The "conventional" tool of central banks is short-term interest-rate-setting through open-market operations on a limited class of assets (typically, sovereign bonds). Unconventional monetary policy mostly refers to QE; i.e., the purchase of assets on financial markets with newly created central bank reserves. When asked about the distributive impact of conventional monetary policy, central bankers have various answers that do not sit well together.

First, Wilkins from the BoC resurrects the idea that an alleged neutrality of money implies that monetary policy cannot affect a structural property such as inequality: "monetary policy – which is neutral in the long run – cannot fix structural problems."[17] Second, and in a move difficult to square with Wilkins' claim about money neutrality, in its 2016 policy review the BoC provided an estimate of the redistributive impact of increasing its inflation target from 2 percent to 3 percent (Bank of Canada, 2016, Box 4; see also Amano et al., 2017). The estimated effects vary between −2.69 percent and +1.14 percent of net wealth across wealth and age groups and thus clearly show that, according to the BoC's own models, the choice of monetary policy does have distributional consequences.[18] Furthermore, it indicates that the overall distributional impact of a monetary policy is a composite effect of changes affecting different groups in opposite directions. It is thus not a question that can be answered easily by pointing to one factor.

Yet, and this is their third typical reply, central bankers tend to quickly brush aside the question by pointing to a factor that puts them in a good light. For instance, Fed officials like to point to their goal of maximum employment as being good for the poor, and they draw invalid conclusions on that basis: "No, we don't think monetary policy is exacerbating inequality. We think, in fact, it is helping those who didn't have jobs get jobs."[19] The dynamic is not necessarily that simple: even if some jobs are created, inequality can still go up if the well-off get a disproportionate part of the newly baked pie.

In sum, central bankers seem to think that the distributional effects of conventional monetary policy are barely worth discussing. By contrast, in our previous analysis for the period between 2007 and 2015 (Fontan et al., 2016, pp. 333–335), we found that many central bankers were more concerned about the unequal impacts of their actions when it came to *unconventional* monetary policy. Based on early research (e.g., Bank of England, 2012; Coibion et al., 2012), central bankers maintained that, although QE had adverse distributive effects, the extraordinary situation of the GFC implied that these unintended side-effects had to be tolerated.

Since 2015, the position of central bankers on the distributive effects of QE has been informed by new research on the topic by central bank staff and academic economists. We expose several reasons to worry about some strands of this research and its uses by central bank officials.[20]

According to a review of this literature, two main channels with opposite effects explain why some models conclude that QE increases economic inequality while other models conclude the opposite (Colciago et al., 2019). In the case of income distribution, the main "direct" effect of QE is to increase the value of financial assets, which exacerbates inequality as these assets are disproportionately owned by the wealthy. However, there is also a significant "indirect" effect, reducing inequality by stimulating the economy: an expansionary monetary policy reduces unemployment and stimulates wages, which mainly benefits the less privileged. The relative impact of these two channels on wealth distribution depends on the distribution and composition of household assets and debts.

A recent article has found that central banks, in their own research, tend to measure stronger *indirect* effects of QE compared to studies conducted by independent academics, which implies that they tend to find that unconventional monetary policy helps to decrease inequality more than other researchers do (Fabo et al., 2021). What could explain this difference? The distinction between "direct" and "indirect" effect indicates that one is easier to measure than the other. Direct effects involve the increase in the value of financial assets, a phenomenon that nobody disputes, central bankers included. Indirect effects are about stimulating the economy. Here the attribution of responsibility to monetary policy is much more difficult.

Moreover, the measures of inequality used in the monetary economics literature probably do not correspond to what one would want to call more or less unequal distributions. Take the left-hand panel of Figure 5.4, which is a reproduction from an influential European Central Bank (ECB) study (Ampudia et al., 2018: Figure 4). It reports the results of a simulation of the impact of ECB policies on the distribution of wealth (similar results for income

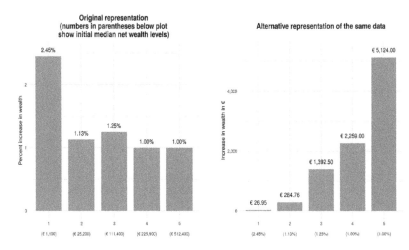

Source: Data and original plot from Ampudia et al. (2018).

Figure 5.4   *Two representations of the alleged effects of the ECB Asset Purchase Programme on the median net wealth by wealth quintile*

can be found in Lenza and Slacalek, 2018: Figure 8). According to the authors, these results should lead us to conclude that the ECB's actions have reduced wealth inequality. The percentage representation hides a huge disparity in growth in monetary values as demonstrated by the right-hand panel in Figure 5.4, which represents the *same* data in a different way: 2.5 percent of €1,100 does not even correspond to an increase of €30 for the bottom quintile, while the median wealth of the top quintile increases by over €5,000! Although this simulated increase is associated with a slight decrease in the Gini index, it does not seem appropriate to celebrate it as a contribution to the decrease in income inequality.

Another weakness of the literature on the distributive effects of monetary policy is the lack of precision as to which counterfactual scenario is considered (Bivens, 2015). Indeed, any causal claim implies a counterfactual scenario: a given monetary policy will have unequal effects *compared to* another policy. For example, one may ask what the effect of the Fed's QE on income distribution was compared to a policy limited to keeping the policy rate as close to zero as possible; that is, a policy that refrained from unconventional measures. The assessment of the distributive effect will not, however, be the same if the counterfactual scenario includes alternative policy measures, such as the substitution of monetary action by a fiscal stimulus or the use of helicopter money[21] instead of QE. In general, the literature assumes the first type of counterfactual scenario (i.e., a scenario of "no policy intervention" rather than "alternative policy intervention"). It thus misleads us to think that we cannot have the positive "indirect" effects without the negative "direct" effects.

All of these considerations imply the need for a nuanced interpretation of where the evidence stands on the issue of the distributive effects of QE. Yet, central bankers at the Fed and the BoC tend to deflect attention to other potential causes of inequalities when their policies – extraordinary or not – are under scrutiny. Back in 2012, then Senior Deputy Governor Tiff Macklem from the BoC asserted that reducing inequality "is a complex subject involving a broad range of factors and the full array of policy frameworks, including education, health, openness to trade, foreign investment, financial development, and fiscal, labour market and environmental policies."[22] The discourse is similar at the Fed with Yellen maintaining that causes of rising inequality are shifts in demand for workers with "higher education and a more versatile skill-set, [...] changes in the minimum wage, declining unionization and executive compensation practices,"[23] while Jerome Powell, Chairman of the Fed's Board, later added "low mobility," declining "labor force participation among prime-age males," and the "opioid crisis."[24] While central bankers are certainly right in pointing out that there are multiple causes underpinning rising inequality, their position that monetary policy is not among them rests on shaky foundations.

6.   SHOULD CENTRAL BANKS FIGHT INEQUALITY?

This last line of reply to the question of whether monetary policy causes inequality is used by central bankers to deflect the next question, about who should address inequality:

> [Rising inequality] unfortunately reflect[s] structural challenges that lie substantially beyond the reach of monetary policy. Monetary policy cannot, for instance, generate technological breakthroughs or affect demographic factors that would boost real GDP [gross domestic product] growth over the longer run or address the root causes of income inequality. And monetary policy cannot improve the productivity of American workers. Fiscal and regulatory policies – which are of course the responsibility of the Administration and the Congress – are best suited to address such adverse structural trends.[25]

The most common position of Fed and BoC central bankers from 2015 to 2020 was thus that fighting inequality was best left to other institutions. The reasons that we highlighted in our analysis of the previous period (Fontan et al., 2016, pp. 340–345) are voiced again. Most importantly, central bankers claim that their tools are too blunt. They allegedly "don't have tools in monetary policy to target particular groups."[26] Although it might have been somewhat plausible in the early 2000s, this claim seems quite a stretch now, especially since the creative response to the COVID-19 pandemic (see the next section). But, even during the inter-crisis period, the claim that monetary policy is too blunt was in tension with other parts of the discourse of central bankers.

Recall that, in the context of reviewing its monetary framework for the 2016 mandate renewal, the BoC studied the "Redistributive Effects of the Transition to a Higher Inflation Target" (Bank of Canada, 2016, Box 4). Inflation-targeting through "conventional" monetary policy is the bluntest arrow in the central banker's quiver. Yet, if we are to believe this study, there are measurable distributive effects of a change of the inflation target. There is a potential to affect inequality, but the BoC's reasoning suggests that it is not seriously interested in exploring this potential.

Instead of thoroughly analyzing the issue, the BoC's study takes a shortcut to conclude that the status quo – i.e., its 2 percent inflation target – is preferable. More precisely, the BoC claims raising the inflation target would be a bad idea because the number of households that would experience net losses in net worth as a result would be bigger than the number of households experiencing gains.[27] This conclusion relies on a highly controversial normative criterion. What normative theory on income and wealth inequality assesses policy proposals by appealing to the *number* of households positively or negatively affected? Standard approaches tend to appeal either to a *utilitarian* criterion – maximize the well-being of the greatest number – or to a *maximin* criterion: maximize the position of the least advantaged (Rawls, 1999). Incidentally, note that on the maximin criterion, the BoC's data may well lead to the opposite conclusion from that presented by the BoC, because the households that would benefit from a rise in the inflation target are poorer, younger households (see Bank of Canada, 2016, Table 4-C). What can we learn from this BoC study? First, even conventional monetary policy is not necessarily too blunt to affect inequality. Second, the BoC needs to refine its position on what kind of inequality matters, and why.

As to the Fed, the key question is to what extent its push for inclusive growth, visible in both its discourse and research during the inter-crisis period, translated into any willingness to do something about inequality. In other words, did "Fed Listens" lead to "Fed Acts" when it comes to inequality, and to a recognition that monetary policy tools may not be too blunt after all?

There are three elements to answering this question. First, Fed officials emphasized the synergies between expansionary monetary policy and promoting inclusive growth. For example, the outcome of the latest policy review by the Fed was to revise and restate the objective of "maximum employment [as] a broad-based and inclusive goal [which] reflects our appreciation for the benefits of a strong labor market, particularly for many in low- and moderate-income communities."[28] In this sense, the Fed acts on inequality in virtue of its mandate. Second, there was a recognition that there are not just synergies between monetary policy and inequality, but also tensions: "Research on the drivers of disparities in labor market outcomes can also help the Federal Reserve better assess potential tradeoffs in monetary policy."[29] Third, and finally, the emphasis on inclusive growth and on the indirect effects of monetary policy on inequality detracted attention from the direct effects of its actions on rising asset prices (see previous section) and policy alternatives. On this subject, the Fed was not listening.

In sum, the analysis of the Fed and the BoC discourse and research on the links between monetary policy and inequality in the inter-crisis period presents us with a paradox. Both central banks acknowledged that inequality is a concern, and recognized the uneven nature of economic cycles. They intensified their research on the distributional dimension of monetary policy with, in the Fed's case, a particular emphasis on the notion of inclusive growth and its capacity to help promote this goal. However, and here lies the paradox, this increased engagement did not translate into an intellectual shift on the links between monetary policy and inequality. Rather, central bankers kept on repeating the arguments that were already put forward by Ben Bernanke before the GFC: the causes for inequality are mostly found in structural factors, and the best that central bankers can do to address the issue is to achieve their traditional monetary goals (Fontan et al., 2016). This position was reinforced by central bank research on QE programmes, which found them to contribute to inequality reduction, but suffered from obvious methodological limitations.

7.   AMBIVALENCE DURING THE COVID CRISIS

The lockdowns implemented to shelter the population from the spread of COVID-19 put intense pressures on the economy as millions of workers faced the threat of job cuts and unemployment. In addition, financial markets gave worrying signs of impending collapse in March 2020 as investors were adjusting to the pessimistic forecasts for the real economy. Against this background, the COVID-19 responses of both the Fed and the BoC have ventured into uncharted waters with the implementation of new unconventional measures (cf. Table 5.1). As we shall see in this section, these actions hold interesting lessons about the willingness and capacity of central banks to affect economic inequality. More specifically, they reveal a tension between the capacity of central bank actions to target specific sectors of the economy on the one hand, and their simultaneous affirmation that this is something they are unable to do on the other hand.

When the economic repercussions of the COVID-19 crisis hit in spring 2020, it became clear very quickly that they would be felt very unevenly by different parts of the population. For example, the risk of unemployment was higher among low-income groups, whereas members of privileged groups were both less likely to lose their job and more likely to be able to shift to virtual work. Central banks were keenly aware of these asymmetries. Powell of the Fed underlined in June 2020 that "low-income households have experienced, by far, the sharpest drop in employment, while job losses of African Americans, Hispanics, and women have been greater than that of other groups. If not contained and reversed, the downturn could further widen gaps in economic well-being."[30]

This sensibility to the hardship faced by disadvantaged groups is now also echoed by the BoC. Governor Macklem stated in the spring of 2021 that:

> This pandemic has had very unequal effects on Canadians. It has particularly affected low-income workers, women, racialized Canadians, new immigrants, youth. So we can't just look at the aggregates. We've got to look under the hood, we've got to look at things on a more disaggregated level.[31]

Another indication that the BoC has recently taken the turn to caring about inequality in terms of marginalized groups and communities is the recent launch of the international Central Bank Network for Indigenous Inclusion,[32] of which the BoC is a founding member.

The observation that the COVID-19 crisis was exacerbating the disadvantageous position of certain groups affected the response of central banks. Recall that during the GFC, the Fed had acted as a "market-maker of last resort" by setting up repurchase facilities (the Primary Dealer Credit Facility, or PDCF; Money Market Mutual Fund Liquidity Facility; Commercial Paper Funding Facility, or CPFF; Term Asset-Backed Securities Loan Facility, or TALF) in order to stabilize problematic market segments, such as derivatives and securitized products (Mehrling, 2011). On 17–18 March 2021, the Fed reactivated three of these facilities to stabilize money markets and to prevent a liquidity crisis. Then, on 23 March and 9 April, the Fed opened up its facilities to a range of brand-new economic players, including corporations, community banks providing loans to small firms, and municipal and state authorities.

In the same vein, the BoC implemented for the first time in its history a QE programme by purchasing federal bonds. It also launched the Bankers' Acceptance Purchase Facility (BAPF), which supported lending to small and medium-sized enterprises; the Provincial Money Market Purchase Program (PMMP), where the BoC purchased provincial debt on the primary market, thus directly financing government expenditure; and the Standing Term Liquidity Facility (STLF), which helped commercial banks manage their liquidity risks while "provid[ing] loans to households and businesses when they need it most."[33]

Table 5.1   *The COVID-19 lending facilities of the Fed and the BoC*
                 (maximum outstanding amount allotted on 31 May 2021)

Federal Reserve	Fed (US $)	BoC (Can $)	Bank of Canada
Corporate Credit Facilities (ended 31 December 2020)	13,757,437,107	220,000,000	Corporate Bond Purchase Program (ended 25 May 2021)
Term Asset-Backed Securities Loan Facility (ended 31 December 2020)	1,733,270,661	2,993,000,000	Commercial Paper Purchase Program (ended April 2021)
Municipal Liquidity Facility (ended 31 December 2020)	5,508,000,000	19,018,000,000	Provincial Bond Purchase Program (ended 6 May 2021)
Main Street Lending Program (ended 8 January 2021)	16,281,636,338	7,629,000,000	PMMP (ended 16 June 2021)
Paycheck Protection Program Liquidity Facility (ended 30 July 2021)	84,226,254,222	38,766,000,000	BAPF (ended November 2021)

Sources: www.federalreserve.gov/econres/feds/files/2021035pap.pdf; www.bankofcanada.ca/2021/06/bank-canada-publishes-transaction-level-data-discontinued-asset-purchase-programs.

What is noteworthy about these respective policy responses is that they explicitly and intentionally target specific sectors of the economy. This approach stands in marked contrast with central bank interventions prior to the COVID-19 crisis, and operates through two different channels. First, a direct channel through which the central bank funnels liquidity directly to a variety of economic actors; for example, the Fed implemented the Paycheck Protection Program (PPP), which was aimed at providing "critical support to small businesses" and to specific communities that are often beyond the reach of conventional monetary policy. Speaking in front of representatives of community banks, Lael Brainard of the Fed acknowledged that "Your firsthand experiences of working with minority borrowers and your knowledge of local communities make you essential partners in better targeting our tools to assist low-income and minority small businesses and communities."[34] In other words, the Fed carefully set up its liquidity facilities to make sure that its credit lines would be accessible to a very wide range of economic actors, especially those lending to the minorities that were the most affected by the crisis. Similarly, the Fed's Main Street lending program targeted "medium-sized companies and smaller companies that sort of fall between the PPP program and the corporate credit facilities [and] we had to create standardized products that would meet the needs of as broad as possible a range of companies." In fact, this program was able to reach very specific economic players, including "small and medium-sized nonprofit organizations, such as hospitals and universities."[35] Interestingly, Powell went out of his way to underscore the unusual character of these programs. Powell underlined that the Fed was in a good position because it has "very specific powers, which are lending powers [...] that we have used to a completely unprecedented extent here." Indeed, by creating specific facilities for specific kind of borrowers, the Fed "worked hard" to respect the "maximum employment" objective of its double mandate because "it's not so simple (to reach) Main Street" with regular monetary tools (Powell, 2020).

The BoC created similarly targeted programs to ensure continued direct access to liquidity for businesses and households with its BAPF, the STLF, and the Canada Mortgage Bond Purchase Program. Once again, these tools provided localized access to liquidity that conventional monetary policy instruments are unable to provide. Because they are tailored to the needs of those most adversely affected by the COVID-19 crisis, the Fed's and the BoC's policies have arguably helped to contain inequality.

The second channel through which central banks have injected liquidity in response to the COVID-19 crisis is by boosting public finances at different levels of government. Not only did they use QE – for the first time in the BoC's case – to buy government bonds on secondary markets, but some of their new programs broke the taboo against direct government financing through the purchase of bonds on primary markets (Turner, 2016, chapter 14).[36] Both the Fed's Municipal Liquidity Facility and the BoC's PMMP directly bought both state/provincial and municipal bonds. To the extent that the different levels of governments used these funds for measures designed to mitigate the K-shaped recovery,[37] the central banks contributed to containing inequality through this channel, too.

In sum, in response to the COVID-19 crisis, both the Fed and the BoC have taken measures to cushion the inegalitarian fallout from the crisis. Two caveats should be added here. First, many of these measures were temporary and discontinued within 12 months of the onset of the crisis. Second, the lending rate attached to these facilities was "based on a rate that is a premium to normal market," the Fed's justification for this premium being that the central bank should act as "a backstop lender (and) not as a first stop that replaces private capital" (Hiteshew, 2020). These specific settings explain why most of these facilities were actually not used much by the economic players,[38] with the exception of the PPP. These two caveats notwithstanding, the measures clearly demonstrate that unconventional monetary policy *can* target specific economic sectors or subgroups of the population.

In stark contrast with these actions as well as with some of the justifications provided for them, representatives from both central banks have recently gone out of their way to reaffirm old discursive tropes about the alleged bluntness of monetary policy and its *in*capacity to target specific economic sectors. For instance, when asked by a member of Congress about what the Fed could do to help African American communities in the midst of the pandemic, Powell acknowledged first that, despite the new Fed facilities, "there are persistent [employment] gaps and they are very troubling." However, he then went on to say:

> [These gaps] are not, in the long run, something that monetary policy can address. It really is up to other policies, by governments, State and local governments, the Federal Government, and frankly businesses, to do what they can to close that gap. What we have is an interest rate tool, and what we can do is support the goals you have given us: maximum employment; and stable prices. We see positive effects from that. But over the longer run, broader policies of education and other things would help with that issue.[39]

The BoC policymakers expressed a similar degree of unease when providing a rationale for their new facilities. On the one hand, when speaking to the considerations that enter the choice of a monetary policy framework, Governor Macklem recognized that "[w]hen it comes to other objectives – climate change, income inequality – income inequality is certainly something we can take into account when we pick a framework."[40] On the other hand, despite this increased awareness and openness to consider distributive issues, Macklem immediately underlined that "monetary policy is a blunt instrument and can't pick and choose where growth happens." Put differently, "we know that monetary policy is a broad macroeconomic instrument that cannot target specific sectors or workers."[41] In short, what central banks including the BoC seem to be saying is: Look, even if you wanted us to act on inequality (read: even if you changed our mandate), there is no point because our policy instruments are just not cut out for this task.

Given their COVID-19 response and its demonstration to the contrary, these statements by the Fed and the BoC are puzzling to say the least. To claim that they cannot act on inequality is bizarre, because they just *did* act on inequality. Nor is the insight about this possibility new. The French economist Richard Cantillon (1755) observed in the 18th century that liquidity injections into the economy benefit some more than other, depending on where in the economy the liquidity is injected and how the stimulus is designed.

Given the incentives structure of central bankers to preserve their independence, they perhaps want to claim that central banks *should not* act on inequality, but that,[42] as we have seen in Section 4, is a different question.

8.   CONCLUSION

We have argued in this chapter that while the Fed and the BoC have come a long way in their discourse on inequality, and even to some extent in their actions to contain inequality, their positions on the issue still suffer from a number of inconsistencies and shortcomings.

During the inter-crisis period from 2015–2020, the Fed and the BoC devote more and more attention to the issue of inequality. With its emphasis on inclusive growth, the Fed in particular implicitly recognizes that inequality matters not just for instrumental reasons, but for its own sake. While this should certainly be welcomed as progress, the case of the BoC vividly illustrates that central bankers still get themselves into a conceptual muddle when probed about the inegalitarian impact of their own policies. One particularly important shortcoming of their discourse on this issue is their failure to compare their actions to alternative policies rather than simply to no intervention at all. Finally, our analysis shows both the Fed's and the BoC's conviction prior to COVID-19 that monetary policy has no role to play in fighting inequality, in large part because its instruments are too blunt for the task.

Their crisis response to COVID-19 reveals a deep tension in their position, because it demonstrates that, contrary to what central bankers have claimed and continue to claim, unconventional monetary policy *can* target specific economic sectors and, thus, *can* contribute to contain inequality.

Someone might object that the COVID-19 response is not really about monetary policy alone, but monetary policy cum fiscal policy, and that the distributive impact comes from the fiscal component. That may be correct with respect to some of the programs – e.g., with respect to buying provincial debt on the primary market – but note that this aspect is contingent. Just think of so-called helicopter money as one potential illustration. The distributive impact of a liquidity injection by helicopter drop is highly likely to be less inegalitarian compared to a liquidity injection by QE.

Finally, even if new monetary facilities can temporally alleviate the economic hardship faced by the least well-off, do they have the potential to create similar effects in the middle and long term? After all, Powell mobilized this argument to pass the hot potato to the government (cf. the previous section). However, if the long-run neutrality of money is intellectually dead, as we mentioned earlier, why would not it be the same for these new facilities? First, even if these new facilities are temporary, they have surely triggered *long-term* positive effects by preventing short-term job losses and business foreclosures and, in turn, middle- and long-term economic hardship.[43] Second, if economic inequality has a structural component and these new facilities help to reduce employment gaps as central bankers themselves acknowledge, why not make

them permanent? Central bankers tend to assign the responsibility for economic inequality to various governmental policies (education, fiscal policy,
labor market policy, etc.). Yet, even if they were right on this issue, which is far
from obvious, why would we, as a society, refrain from using other tools, such
as monetary policy, to decrease economic inequality? Central bankers might
answer that this is not in their mandate or that it induces undesirable tradeoffs
(such as a lower independence level or suboptimal performance on price
stability), but this answer opens the debate rather than closes it (Dietsch et al.,
2018). Our goal here is not to advocate a specific set of alternative policies. It
is merely to point out that the BoC's and the Fed's responses to the COVID-19
crisis illustrate what *can* be done and, thus, belie their discourse that monetary
policy is too blunt a tool to address inequality. Perhaps conventional monetary
policy was indeed too blunt to do that, but policy innovation in response to the
COVID-19 crisis has shown that unconventional monetary policy can certainly
be one tool among others when it comes to reducing inequality. The cat is out
of the bag, and we need to think constructively about how to manage it.

NOTES

1.   The chapter can be interpreted as a continuation of our work on the Fed, the
      European Central Bank, and the Bank of England and their response to the finan-
      cial crisis of 2007 (see Fontan et al., 2016).
2.   See https://doi.org/10.5281/zenodo.5579878.
3.   For example, we shall see in Section 4 that the Bank of Canada explicitly
      appealed to the idea of neutrality as recently as 2017.
4.   This three-way distinction also informed the structure of some of our previous
      work on the relation between central banks and inequality. See Fontan et al.
      (2016).
5.   For the general review process, see www.bankofcanada.ca/core-functions/
      monetary-policy/agreement-inflation-control-target/. For information on the
      latest round of reviews, see www.bankofcanada.ca/toward-2021-renewing-the
      -monetary-policy-framework/toward-2021-outreach/.
6.   Bernanke, 6 February 2007.
7.   Wilkins, 18 April 2017.
8.   Powell, 17 July 2018.
9.   A parallel, albeit much earlier, shift can be observed in the philosophical litera-
      ture on inequality over the last half century, where the assumptions of liberalism
      have been criticized for implicit bias in terms of race (e.g., Mills, 1997), gender
      (e.g., Okin, 1989), or ethnic minority (e.g., Kymlicka, 1995).
10.   Yellen, 22 June 2016. For a concrete example of the kind of research done at the
      Fed and its regional offices in this regard, see, for example, Gerardi et al. (2020).
11.   The campaign was led by the Center for Popular Democracy; see http://
      whatrecovery.org/.
12.   Transcript from the *Wall Street Journal* Pro, 26 August 2016.
13.   Ibid.
14.   Ibid.

15. Yellen, 28 March 2017.
16. Clarida, 5 June 2019.
17. Wilkins, 18 April 2017.
18. Wilkins explicitly grants this point elsewhere: "Different monetary policy frameworks can have different implications for [...] the distribution of income and wealth" (Wilkins, 20 November 2018).
19. Powell, 18 July 2018.
20. Most of the critical assessment of recent research on the distributive effects of quantitative easing in the rest of this section is a translation from our article in French (Fontan et al., 2019).
21. "Helicopter money" refers to a hypothetical scenario where the central bank would directly deposit money into citizens' accounts in order to boost aggregate demand.
22. Macklem, 12 March 2012.
23. Yellen, 17 November 2016.
24. Powell, 17 July 2018.
25. Yellen, 3 March 2017.
26. Yellen, 22 June 2016.
27. Another consideration that might play a role in the background here is that the BoC has sometimes emphasized that *any* change to its policy framework risks undermining the credibility of its inflation target and, as such, needs to be backed by strong reasons in its favour. Consider former Deputy Director Agathe Côté, who stated in 2014 that "any modification to the framework must be thoughtfully researched and carefully considered. This doesn't mean there is no room for improvement, just that [...] the bar for change is high" (Côté, 18 November 2014).
28. Powell, 27 August 2020.
29. Brainard, 27 September 2017.
30. Powell, 16 June 2020.
31. Citation from the *Globe and Mail* (Rendell, 2021). See also Macklem and Wilkins, 26 November 2020, for an unequivocal concern voiced by BoC officials "that this pandemic is widening divides in society."
32. See www.bankofcanada.ca/2021/04/bank-canada-becomes-inaugural-member-of-new-international-central-bank-network-indigenous-inclusion/.
33. See www.bankofcanada.ca/markets/market-operations-liquidity-provision/covid-19-actions-support-economy-financial-system/.
34. Brainard, 15 October 2020.
35. See www.federalreserve.gov/newsevents/pressreleases/monetary20200717a.htm.
36. Contrast this with the response to the GFC. When a member of the Fed Board was asked back in 2009 why the Fed did not intervene in the municipal bond markets then, he answered: "the Federal Reserve has important misgivings about assuming such a role in light of the potential for decisions about the provision of credit to states and municipalities to assume a political dimension."
37. A K-shaped recovery happens when there are strong divergences in the performances of economic sectors after a crisis.
38. The lack of use of these facilities does not mean that they were useless: their mere announcement was instrumental in stabilizing the targeted markets.
39. Powell, 11 February 2020.
40. Macklem and Wilkins, 26 November 2020.

41. Macklem, 10 September 2020.
42. For the opposite position, see, for example, Hockett and James (2020).
43. This argument is similar to the *hysteresis effect* put forward by Blanchard and Summers (1992).

REFERENCES

Amano, R., Carter, T., and Y. Terajima (2017), "Redistributive effects of a change in the inflation target." *Staff Analytical Note*, 2017–13. Bank of Canada, Ottawa.

Ampudia, M., Georgarakos, D., Slacalek, J., Tristani, O., Vermeulen, P., and G. Violante (2018), "Monetary policy and household inequality." *Discussion Papers*, 2170, ECB Working Paper Series. European Central Bank, Frankfurt.

Bank of Canada (2016), *Renewal of the Inflation-Control Target: Background Information*. Bank of Canada, Ottawa.

Bank of England (2012), "The distributional effects of asset purchases." Bank of England, London.

Best, J. (2018), "Technocratic exceptionalism: monetary policy and the fear of democracy." *International Political Sociology*, 12 (1), pp. 328–345. https://doi.org/10 .1093/ips/oly017.

Bivens, J. (2015), "Gauging the impact of the Fed on inequality during the Great Recession." *Hutchins Center Working Papers*.

Blanchard, O.J., and L.H. Summers (1992), "Hysteresis in unemployment." In Garonna, P., Mori, P., and P. Tedeschi (eds), *Economic Models of Trade Unions: International Studies in Economic Modelling*. Dordrecht: Springer Netherlands, pp. 235–242. https://doi.org/10.1007/978-94-011-2378-5_11.

Cantillon, R. (1755), *Essay sur la nature du commerce en géneral*. London: Fletcher Gyles.

Coibion, O., Gorodnichenko, Y., Kueng, L., and J. Silvia (2012), "Innocent bystanders? Monetary policy and inequality in the U.S." *NBER Working Papers*, 18170, June. https://doi.org/10.3386/w18170.

Colciago, A., Samarina, A., and J. de Haan (2019), "Central bank policies and income and wealth inequality: a survey." *Journal of Economic Surveys*, 33 (4), pp. 1199–1231. https://doi.org/10.1111/joes.12314.

Dietsch, P., Claveau, F., and C. Fontan (2018), *Do Central Banks Serve the People?* Cambridge: Polity Press.

El-Erian, M. A. (2017), *The Only Game in Town: Central Banks, Instability, and Avoiding the Next Collapse*. New York, NY: Random House.

Fabo, B., Jančoková, M., Kempf, E., and L. Pástor (2021), "Fifty shades of QE: comparing findings of central bankers and academics." *Journal of Monetary Economics*, 120 (May), pp. 1–20. https://doi.org/10.1016/j.jmoneco.2021.04.001.

Fontan, C., Claveau, F., and P. Dietsch (2016), "Central banking and inequalities: taking off the blinders." *Politics, Philosophy & Economics*, 15 (4), pp. 319–357.

Fontan, C., Dietsch, P., and F. Claveau (2019), "Les banques centrales et la justice sociale." *Éthique publique* [online], 21 (2). http://journals.openedition.org/ ethiquepublique/4856; https://doi.org/10.4000/ethiquepublique.4856.

Gerardi, K., Willen, P., and D.H. Zhang (2020), "Mortgage prepayment, race, and monetary policy." *Working Papers of the Federal Reserve of Boston*, pp. 20–27.

Hiteshew, K. (Federal Reserve) (2020), Testimony before the Congressional Oversight Commission, Washington, DC, 17 September. www.federalreserve.gov/newsevents/testimony/hiteshew20200917a.htm.

Hockett, R., and A. James (2020), *Money from Nothing: Or, Why We Should Learn to Stop Worrying about Debt and Love the Federal Reserve*. New York, NY: Melville House.

Ingham, G.K. (2004), "The nature of money." *Economic Sociology: European Electronic Newsletter*, 5, pp. 18–28.

Ingham, G.K. (2020), *Money: What Is Political Economy?* Cambridge: Polity Press.

Kymlicka, W. (1995), *Multicultural Citizenship: A Liberal Theory of Minority Rights*. Oxford and New York, NY: Clarendon Press and Oxford University Press.

Lenza, M., and J. Slacalek (2018), "How does monetary policy affect income and wealth inequality? Evidence from quantitative easing in the Euro Area." *ECB Working Paper*, 2190, European Central Bank, Frankfurt am Main.

Macklem, T. (Bank of Canada) (2020), "Economic progress report: a very uneven recovery at the Canadian Chamber of Commerce," 10 September. www.bankofcanada.ca/2020/09/economic-progress-report-a-very-uneven-recovery/.

Mehrling, P. (2011), *The New Lombard Street: How the Fed Became the Dealer of Last Resort*. Princeton, NJ: Princeton University Press.

Mills, C.W. (1997), *The Racial Contract*. Ithaca, NY: Cornell University Press.

Minsky, H. (1993), "On the non-neutrality of money." *Federal Reserve Bank of New York, Quarterly Review*, 18 (Spring), pp. 77–82.

Okin, S.M. (1989), *Justice, Gender, and the Family*. New York, NY: Basic Books.

Powell, J. (Federal Reserve) (2020), "Semiannual Monetary Policy Report to the Congress," at Hearing before the Committee on Banking, Housing, and Urban Affairs, US Senate, 16 June. www.federalreserve.gov/newsevents/testimony/powell20200616a.htm.

Rawls, J. (1999), *A Theory of Justice* [Revised Edition]. Cambridge, MA: Harvard University Press.

Rendell, M. (2021, 13 May), "Canadian economy won't fully recover until inequality addressed, BoC's Macklem says." *Globe and Mail*. www.theglobeandmail.com/business/economy/article-canadian-economy-wont-fully-recover-until-inequality-addressed-bocs/.

Rochon, L.-P., and S. Yinka Olawoye (eds) (2012), *Monetary Policy and Central Banking: New Directions in Post-Keynesian Theory*. Cheltenham, UK and Northampton, MA: Edward Elgar Publishing.

Tobin, J. (1972), "Friedman's theoretical framework." *Journal of Political Economy*, 80 (5), pp. 852–863. https://doi.org/10.1086/259941.

Tucker, P. (2018), *Unelected Power: The Quest for Legitimacy in Central Banking and the Regulatory State*. Princeton, NJ: Princeton University Press.

Turner, A. (2016), *Between Debt and The Devil: Money, Credit, and Fixing Global Finance*. Oxford: Princeton University Press.

Wall Street Journal Pro (2016, 26 August), "Transcript: Fed officials meet with Fed up activists at Jackson Hole." *Wall Street Journal*. www.wsj.com/articles/transcript-fed-officials-meet-with-fed-up-activists-at-jackson-hole-1472234174.

Wilkins, C.A. (Bank of Canada) (2018), "Choosing the Best Monetary Policy Framework for Canada," at the McGill University Max Bell School of Public Policy, Montreal, 20 November. www.bankofcanada.ca/2018/11/choosing-best-monetary-policy-framework-canada/.

APPENDIX I: CITED DOCUMENTS FROM OUR CORPUS

Bernanke, B. (Federal Reserve) (2007), "The Level and Distribution of Economic Well Being," before the Greater Omaha Chamber of Commerce, 6 February, Omaha, Nebraska. www.federalreserve.gov/newsevents/speech/bernanke20070206a.htm.

Brainard, L. (Federal Reserve) (2017), "Labor Market Disparities and Economic Performance," at Banking and the Economy: A Forum for Minority Bankers, Federal Reserve Bank of Kansas City, 27 September, Kansas City, Missouri. www.federalreserve.gov/newsevents/speech/brainard20170927a.htm.

Brainard, L. (2020), "Modernizing and Strengthening CRA Regulations: A Conversation with Minority Depository Institutions," to the National Bankers Association, 15 October. www.federalreserve.gov/newsevents/speech/brainard20201015a.htm.

Clarida, R.H. (Federal Reserve) (2019), "The Federal Reserve's Review of its Monetary Policy Strategy, Tools, and Communication Practices," at the Conference on Monetary Policy Strategy, Tools, and Communication Practices (Fed Listens Event), hosted by the Federal Reserve Bank of Chicago, 5 June, Chicago, Illinois. www.bis.org/review/r190607f.htm.

Côté, A. (Bank of Canada) (2014), "Inflation Targeting in the Post-Crisis Era," at the Calgary CFA Society, 18 November, Calgary, Alberta. www.bankofcanada.ca/2014/11/inflationtargeting-post-crisis-era/.

Macklem, T. (Bank of Canada) (2012), "Promoting Growth, Mitigating Cycles and Inequality: The Role of Price and Financial Stability," at the Brazil-Canada Chamber of Commerce, 12 March, São Paulo, Brazil. www.bankofcanada.ca/2012/03/promotinggrowthmitigating-cycles-and-inequality/.

Macklem, T. (Bank of Canada) and C.A. Wilkins (Bank of Canada) (2020), Testimony before the Standing Committee on Finance, House of Commons, Government of Canada, 26 November. www.ourcommons.ca/DocumentViewer/en/43-2/FINA/meeting-7/evidence.

Powell, J. (Federal Reserve) (2018), "Federal Reserve's Second Monetary Policy Report for 2018," at Hearing before the Committee on Banking, Housing, and Urban Affairs, US Senate, 17 July. www.govinfo.gov/content/pkg/CHRG-115shrg32517/html/CHRG115shrg32517.htm.

Powell, J. (Federal Reserve) (2018), "Monetary Policy and the State of the Economy," at Hearing before the Committee on Financial Services, US House of Representatives, 18 July. www.govinfo.gov/content/pkg/CHRG-115hhrg31509/html/CHRG-115hhrg31509.htm.

Powell, J. (Federal Reserve) (2020), "Monetary Policy and the State of the Economy," at Hearing before the Committee on Financial Services, US House of Representatives, 11 February. www.govinfo.gov/content/pkg/CHRG-116hhrg42819/html/CHRG-116hhrg42819.htm.

Powell, J. (Federal Reserve) (2020), "Semiannual Monetary Policy Report to the Congress," at Hearing before the Committee on Banking, Housing, and Urban Affairs, US Senate, 16 June. www.federalreserve.gov/newsevents/testimony/powell20200616a.htm.

Powell, J. (Federal Reserve) (2020), "New Economic Challenges and the Fed's Monetary Policy Review," at Navigating the Decade Ahead: Implications for Monetary Policy, Federal Reserve Bank of Kansas City economic policy sympo-

sium, 27 August, Jackson Hole, Wyoming. www.federalreserve.gov/newsevents/
speech/powell20200827a.htm.

Wall Street Journal Pro (2016), "Transcript: Fed Officials Meet with Fed Up Activists
at Jackson Hole," meeting held on 25 August 2015 at Jackson Hole, Wyoming. www
.wsj.com/articles/transcript-fed-officials-meet-with-fed-up-activists-at-jackson
-hole1472234174.

Wilcox, D. (Federal Reserve) (2009), "Municipal Finance," before the Committee on
Financial Services, US House of Representative, 20 May, Washington, D.C. www
.federalreserve.gov/newsevents/testimony/wilcox20090521a.htm.

Wilkins, C.A. (Bank of Canada) (2017), "Blame It on the Machines?" before the
Toronto Region Board of Trade, 18 April, Toronto. www.bankofcanada.ca/2017/04/
blame-it-on-the-machines/.

Wilkins, C.A. (Bank of Canada) (2018), "Choosing the Best Monetary Policy
Framework for Canada," at the McGill University Max Bell School of Public Policy,
20 November, Montreal. www.bankofcanada.ca/2018/11/choosing-best-monetary
-policy-framework-canada/.

Yellen, J. (Federal Reserve) (2016), "Monetary Policy and the State of the Economy," at
Hearing before the Committee on Financial Services, US House of Representatives,
22 June. www.govinfo.gov/content/pkg/CHRG-114hhrg25848/html/CHRG
-114hhrg25848.htm.

Yellen, J. (Federal Reserve) (2016), "The Economic Outlook," at Hearing before the
Joint Economic Committee, Congress of the United States, 17 November. www
.govinfo.gov/content/pkg/CHRG-114shrg23027/html/CHRG-114shrg23027.htm.

Yellen, J. (Federal Reserve) (2017), "From Adding Accommodation to Scaling It
Back," at the Executives' Club of Chicago, 3 March, Chicago, Illinois. www
.federalreserve.gov/newsevents/speech/yellen20170303a.htm.

Yellen, J. (Federal Reserve) (2017), Addressing Workforce Development Challenges
in Low Income Communities," at Creating a Just Economy, the 2017 annual conference of the National Community Reinvestment Coalition, 28 March, Washington,
DC. www.federalreserve.gov/newsevents/speech/yellen20170328a.htm.

6. Making environments safer: a safe asset for a green (and financial) new deal and for more responsible central banks – what could, and should, the ECB do?

Massimo Amato and Lucio Gobbi

1. THE BASIC STRUCTURE OF FINANCIAL MARKETS AND THE STABILISING ROLE OF CENTRAL BANKS

1.1 The Pandemic Crisis, and the Role of Debt and of its Responsible Financing

At the end of February 2020, the European Union (EU) was hit by the first wave of the Covid-19 pandemic. Despite the vaccination campaigns conducted by all member countries and the implementation of extraordinary fiscal and monetary policies by European governments and institutions, the cyclical waves of contagions and the sustained fall in global production do not yet allow us to claim that we are in a post-Covid phase.

The only thing we have learned is that, to paraphrase Hyman Minsky (1982), a crisis of this magnitude can only be tackled with the joint intervention of a 'Big Government' and a 'Big Bank'. This seems to have been the path taken by the European Commission, the European Central Bank (ECB) and all EU countries over the last year and a half.

Unlike the financial crisis of 2007–2009, fiscal policy was the first economic instrument put in place to try to contain the spread of the virus, to adapt national health systems to the emergency, and to manage the trade-off between health and employment goals. This involved the use of discretionary spending and the activation of automatic stabilisers to an unprecedented extent. Figure 6.1 compares the discretionary spending made by eurozone countries during the 2007–2009 crisis with that in the first year of the Covid crisis. As can be seen, with the exception of Spain, Luxembourg and Cyprus, the level of such expenditure has been significantly higher.

The aggregate impact of the pandemic on the public deficits of eurozone countries in 2020 resulted in a deficit-to-GDP (gross domestic product) ratio of 7.3 per cent, while in 2019 the ratio was 0.7 per cent. As regards the future, the vaccination campaign is likely to prevent new lockdowns, and this is expected to reduce eurozone deficits to 3.4 per cent in 2022 and 2.6 per cent in 2023 (ECB, 2021b), but in any case, still at a level markedly above the pre-crisis level.

Although the pandemic is a common exogenous shock, its effect on the various economies has been asymmetric. This was inevitable given the diversity of the production structures of countries, which had already increased during the 2011–2012 sovereign debt crisis and is set to increase further.

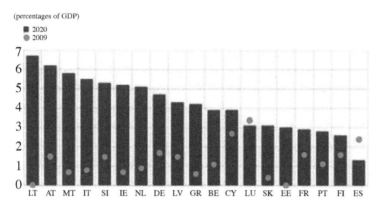

Source: ECB, 2021a.

Figure 6.1   *Comparison of the percentages of GDP consisting of non-discretionary expenditure by EU countries in 2009 and 2020*

An extraordinary increase in public deficits cannot fail to affect the general level of public debt in the countries of the Union. Figure 6.2 clearly shows this phenomenon, as well as the fact that the main European economies (France, Germany, Italy and Spain) are above the levels required by the Stability and Growth Pact (SGP). With the exception of Germany, the slippage in the major economies is significantly high and is of great concern to European policy-makers. At the moment, the constraints on national fiscal policies have been suspended by the European Commission's activation of the general escape clause. The European Commission's measure no. 123 (European Commission, 2020a, p. 2) states that:

> The EU must continue to respond quickly, forcefully and in a coordinated manner to this fast-evolving crisis. During the video conference with members of the European Council of 17 March 2020, the President of the Commission announced the imminent activation of the so-called general escape clause. The clause was introduced as part of the "Six-Pack" reform of the SGP in 2011, which drew the lessons of the economic and financial crisis. Notably, that experience highlighted the need for specific provisions in the EU's fiscal rules to allow for a coordinated and orderly temporary deviation from the normal requirements for all Member States in a situation of generalised crisis caused by a severe economic downturn of the euro area or the EU as a whole.

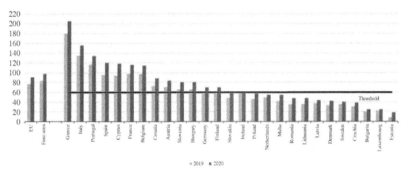

Source: ECB, 2021a.

Figure 6.2   Public debts of the European Union countries

The Commission did not limit itself to suspension of the SGP; it also provided active support to national economies. In a first phase, several anti-crisis instruments were activated: for instance, the possibility given to each country to access, in order to finance healthcare expenditure, the European Stability Mechanism (ESM) for a percentage equal to 2 per cent of GDP in 2019; the activation of an unemployment support programme for 100 billion euros (SURE); and an extension of the guarantee to corporate loans by the European Investment Bank (EIB) for 200 billion euros. Subsequently, the European Parliament decided to launch the NextGenerationEU (NGEU) programme for 750 billion euros to support the economies of the Union, divided into 390 billion in subsidies and 360 billion in loans.[1] The programme will support research and innovation within the framework of the Horizon Europe programme: the fight against climate change, for which 30 per cent of the funds will be reserved; the Digital Europe programme; policies aimed at closing the gender gap; and agricultural policy.

With regard to monetary policy, the ECB used the unconventional instruments already activated in response to the sovereign debt crisis, and added new ones. In particular, the main interventions were the activation of extraordinary long-term financing operations (PELTRO) in addition to the extension of long-term refinancing operations (TLTRO III). With regard to asset purchases by the ECB, the PEPP programme was established, the peculiarity of which consisted of abandoning the capital key rule (i.e., the obligation of the ECB to purchase government bonds in proportion to their capital in the Bank), which, instead, had not been waived in the previous programme of purchases of sovereign debt (PSPP) within the asset purchase programme (APP).

The abandonment of the capital key rule and the activation of the escape clause have substantially transformed the European architecture, although not necessarily to a definitive extent. However, the unsustainability of European public debts under the current treaties makes a pure and simple return to what we might call the 'old normal' highly unlikely. This de facto situation could trigger a process of revision of the treaties. The challenge for economists and policy-makers is therefore to design the mix of national and European fiscal policies (NGEU) together with the refinancing and management of national public debts.

In the following sections, after presenting our theoretical framework of reference, we will illustrate the specificities of the European case.

1.2   The Role of Markets: Efficiency and Inefficiency in the Valuation of Public Debts after the Crisis

There are still two main contrasting views on how financial markets operate and on their degree of efficiency. Analysing the efficiency of markets is important for interpretation of the price and yield trends of European sovereign debt, especially in order to design appropriate policy proposals. The concept of efficiency, which is mainly associated with neoclassical theory, assesses how financial market participants make use of their resources provided that: (1) they are scarce with respect to the possibilities of use, (2) alternative uses can be made of them and (3) it is possible to order them with respect to those alternative uses.

According to neoclassical theory, a necessary condition for efficiency is that all actors are endowed with perfect rationality and perfect information with respect to all the events that may affect the performance of markets. Moreover, all agents must adopt the same interpretative model to analyse information.

The theory of perfect markets, which emerged powerfully in the second half of the 1970s, became the benchmark for either adherence to, or criticism of, the neoclassical theory. Criticisms were not long in coming. In particular, Shiller (1979) showed that stock prices are characterised by an excess of volatility compared to that of the fundamentals. This implies that fundamentals cannot fully explain stock price movements. In turn, Tversky and Kahneman (1982) emphasised that investors' cognitive limitations render them unable to make decisions under uncertainty using the calculus of probabilities in a rational manner. Rather, agents' decisions tend to follow heuristic rules that cannot be traced back to those of perfect rationality. Minsky (1982) showed the existence of a financial cycle that assumes the non-perfect rationality and information of investors.

However, the notion that deviation from fundamentals depends on the view prevailing among imperfectly informed investors was already at the heart of Chapter 12 of the *General Theory* (Keynes, 1936). In his 1937 article in response to the first criticisms of the *General Theory*, Keynes highlighted that the cognitive capacities of agents are not such that the assumption of perfect information can be considered valid (Keynes, 1937).

It is evident that the cleavage between the two theories arises from the different interpretations that they offer of the efficiency of financial markets: the first theory presupposes a radical autonomy of market agents able by themselves to produce all the stability that markets need; the other theory instead highlights that expectations can systematically deviate from fundamentals, thus determining the possibility of multiple equilibria, with respect to which only a viewpoint external to that of private actors can provide a reference point for their calculations. The latter is an institutional perspective which we can already find in Chapter 12.

But before doing so, it is worth reading the European sovereign debt crisis in its light. From 2007–2009, international and European investors began to attribute greater risk to the sovereign debts of southern European countries. This dynamic was justified by the fact that southern economies, albeit in different ways, were struggling to recover from the shock generated by the Global Financial Crisis (GFC). In the autumn of 2009, the Greek prime minister announced that the official data on Greece's public debt had been manipulated by the previous government. The announcement caused panic among investors and capital flight. Within a short period of time, all southern European countries found it difficult to refinance their debts. The change in investor market sentiment led to a situation that could be described as a 'bad equilibrium'; i.e., a potentially widening spread between the yields of safe and risky countries. The mix of high financing costs of sovereign debt and austerity policies caused a concentration of capital flows towards northern economies. This crisis shows how the European sovereign bond markets were not characterised by allocative efficiency, given the inability of investors to assess the risk of investments both *ex ante* and *ex post*. This was because herding behaviour phenomena accentuated the fall in the value of the debts of southern countries to well below the value indicated by the fundamentals.

1.3 Private Expectations and Socialisation: The Role of Chapter 12 in *General Theory*

As is well known, Chapter 12 of *General Theory* provides an interpretation of the structural instability of financial markets, which is linked to the role played by expectations. Many of the subsequent developments in the theory of financial markets discussed in the previous section can be read as responses to the issues raised in that chapter.

The focus of Chapter 12 has primarily to do with the way financial market practice, even before theory, normally treats expectations; or better still, with the way it tries to normalise them. There is a deep-lying reason for this attempted normalisation. It first of all concerns the conduct of market actors; i.e. their attempt to evade an elementary fact of reality which Keynes encapsulates in the formula 'uncertainty about the future', a formula which recurs in crucial passages of the *General Theory*.

For many, it is precisely this flight from reality which haunts the financial markets that is the fundamental reason for the instability of modern capitalist economic systems and their tendency not to converge towards stable full-employment equilibria. Thrown out of the door, uncertainty returns through the window in the form of a systemic risk affecting the relationship between debtors and creditors, and which cannot be dealt with exhaustively by macro-prudential models.

The point is that uncertainty, which a year after the publication of the *General Theory* Keynes defined as constitutively irreducible 'at the same calculable status as that of certainty itself' (Keynes, 1937, pp. 112–113), sets a preventive limit on calculation: it is this *preventive* limit that makes political economy a moral science and the construction of models something whose application, as Keynes writes to Harrod, must always be corrected by 'intimate and messy acquaintance with the facts to which his model has to be applied'; i.e., by a non-modelling screening (Keynes, 1938, p. 300).

The interpretation of Chapter 12 has given rise, at least in the heterodox sphere, to numerous strands of critical interpretation (the last in order of time and undoubtedly the most complete being that of Carabelli, 2021). In a 2011 speech, Paul Krugman ironically referred to the supporters of this interpretation as the 'chapter 12ers', in order to oppose them to the 'part 1ers', among whom he included himself (Krugman, 2011). This division, which largely overlaps with the division between heterodox and orthodox readings (starting with Hicks and Samuelson, cited by Krugman himself) of Keynes, is very interesting, because what is at stake is detection of the origin of instability in modern economic systems, as well as the nature of the answers that economic policy can and must give to such instability, and therefore of the role and responsibility of economic institutions – first and foremost central banks.

Krugman identifies this origin in the constitutive flaws in Say's law, which Keynes criticises in the first part of *General Theory*. At stake is obviously, on the one hand, the role of real wages as a structural adjustment variable, and of monetary policy as a support to this adjustment, and on the other, the role of effective demand in determining saving and investment choices. From Keynes' criticism of Say's law, Krugman derives the possibility of stable unemployment equilibria and therefore the necessity that deficit fiscal policies put back on the path to full employment a system that left to itself not only tends not to converge, but even risks falling into permanent deflationary traps.

What counts for Krugman is, in particular, the specificity of the role that public debt can play, and the fact that it *cannot* be likened to private debt, and indeed in some cases can and should validly replace it: 'all debt isn't created equal – which is why borrowing by some actors now can help cure problems created by excess borrowing by other actors in the past'.

This perspective has recently started to be reaffirmed even in the mainstream, if one only thinks of the title of the latest work by Eichengreen et al. (2021),[2] *In Defense of Public Debt*, in which the positive role of public debt is assessed in relation to its ability in regard to addressing national emergencies, as well as to funding essential public goods and services, without forgetting the contribution of public debt to the development of private financial markets and, through this channel, to modern economic growth.

The theme of infrastructure is particularly important for our purposes here. Let us quote Krugman once more:

> Suppose, in particular, that the government can borrow for a while, using the borrowed money to buy useful things like infrastructure. The true social cost of these things will be very low, because the spending will be putting resources that would otherwise be unemployed to work. And government spending will also make it easier for highly indebted players to pay down their debt.

Translating that remark into Chapter 12 language: in a market capitalist system based on the decisions of private investors, the crucial risk is that the both stabilising and dynamising role of infrastructure investments is lost precisely because such investments are not regarded as essentially the responsibility of the public. The fact remains, however, that the role of the state and its specific mode of borrowing are crucial in crisis resolution for counteracting uncertainty and flight from uncertainty; i.e., the base structures of long-term expectations and financial markets, respectively.

There is a further aspect that should be highlighted. After describing in various ways the dilemma of financial markets – that is, the fact that their presence 'sometimes facilitates investment but sometimes adds greatly to the instability of the system' (Keynes, 1936, pp. 150–151) – and after pointing out that the dilemma is destined not to be solved, Keynes indicates what could be remedies for the instability that it determines.

In particular, he points to public investments as a remedy:

> there is a growing class of investments entered upon by, or at the risk of, public authorities, which are frankly influenced in making the investment by a general presumption of there being prospective social advantages from the investment whatever its commercial yield may prove to be within a wide range. (p. 163)

1.4   What Does 'Socialising Investments' Mean?

The theme of the socialisation of investments, which is taken up in the final considerations of Chapter 24, is well known. But it is in Chapter 12, even more than in Chapter 24, that the justification of such investments is linked to the different time horizon in which the subject that implements socialisation can move. Not only can the socialisation promoted by public actors generate social advantages that escape private calculations, but in doing so it can mobilise resources that private investment and indebtedness cannot, because socialisation can operate 'without seeking to be satisfied that the mathematical expectation of the yield is at least equal to the current rate of interest' (p. 163).

Socialisation of investment has to do with a *political* transformation of the time horizon of investment; that is, a socialisation of the relationship with time and uncertainty. However much political cycles may induce public decision-makers to make short-sighted choices, the basic characteristic of socialisation is that it escapes the 'accountant's nightmare' that Keynes evokes in *National Self-Sufficiency* (Keynes, 1933), and which well illustrates the logic of *socialised* infrastructure investment:

> Instead of using their vastly increased material and technical resources to build a wonder city, the men of the nineteenth century built slums; and they thought it right and advisable to build slums because slums, on the test of private enterprise, 'paid', whereas the wonder city would, they thought, have been an act of foolish extravagance, which would, in the imbecile idiom of the financial fashion, have 'mortgaged the future' – though how the construction to-day of great and glorious works can impoverish the future, no man can see until his mind is beset by false analogies from an irrelevant accountancy. (p. 241)

However, the point made by Keynes is only half grasped if one stops at the effects of public expenditure as not bound to the criterion of private profitability without dwelling on how such expenditure must be financed, precisely because it implies a socialisation of the relationship with time and uncertainty.

In short: the socialisation of the relation with time and uncertainty that public investments imply must be extended also *to how they must be financed.* Keynes is well aware of this and – after showing that for these investments the condition 'that the mathematical expectation of the yield is at least equal to the current rate of interest' structurally does not apply – he adds an equally structural restriction: 'the rate which the public authority has to pay may still play a decisive part in determining the scale of investment operations which it can afford' (pp. 163–164). The corollary is clear: the socialisation of the relationship with time (i.e., with uncertainty) implied by socialisation *should apply also on the financial side.*

The question is, in fact, this: to what extent is it *logically* legitimate to leave to those same markets that prove themselves unable to assess the social profitability of infrastructure investments the task of assessing the 'credit risk' of a public debt that arises precisely because of the need to replace the market agents in those investment decisions? Should not such an assessment be prevented from falling prey to a market sentiment that is always on the verge of assessing debts not on the basis of their fundamental risk but on the basis of their 'liquidity', in a context where the liquidity preference may become insensitive to any stimulus whatsoever coming from monetary policy? Are not central banks, precisely as monetary policy-makers, called into question here?

In a well-known article of March 2020, Draghi drew a parallel between the Covid emergency and the state of emergency represented by a war (Draghi, 2020). And in fact, if we look at its history, modern public debt was born, after some important precedents in Italy in the 16th century, in England at the end of the 17th century. Its purpose was essentially to finance warfare (only later in the 20th century would public spending also deal with welfare), with the specific concern that the financing of such spending should not be excessively expensive for the state nor excessively risky for its creditors. This is why the Financial Revolution of the end of the 17th century was characterised by the simultaneous emergence of three actors: the Treasury as the issuer of public debt, the private markets of its creditors, and a *third* actor, private in its operation, but with the public mission to mediate between the first two: the central bank. The Bank of England was created in 1694 with the precise purpose of mediating between the state and the financial markets, in a triangulation where it was in a position of summit and arbiter (see Dickson, 1967; Amato, 2008; Amato and Fantacci, 2012).

1.5   The Primary Social Responsibility of a Central Bank

A central bank is established as that debtor which is able to induce market actors to accept its liabilities as currency – i.e., as a legal tender for the payment of all other debts (Greenspan, 1997) – and therefore operates in a time horizon that is wider and deeper than that of any private speculator. Precisely for this reason it is the actor that can mediate between the profitability needs of private investors and the sustainability needs of servicing public debt, which from its origins was not made to be *repaid*, but indefinitely refinanced.

But this means that a responsible central banker *cannot* do whatever he or she wants, but *must* instead do whatever it takes to preserve long-term balances whose social and systemic value may not be seen or taken into account by private actors, driven as they are by money-making motives and bound to the shorter-term profitability of their investments.

This then is the primary social responsibility of a central bank: to ensure the socialisation of stable expectations not only on the price level but also on the resilience of public assets, which precisely for this reason become safe; i.e., capable of ensuring the resilience of the system as a whole, to the extent that they, and only they, can constitute that 'simple debt instrument that is expected to preserve its value during adverse systemic events' (Caballero et al., 2017, p. 29).

A 'twofold safety' is therefore involved in public investments in infrastructures and, in particular, in the infrastructures required by the Green New Deal (GND): the 'real' safety of the economic system, which the infrastructural investments intend to secure; and the 'monetary' safety of the financial system called upon to support these investment programmes under the safest possible conditions. With a further advantage, implied by the safe assets: that every other private investment, by definition riskier, can be financed by collateralising it with public assets.

Apparently simplistic, Caballero's definition tells us that only *public* assets can be properly safe, since in the case of 'adverse systemic events' only the repayment capacity of a state, linked to its ability to last over time, can enable market operators to exclude a generalised risk of insolvency.

What that definition does not tell us is that the public entity which can safely assume this view is precisely the central bank. Since the 2007–2009 crisis, and even more so with the Covid crisis, what we have witnessed is an expansion of central bank balance sheets which, far from generating instability, has allowed both a stabilisation of financial markets and a substantial growth of public debts, to which correspond precisely those public policies aimed at compensating for the lack of incentives for private initiative and even more so those public policies aimed at making possible investments made 'social' simply by their time horizon, as is the case of infrastructural investments.

Without having to call into question the independence of central banks, it is possible to argue in favour of a duty of compliance on the part of the latter with respect to the public mission of stabilising expectations.

2.   A FOCUS ON THE EUROPEAN CASE

2.1   Financing the Green New Deal and the Role of Public Institutions

That recent climate change developments have accelerated climate conversion projects is beyond doubt, at a global level (IMF, 2021) as well as within the EU (European Commission, 2020b, 2021), where this acceleration is reflected by the role that green investments play in the NGEU. The debate on the net macroeconomic impact of the green conversion plans of economies is still open, and it is marked by strong uncertainty. Nevertheless, we can already put forward some considerations on the role of investment, and in particular of public investment in the strategic framework of a global NGEU.

In a 'militant' yet very rigorous book (Pettifor, 2019), Ann Pettifor, in dialogue with the American positions on the GND (Ocasio-Cortez, 2019) has no doubts in supporting the centrality of the role of the public in *guiding* investment decisions. We insist on this notion, because, as we pointed out earlier, the socialisation of investment does not necessarily imply centralisation. Indeed, within certain limits, it excludes it: 'the transformation of the economy requires more than the collective efforts of the state. Market transactions will complement, support and gain from the activities of the state [...] The GND is best delivered by a mixed economy' (Pettifor, 2019, p. 99).

Obviously, precisely because we are talking about infrastructural reconversion plans, the short- and medium-term macroeconomic effects may also be adverse (Pisani-Ferry, 2021). On the other hand, the ability of infrastructural investments in the environmental field to trigger new waves of technological investment has long been underlined (Acemoglu et al., 2012). Their effect could be such that they increase the overall share of investment, bringing it back from the 24.3 per cent of the 2010–2019 decade, marked by the difficult recovery from the GFC, to the levels of the 1980–1989 decade (25.7 per cent), characterised by high rates of technological innovation (Pisani-Ferry, 2021).

Since 'the level of output and employment as a whole depends on the amount of investment', given 'the psychology of the public' (Keynes, 1937, p. 121), and since the public part of infrastructure investments will have to be financed by deficits rather than by green taxes (largely regressive, and therefore unsustainable and destabilising from a political point of view), the question becomes precisely how to stabilise the psychology of financial investors.

The current situation is characterised by huge world private savings seeking outlets for long-term investments, the stability of which can be guaranteed by public intervention on the one hand, and by the intervention of central banks on the other, in order to avoid an excessive centralisation of decision-making processes:

> to support government borrowing, central banks can transparently intervene in bond markets, and can purchase government bonds for new finance. By so doing the central bank can lower the yield on that borrowing. They do this by purchasing and removing bonds or treasury bills from the market. This makes much-sought-after sovereign bonds scarce, which raises the price of the remaining bonds. (Pettifor, 2019, pp. 142–143)

Under what conditions could this strategy be implemented in Europe? Let us take a further step in the direction indicated by Pettifor and ask ourselves whether what is missing in Europe is not precisely a public bond at the European level; i.e., a 'Eurobond'.

2.2 Eurobonds as a Safe Asset

The sovereign debt crisis of 2010–2012 exacerbated two major problems that had begun to emerge during the GFC: the lack of a European safe asset, and the cost of refinancing public debt for southern European countries.

The scarcity of safe assets in the European financial market began with the GFC and increased considerably over the following years. After the introduction of the single currency, a direct flow of capital from northern European economies to southern economies was observed (Merler and Pisani-Ferry, 2012). It was determined by the fact that assets issued by southern European countries recorded slightly higher yields than in northern countries, against a limited risk stemming from those countries' membership of the euro area. Therefore, until 2007 the European financial system was able to enjoy a supply of safe or quasi-safe public assets (sovereign bonds of Germany, France, Italy and Spain) adequate to its needs. After 2007, however, the effects of the crisis significantly worsened the state of public budgets in all member countries. This dynamic was exacerbated by the austerity policies imposed by the European Commission on the most distressed countries, and which triggered capital flights from southern to northern European countries, in particular to Germany. This 'flight to quality' was the manifestation of investors' fears that the fiscally weaker countries might become insolvent. The process of capital centralisation that followed abruptly increased the spread between the yield on German Bunds and that on Italian, Irish, Spanish, Greek and Portuguese bonds. The immediate consequences were a drastic reduction in the supply of safe assets in Europe, a rise in the cost of refinancing sovereign debt for countries hit by capital flight, the emergence of a doom-loop between national banking systems and their sovereign debt, and the credit crunch that followed.

Since the GFC, the debate on the need for a European safe asset has therefore become of central importance. Here we limit ourselves to presenting the main contributions that have been made in recent years. We group them according to their shared features.

A first group is characterised by a safe asset not guaranteed by any kind of European mutual fund (Brunnermeier et al., 2011, 2017) but issued by a special institution that will present on the assets side of its balance sheet a pool of European sovereign debt and, on the liabilities side, European bonds divided into two tranches. The first tranche will be composed of senior bonds (European Senior Bonds, ESB), the second of subordinated bonds (European Junior Bonds, EJB). A system of this kind has certainly the advantage of creating a safe asset without the need for public guarantees, since it performs risk filtering by diversifying the underlying assets portfolio and through tranching. Nevertheless, three main problems may arise in this context (De Grauwe and Ji, 2018; Gabor and Vestergaard, 2018):

1. Without a public guarantee, there is no assurance that the senior tranche can remain a safe asset in the event of a systemic shock.
2. The EJB market could easily become illiquid during turmoil, thus creating problems in refinancing the outstanding public debt.
3. The creation of a safe asset market is parallel to public debt securities markets. The evaluation of the senior tranche as equally safe as the highly rated sovereign bonds is very questionable and cannot prevent flight to quality during turmoil.

A second group of contributions is characterised by a tranching of national debts, whose main features are:

1. Implicit tranching. A common issuer (CI) would issue a safe asset backed by a diversified portfolio of European public debts bought at their face value. The debt-servicing costs of the safe asset would then be charged to the sovereigns in proportion to the amount of each national debt purchased by the CI. Here, risk filtering occurs through the preferred status of the CI and the diversification of the sovereign debts portfolio. The implicit tranching is due to the fact that the preferred status introduces the juniority effect on the portion of the debt not included in the CI (Juncker and Tremonti, 2010; Monti, 2010).
2. Tranching implemented at the national level in two forms: senior debt issued by the states on the market and purchased entirely by the CI (Leandro and Zettelmeyer, 2018a); senior debt resulting from a CI loan (Giudice et al., 2019).

3.   Tranching of sovereign debt implemented by the state and then bought by institutional investors (Wendorf and Mahle, 2015).

There is finally a third type of Eurobond. This operates very differently, since it eliminates tranching and institutes CIs (Leandro and Zettelmeyer, 2018b).

Before the pandemic crisis, the Eurobond debate seemed to have exhausted its force and scope. However, the need to expand Europe's public budgets on an unprecedented scale, triggered by the Covid crisis, has once again put the question of their financing back at the heart of the debate.

2.3   The NGEU and the Eurobonds

It is in the light of the revival of the Eurobond debate that it is important to analyse how the European institutions have conceived the funding of the NGEU, so crucial to the European green deal debate.

During the first half of 2021, the member countries of the Union drew up their recovery plans and submitted them to the Commission. As shown in Figure 6.3, the countries with the highest funding requests are Italy and Spain. Considering that Germany and France are the most populous countries in the EU, what clearly emerges from the graph is that the countries most in need of recovery resources are those hit by austerity in the pre-pandemic period. Moreover, Figure 6.3 shows that green expenditures are predominant in the plans that have been submitted (Bruegel, 2021).

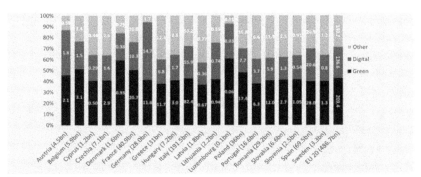

Source: Bruegel, 2021.

Figure 6.3   *Amount and composition of expenditure on the recovery fund, by country*

The resources needed to finance the NGEU will be raised on the financial markets in the period between mid-2021 and December 31, 2026. However, no kind of rollover is envisaged for the bonds issued by the EU, which will be fully repaid in 2058. Each year the Commission will set the total value of the bonds to be issued as well as their maturity. These decisions will be taken in light of the evolution of both the EU budget and the pandemic crisis. At present, the financial instruments envisaged are EU bonds and EU bills. The former are bonds with long-term maturities ranging from 3 to 30 years. This kind of bond has already been issued to finance the SURE unemployment programme (maturity: 5–30 years). The latter are bonds with short-term maturities (1, 3, 6 and 12 months) issued in order to meet the Commission's liquidity needs. About one-third of the long-term bonds issued will be called 'Green Bonds', meaning that the funds raised will be used exclusively to finance the European 'Green New Deal'. The value of the bonds issued will be 5 per cent of the Union's pre-pandemic-crisis GDP.

The response to the pandemic will thus be financed through Eurobonds to a not inconsiderable extent. This in itself shows that a European fiscal policy is not only desirable but also possible. In fact, such a financial architecture enables the European institutions to control the spending choices of the EU member states, preventing political cycles from interfering with the implementation of a sound fiscal policy.

At present, the institutionalisation of a stable and permanent European taxation mechanism seems more of a mirage than a realistic prospect, given the disproportion between national public debts and the debts issued by the Union. Fears that moral hazard mechanisms will be triggered by the countries of southern Europe are still very strong. Nevertheless, this is an inescapable issue, one which will come to the fore as soon as an attempt is made to return to a non-emergency mode, and the problem of rollover of debt issued by the Commission arises. In sections 2.6 and 2.7 we will explain how these problems can be successfully handled by a European Debt Agency (EDA). In view of these problems and objectives, it is perhaps useful to briefly review the history of European public debt since the establishment of the euro.

2.4   European Public Debt and the Misconstruction of Monetary Unification

For a general consideration on the role of debt in capitalism, we may quote the words of the historian Marc Bloch (Bloch, 1954, p. 77): 'Delaying payments or repayments and making such delays perpetually overlap each other: this seems to be, ultimately, the great secret of the modern capitalist regime, the most exact definition of which might perhaps be "a regime that would die in the event of a simultaneous closure of all accounts."'

We can 'translate' this text written in 1935 by acknowledging that capitalism is a regime characterised by debts, which *formally* have to be paid, but which are in fact systematically rolled over. This applies in particular to public debts. As we have said above, since the English 'Financial Revolution' that is the way things have gone. Central banks exist and can exert 'soft power' over financial markets only because public debts exist, and vice versa.

Another historian, Adam Tooze, has recently had no difficulty in recognising this:

> To the horror of conservatives everywhere, the arena in which central banks perform this balancing act is the market for government debt. Government IOUs are not just obligations of the taxpayer. For the government's creditors, they are the safe assets on which pyramids of private credit are built. This Janus-faced quality of debt creates a basic tension. Whereas conservative economists anathematise central banks swapping government debt for cash as the slippery slope to hyperinflation, the reality of modern market-based finance is that it is based precisely on this transaction-the exchange of bonds for cash, mediated if necessary by the central bank. (Tooze, 2020)

Actualising Bloch's thesis, Tooze introduces the real underlying theme of the Covid crisis in Europe: the growing public eurozone debt and the methods of its financing. The issue to be addressed is this: if correctly managed, European public debt could be the potential origin of a European safe asset able to sustain financial markets' stability, which is constantly menaced by the risk of equilibria not anchored to 'fundamentals' but potentially distorted by expectations.

As mentioned in Section 1, since 2020 debt has expanded for all EU countries because of a common, global shock. There have been many proposals for cancellation of the Covid debt, whose admitted purpose is to lighten the burden of European public debt, as if the only debt to cancel could be that caused by the EU's emergency extra-expenses.

Pending a decision on the financing of the Next Generation EU, these expenses have been essentially financed by the issuance of national bonds purchased overwhelmingly by the ECB, under the PEPP.

Since the purchase programmes were already in operation even before the pandemic (PSPP), the ECB now holds large amounts of European public debt. If rolled over at maturity, these debts are in fact hedged against the vagaries of market sentiment, and hence lead to a substantial mitigation of volatility. The clear, and for some surprising, novelty in recent months is that the 'scary' increase in public debt and Europe's debt/GDP ratio has not scared anyone at all. It has instead been accompanied by a *mitigation* of the yield on 'govies'.

Clearly, behind the expansion of debts and deficits is the suspension of the stability pact, and behind the PEPP is the suspension of the capital key rule. The problem is therefore understanding what will happen to this suspension, given that we cannot even remotely hope that the 'new normal' can be an indefinite procrastination of suspensions. If there is something to procrastinate, it is not the suspension of the rules, but the payment of the debt. But the procrastination of payment has to be performed in such a way as not to undermine the sustainability of its servicing; hence it requires *rules*. It is in this perspective that the social responsibility of the central bank comes to the fore.

Certainly, under the treaties, the indefinite maintenance of public debt securities on the ECB's balance sheet would be equivalent to its cancellation. This choice would respond to various proposals recently made to transform public debts linked to the pandemic into perpetual debts, exactly as happened during the wars of the last century. These proposals can rely on the blessing, if not of Robert Barro, certainly of David Ricardo and Luigi Einaudi. The perpetuation of the quantitative easing (QE) would lead to an effective lightening of the debt burden able to produce expansionary effects on the real economy. However, this perpetuation would presuppose the definitive superseding of the ECB capital key rule, because it would imply that the ECB's purchase decisions for securities are linked to a stability objective and not to a formal distribution rule.

However, if it is true that we are only at the beginning of a new season of systematic expansion of public debt for infrastructure spending, of which the Green New Deal is but the spearhead, what we face is a permanent need for public debt growth. If that is the case, an institutionalisation of QE would overload the ECB with a weight that is already excessive for some, because it concentrates fiscal policy decisions in the hands of the monetary policy-maker, which by definition is independent from the decisions of democratically elected and politically responsible governments. Here we face a trade-off between efficiency and responsibility; a trade-off that has been traditionally ruled in the framework of the interaction between treasury and central bank. This already applies to the US, the UK and Japan, to name only the most relevant cases.

How can the ECB play its role in this eventuality, irrespectively of, or even simply before, the possibility of an institutional reform of the EU in a federal sense?

2.5   The Possible Joint Role of the European Central Bank and a European Debt Agency

In what follows, we take up the guidelines for the design of an EDA set out in Amato et al. (2021). The EDA can be read both as an efficient means to manage national public debts in the context of the existing treaties, and as a first step towards coordinated, cooperative and ultimately federal forms of management of European public debt.

Here we will focus on this second aspect, trying to show how the infrastructural instance embodied by the GND requires a rethinking of the overall relations among public investment, public debt, financial markets and the central bank. As regards the central bank, its independence cannot mean its isolation from other economic forces. The events of the last decade, to which the Covid crisis and the climate crisis have given only a final push, have decreed the end of the 'cult of the independent central bank' (Krugman, 2011), isolated from political pressures, concentrated on the management of the cycle on the assumption that all the rest can be managed by efficient markets, in the sense of not needing external indications for their operations.

If this is true in general, it is even more true for the ECB, which was established at the beginning of the millennium on the basis of unconditional compliance with the dogma of efficient markets (Abdelal, 2009). At stake with the GND, and in general with the re-infrastructuring of economies, is a reformulation of the triangulation that since the Financial Revolution has existed among public debt, financial markets and central banks (cf. Amato, 2008).

The pivot of this reformulation is the role that safe assets are called upon to play in modern financial markets. On the one hand, markets and systemic market players experience, and therefore express, a growing demand for safe assets. On the other, the stability of long-term expectations that characterises the yields of safe assets makes government bonds the elective assets because of this need for stability. This is why, as Tooze pointed out, central banks once again find themselves tasked with the mission of mediating between public debtors and private creditors.

On the one hand, the sustainability of public deficits has to be ensured by acting on the real interest rate in such a way that it is lower than the growth of the economy as a whole. It has been abundantly proven that this condition does not occur 'naturally' (Piketty, 2014); rather, it is the outcome of the prudent and decisive – i.e., responsible – operation of central banks. On the other hand, it is precisely this rate-governance action by central banks that can provide private markets with a benchmark for their calculations.

In the European context, and given the current constraints of the treaties, an EDA could make it possible to achieve this twofold objective.

2.6   The Operational Structure of the European Debt Agency

Referring to (Amato et al., 2021) for details, we can summarise the European Debt Agency's functioning as follows.

The EDA is conceived as a European institution which (1) addresses the market to raise liquid funds by issuing plain vanilla bonds with a finite maturity, which are effectively Eurobonds; (2) uses these funds to finance the national debts of individual states with loans of infinite maturity; and (3) ensures an adequate level of capitalisation against the risk of insolvency by relying on an insurance-type solvency mechanism.

The EDA does not purchase floating debt securities in the secondary market, but directly finances new debt or debt to be rolled over, according to cost formulas based on the fundamental risks of individual states.

Because it is held in perpetuity, the portion of government debt financed through EDA loans (which will grow progressively as floating debt securities mature) is structurally hedged from liquidity risk, which is linked precisely to the volatility of market sentiment at the time of refinancing.

Since it filters the market liquidity spread risk, the EDA receives from each member state an annual instalment calculated considering only the fundamental risk; i.e., its credit risk anchored to its rating, which in turn depends on the compliance of each state with the budgetary rules in force – rules which, however, as is the case today in Europe, are expected to be reintroduced with some important modifications. The total flow of instalments, net of prudential provisions, enables the EDA to remunerate its creditors at a rate in line with its high credit standing, and which will therefore be lower than, or at most equal to, the fundamental cost of each member state (cost of the underlying portfolio). The EDA thus finds its financial equilibrium on terms more advantageous than those of any portfolio manager in the market.

An EDA conceived in this way would enable member states to finance themselves from an entity that acts with a *private* logic when interfacing with the markets, but which has the *public* mission of minimising the financial burden for the states themselves.

Precisely because the EDA effectively filters liquidity risk, it is also able to impose on individual countries rates that respond to the fundamental risk of each country according to criteria of pure proportionality. The advantage of this solution is that it avoids by definition any form of mutualisation and therefore prevents any form of moral hazard.

However, this aspect of its operation, although reinforced by the risk-absorbing insurance mechanism, is not by itself capable of guaranteeing an intertemporal balance for the agency; i.e., it does not guarantee that the cash flows from the payment of instalments will enable the agency to pay the markets the returns that they have been promised. And it is precisely here that the ECB could exercise the mediating action that we discussed earlier, in full compliance with the treaties, even more so than in the various forms of QE put in place so far.

The ECB could indirectly support the activity of the EDA by using its instruments to ensure the alignment of the yields of the new European 'safe asset' with the risk-free interest rate. It could do this in two ways: (1) by remunerating at an ad hoc director rate the reserves that the EDA would progressively be able to accumulate (the accumulation of reserves is a direct function of the non-occurrence of default events by states over time) and (2) by acting in the primary market to bring the yield on bonds issued by the EDA in line with the nominal interest rate offered through a policy of targeted purchases. In particular, this intervention would be justified by the fact that it would apply to a bond that is common but does not imply any mutualisation.

The EDA would thus be able to issue Eurobonds which could play the role of safe assets in the markets, also thanks to the stabilising and mediating action of the central bank – exactly as happens today in the institutional contexts which we mentioned above.

Moreover, given that the absorption of the floating debt of states by the EDA takes place over time, the interregnum could also be managed by the ECB in full compliance with the existing treaties. Indeed, it could reduce the volatility of spreads on debt outside the EDA, continuing the PSPP. In this support action, the ECB could also free itself from the constraint of capital keys, as is already the case with the PEPP, since it would be a residual support (the share of the free float would gradually decrease), and for a limited time (because even the float purchased would flow to the EDA at maturity).

2.7 The European Debt Agency and Green Investment Financing

What we have described can be read as a process of technical optimisation in the management of public debts accumulated so far. Also the debts related to the management of the pandemic could be reabsorbed by the EDA, but what we are interested in showing now is the active role that the agency could play in the design of a *European* infrastructure investment strategy in view of the responses that the current infrastructural challenges require. The GND is undoubtedly the cutting edge of this need, but it is not the only area in which the restructuring of economic systems requires significant forms of public investment.

First, the EDA, which in its functioning does not presuppose any form of mutualisation, could introduce risk mutualisation should the political conditions for it actually arise. As is evident, a mutualistic management of European public debt would reduce the average total burden for the member states.

While mutualisation does not have much political basis for being applied to *past* debts relating to choices already made in terms of national economic policy, it may, on the other hand, appear plausible when future investment plans are envisaged, involving cooperation among countries with a view to obtaining common systemic advantages.

Most green investments, clearly infrastructural in nature, require important forms of coordination and cooperation among countries. In this case the part of public debt linked to these investments could be financed on the basis of mutualistic schemes. The EDA can in fact build segregated portfolios, managed according to different rules and according to the political objectives of fiscal policies.

Mutualistic management of common investment projects could then be reinforced by the introduction of ad hoc taxes at the European level, which would further contribute to strengthening the credibility of EDA issues (with the only caveat that particularly regressive taxes should be avoided).

Again, the central bank would play its mediating role by ensuring the intertemporal equilibrium condition of the EDA through ad hoc benchmark rates.

Finally, the EDA could become the vehicle for financing the NGEU. As we have seen, the NGEU already provides for its own financing through the issuance of securities by the Commission. However, these securities are issued to be repaid. The EDA could be the elective vehicle for a systematic rollover of the NGEU's debt as well, which even more than pooled national debts would enjoy top-notch ratings and credibility. And even in this case, the ECB would not have to do anything other than what all sovereign central banks do; i.e., guarantee the long-term stability of public bond yields, making them full-fledged safe assets.

In making possible both a 'transmigration' of national debts into the EDA and an orderly growth of common debts backed by European taxes, the ECB would not only be performing the institutional task entirely in keeping with its nature, but it could also divest itself of the programmes that it has so far deployed to reduce the volatility produced by market expectations increasingly detached from fundamental values.

But this would mean that responsibility for fiscal policy decisions would remain firmly in the hands of the states, and only eventually in the hands of a European Commission able to devise its own fiscal strategy. The ECB would not stop doing 'whatever it takes'. But it would do so in a manner more in keeping with its nature, which is not to judge the viability of fiscal policies, but only to ensure the right conditions for their financing. It would exercise a social responsibility more appropriate to its mandate.

At the same time, fiscal policy, and in particular budget expansions linked to infrastructure policy choices, could rely on financing conditions that are as little biased as possible by the 'sentiment' of markets left to themselves. For their part, the markets would have, precisely thanks to public infrastructure policies, the safe assets that they sorely need simply to operate in stable conditions.

The triangulation would start to be virtuous again, and austerity would stop being the only viable recipe. In short, we would definitely stop hiding behind the excuse that the GND, as important as it is, cannot be implemented because 'there is no money'.

NOTES

1. To date, the plan has reached a level of 806.9 billion euros. See https://ec.europa
    .eu/info/strategy/recovery-plan-europe_en.
2. See also Eichengreen (2021): 'Recent years have witnessed a sea-change in how
    elected officials and their constituents view public debt. Anyone over the age of
    50 will recall the 1990s, when there was widespread concern about government
    profligacy and fears that debt was on an unsustainable path. These worries found
    their way into the Maastricht Treaty.'

REFERENCES

Abdelal, R. (2009), *Capital Rules: The Construction of Global Finance*. Cambridge, MA: Harvard University Press.

Acemoglu, D., Aghion, P., Bursztyn, L., and D. Hemous (2012), 'The environment and directed technical change'. *American Economic Review*, 102 (1), 131–166.

Amato, M. (2008), *The Roots of a Faith: For a History of The Relationship Between Money and Credit in the West*. Torino: Bruno Mondadori.

Amato, M., Belloni, E., Falbo, P., and L. Gobbi (2021), 'Europe, public debts, and safe assets: the scope for a European Debt Agency'. *Econ. Polit.*, 38, 823–861. https://doi .org/10.1007/s40888-021-00236-6.

Amato, M., and L. Fantacci (2012), *The End of Finance*. Cambridge, MA: Polity Press.

Bloch, M. (1954), 'Esquisse d'une histoire monétaire de l'Europe'. *Cahiers des Annales*, 9.

Bruegel (2021), *European Union Countries' Recovery and Resilience Plans*. www .bruegel.org/publications/datasets/european-union-countries-recovery-and -resilience-plans/.

Brunnermeier, M.K., Garicano, L., Lane, P., Pagano M., Reis, R., Santos, T., Thesmar, D., Van Nieuwerburgh, S., and D. Vayanos (2011), *European Safe Bonds (ESBies)*. N.p.: Euro-nomics Group. https://personal.lse.ac.uk/vayanos/Euronomics/ESBies .pdf.

Brunnermeier, M.K., Langfield, S., Pagano, M., Reis, R., Van Nieuwerburgh, S., and D. Vayanos (2017), 'ESBies: safety in the tranches'. *Economic Policy*, 32 (90), 175–219.

Caballero, R.J., Farhi, E., and P.O. Gourinchas (2017), 'The safe assets shortage conundrum'. *Journal of Economic Perspective*, 31 (3), 29–46.

Carabelli, A.M. (2021), *Keynes on Uncertainty and Tragic Happiness: Complexity and Expectations*. London: Palgrave Macmillan.

De Grauwe, P., and Y. Ji (2018), 'How safe is a safe asset?' *CEPS Policy Insight*, 2018-08. Brussels: Centre for European Policy Studies.

Dickson, P.G.M. (1967), *The Financial Revolution in England: A Study in the Development of Public Credit 1688–1756*. London: Macmillan.

Draghi, M. (2020), 'We face a war against coronavirus and must mobilise accordingly'. *Financial Times*, March 20. www.ft.com/content/c6d2de3a-6ec5-11ea-89df -41bea055720b.

Eichengreen, B. (2021), 'What to do with public debt in a post pandemic world?' Groupe d'études géopolitiques. https://geopolitique.eu/en/2021/09/09/what-to-do -with-public-debt-in-a-post-pandemic-world/.

Eichengreen, B., El-Ganainy, A., Esteves, R., and K.J. Mitchene (2021), *In Defense of Public Debt*. Oxford: Oxford University Press.

European Central Bank (ECB) (2021a), *Economic Bulletin*, 1. Frankfurt am Main: ECB. www.ecb.europa.eu/pub/economic-bulletin/articles/2021/html/ecb.ebart202101_03 ~c5595cd291.en.html.

European Central Bank (ECB) (2021b), *Economic Bulletin*, 4. Frankfurt am Main: ECB. www.ecb.europa.eu/pub/economic-bulletin/html/eb202104.en.html.

European Commission (2020a), Communication from the Commission to the Council on the activation of the general escape clause of the Stability and Growth Pact. Brussels, March 20. https://eur-lex.europa.eu/legal-content/EN/TXT/PDF/?uri= CELEX:52020DC0123&from=EN.

European Commission (2020b), *2030 Climate Target Plan Impact Assessment*, SWD (2020) 176 final. Brussels: European Commission.

European Commission (2021), *'Fit for 55': Delivering the EU's 2030 Climate Target on the Way to Climate Neutrality*. COM (2021) 550 final. Brussels: European Commission.

Gabor, D., and J. Vestergaard (2018), 'Chasing unicorns: the European single safe asset'. *Competition and Change*, 22 (2), 140–164.

Giudice, G., de Manuel Aramendia, M., Kontolemis, Z., and D.P. Monteiro (2019), 'A European safe asset to complement national government bonds'. *MPRA Paper*, 95748, University Library of Munich.

Greenspan, A. (1997), 'Fostering financial innovation: the role of government'. In Dorn, J.A. (ed), *The Future of Money in the Information Age*. Washington, DC: Cato Institute, pp. 45–50.

IMF (International Monetary Fund) (2021), *Reaching Net Zero Emissions: Note Prepared for the Group of Twenty*, June. N.p.: IMF.

Juncker, J.-C., and G. Tremonti (2010), 'E-bonds would end the crisis'. *Financial Times*, December 5.

Keynes, J.M. (1933), 'National self-sufficiency'. *Yale Review*, 22 (4), June, 755–769 [reprinted in *Collected Writings of John Maynard Keynes XXI*, pp. 233–246].

Keynes, J.M. (1936), *The General Theory of Employment, Interest and Money*. Cambridge: Cambridge University Press.

Keynes, J.M. (1937), 'The general theory of employment'. *Quarterly Journal of Economics*, 51 (2), February [reprinted in *CW XIV*, pp. 109–123].

Keynes, J.M. (1938), *Letter to Roy Harrod*, July 16, in *CW XIV*, p. 300.

Krugman, P. (2011), 'Mr Keynes and the moderns'. *VOX CEPR Policy Portal*, June 21. https://voxeu.org/print/6668.

Leandro, A., and J. Zettelmeyer (2018a), 'The search for a euro area safe asset'. *Peterson Institute for International Economics Working Paper*, 18-3. Washington, DC: Peterson Institute for International Economics.

Leandro, A., and J. Zettelmeyer (2018b), 'Safety without tranches: Creating a "real" safe asset for the euro area'. *Center for Economic and Policy Research Policy Insight*, 93. Washington, DC: Center for Economic and Policy Research.

Merler, S., and J. Pisani-Ferry (2012), *Sudden Stops in the Euro Area*. Bruegel Policy Contribution. Brussels: Bruegel.

Minsky, H. (1982), *Can 'It' Happen Again? Essays on Instability and Finance*. Armonk, NY: M.E. Sharpe.

Monti, M. (2010), *A New Strategy for the Single Market: Report to the President of the European Commission, Jose Manuel Barroso*, May 9. N.p.: European Commission.

Ocasio-Cortez, A. (2019), *Draft House Resolution 109 Recognizing the Duty of the Federal Government to Create a Green New Deal.* Washington, DC: US Congress.

Pettifor, A. (2019), *The Case for the Green New Deal.* New York, NY: Verso.

Piketty, T. (2014), *Capital in the 21st Century.* Cambridge, MA: Harvard University Press.

Pisani-Ferry, J. (2021), 'Climate policy is macroeconomic policy, and the implications will be significant'. *PIIE Policy Brief,* 21-20, August.

Shiller, R. (1979), 'The volatility of long-term interest rates and expectations models of the term structure?' *Journal of Political Economy,* 87 (6), 1190–1219.

Tooze, A. (2020), 'The death of the central bank myth'. *Foreign Policy,* May 13. https://foreignpolicy.com/2020/05/13/european-central-bank-myth-monetary-policy-german-court-ruling/?fbclid=IwAR20r6NogK7qOMx8mMauqPjjTNKC09hcT15jS51M6y1m-Zf0RNn1ctrUGmg.

Tversky, A., and D. Kahneman (1982), 'Evidential impact of base rates'. In Kahneman, D., Slovic, P., and A. Tversky (eds), *Judgment Under Uncertainty: Heuristics and Biases.* Cambridge: Cambridge University Press, pp. 153–160.

Wendorff, K., and A. Mahle (2015), 'Staatsanleihen neu ausgestalten – für eine stabilitätsorientierte Währungsunion'. *Wirtschaftsdienst,* 95, 604–608.

7. Masters of the game: the power and social responsibility of central banks and central bankers in a democracy

Louis-Philippe Rochon and Guillaume Vallet[1]

1. INTRODUCTION

Since at least the financial crisis of 2007–2008 and indeed more recently with the current COVID-19 crisis, monetary policy has come under greater scrutiny with respect to its effectiveness. As interest rates have been pushed back down to the lower bound in many countries, and into negative territory in some others, it has become clear that monetary policy cannot go it alone, and fiscal policy has come back with a vengeance, resulting in unprecedented levels of public debt. More than ever, policy makers are realizing the limits of monetary policy in times of crises, and how indeed you simply cannot push on a string, or force a horse to drink.

Nevertheless, these crises have mobilized central banks to an extent rarely seen in history, not only regarding the near-zero-interest-rate policy implemented in numerous countries, but also with respect to their massive 'assets purchase programs' as central banks and monetary policy try to remain relevant.

In addition, a number of central banks have relaxed their approach to a 'strict' inflation-targeting regime, either by adopting a dual mandate as in New Zealand – or proposing to do so for the European Central Bank (ECB; Marsh, 2020) – or moving to an average inflation-targeting regime in the US.

Through it all, the overall mission of central banks has nevertheless remained the same regardless of whether they follow a strict inflation-targeting policy or a more relaxed one: the production of an alleged public good (low inflation) in the spirit of maximizing prosperity for all and society's net welfare. In this context, inflation is described as an evil (Johnson, 2016) affecting everybody, but in particular the weak and vulnerable, and those in lower income brackets. Central bankers therefore justify and legitimize their policies for this reason: the fight against inflation serves the people, and especially the disadvantaged.

As such, mainstream monetary policy is focused on fine-tuning; that is, the incremental changes in interest rates, up and down, in order to reach a natural rate and in the process influence economic activity with the aim of achieving low and stable inflation around a stated target (Rochon and Vallet, 2019).

While central banks are not poised to give up their inflation obsession anytime soon, in this chapter we wish to explore a different view of monetary policy – different from the mainstream and indeed different from some circles within the post-Keynesian economic camp. This approach, which we explore in the next section, sees monetary policy in terms of its income-distributive consequences, in both the short and long run. This stands in contrast of course to the mainstream emphasis regarding the neutrality of money.

Yet, if monetary policy has distributional consequences in the long run, this then raises important questions about the power of central banks and of central bankers, and their rightful place within a democracy; in other words, we question the role of central banks and of central bankers as unelected bureaucrats with the ability to impose their conception of the role of money vis-à-vis the functioning of the economy and society.

2.   THE INCOME-DISTRIBUTIVE NATURE OF MONETARY POLICY

As discussed above, mainstream theory rests on the notion that monetary policy is a powerful tool of economic policy, and by controlling the rate of interest central bankers somehow hope to fine-tune economic activity in a way that delivers a low and stable inflation rate, around a given inflation target, for a minimum of social costs. The premise therefore is that monetary policy is effective in delivering a target rate of inflation at low cost in terms of unemployment or loss output.

According to this view, incremental changes in the rate of interest will have repercussions that work themselves through a series of transmission mechanisms, usually associated with the notion that changes in interest rates represent a 'cost' in terms of either lending or borrowing. In this sense, increases in rates will typically slow down economic activity, and rate decreases will spur activity – or so the theory goes. The ultimate objective is twofold: to force the convergence of central bank interest rates to their natural level, which in turn will push inflation to its targeted value, which can be seen from the central bank's perspective as the 'natural' rate of inflation.

In this sense, monetary policy may have a short-run impact on economic activity, or unemployment and output, which in turn will impact inflation. This is a common belief among all mainstream economists: monetary policy works through well-behaved IS (investment–saving) and Phillips curves. Yet, the impact is considered short-lived; in other words, monetary policy is neutral in the long run. This is one of the most fundamental and sacrosanct assumptions of mainstream monetary thinking.

This convenient assumption reduces monetary policy to a sterile and quasi-mechanistic operation: if the economy is overheating, you raise interest rates and the job is done. In many ways, it is the very definition of a 'reaction function': central banks simply 'react' to, say, inflationary expectations and adjust rates accordingly. Mainstream thinking is careful to frame this debate in very sterile terms: there are no individual winners and losers, but rather it is society that wins or loses depending on the level of inflation. Monetary policy therefore is seen as delivering a common good, for the benefit of the whole society: everybody wins when inflation is low and stable.

Framing the debate in these terms has a very clear objective: it absolves central bankers from any responsibility regarding any possible antisocial consequences their policy may have, and if they recognize such ills, they are quick to point out that these negative consequences are necessarily short-lived, in the name of the long-run neutrality of money.

This is particularly the case in terms of the relationship between monetary policy and income distribution, which has grown considerably since the 2007 financial crisis (see Kappes, forthcoming, for a survey). The conclusions are very clear: any impact monetary policy has on inequality is (must be) only short-lived, and as such is inconsequential for policy. Such an impact is, in fact, considered simply the inevitable 'side effect' of sound monetary policy. Central banks

> should refrain from engaging in income redistribution, which should be sanctioned by parliaments. This does not imply that monetary policy actions do not have distributive consequences – in fact, they always have. But these are the side-effects of a strategy that aims to ensure price stability, which is by essence neutral as regards income distribution. (Cœuré, 2013)

Post-Keynesian theory, however, takes a radically different view of monetary policy, one where there are clear winners and losers not only in terms of individuals but also in terms of social classes (Lavoie and Seccareccia, 2020) and where central bank policy carries long-lasting effects and possibly leads to structural change in the way economies operate. This said, not all post-Keynesians agree. Rochon and Setterfield (2008) identified two very distinct approaches, which they labelled the 'activist' and the 'parking-it' approaches.

The activist approach is clear: central banks should use incremental changes in interest rates as a way of influencing economic activity, and hit some target, albeit some real variable; perhaps relating to unemployment, growth or capacity utilization. This post-Keynesian approach is not significantly different from the mainstream New Consensus model, for instance, in which central banks change interest rates in order to achieve a monetary target – or an inflation target, which is now the dominant central bank approach. In both views, the power of the central bank should be utilized in order to minimize the cost of achieving some targeted variable; and in both approaches, monetary policy relies on some very traditional transmission mechanisms, usually focused on demand.

In some way, it is perhaps understandable why some post-Keynesians would want to see an activist central bank: after all, post-Keynesians are united in advocating for activist institutions, especially fiscal policy, as a way of righting the wrongs of free markets, and an activist central bank using monetary policy as an unemployment and growth strategy would be a natural extension of this thinking.

Yet, the reason post-Keynesians advocate for an activist *fiscal* approach, for example, is because there is ample empirical evidence to support the notion that it works – that higher fiscal spending reduces unemployment, for example. Studies have clearly identified important fiscal multiplier effects benefiting economic activity (see Qazizada and Stockhammer, 2015).

As for monetary policy, its success in terms of achieving a given target as a result of fine-tuning is not clear. Indeed, many have pointed out the limitations of a countercyclical monetary policy, where consumption and investment may not respond to incremental changes in interest rates. For instance, Cynamon et al. (2013, p. 13) have argued that

> The transmission mechanism from monetary policy to aggregate spending in new consensus models relies on the interest sensitivity of consumption. It is difficult, however, to find empirical evidence that households do indeed raise or lower consumption by a significant amount when interest rates change. Some authors have generalized the link to include business investments (see Fazzari, Ferri, and Greenberg, 2010 and the references provided therein) but a robust interest elasticity of investment has also been difficult to demonstrate empirically.

Moreover, according to Sharpe and Suarez (2015, p. 1), 'a large body of empirical research offers mixed evidence, at best, for substantial interest-rate effects on investment. [Our research finds] that most firms claim their investment plans to be quite insensitive to decreases in interest rates, and only somewhat more responsive to interest rate increases' – what Krugman (2018) called the profession's 'dirty little secret'. In the end, there may not be any empirical support for an activist central bank nor an activist monetary policy.

2.1   Monetary Policy as Income Distribution

It is largely because of the ineffectiveness of monetary policy that some
post-Keynesians – close to the revolutionary endogenous money tradition (see
Rochon, 1999) – have proposed a new channel of transmission: the income distribution channel (see, for instance, Rochon and Seccareccia, 2021). This is in
line with Rochon and Setterfield's work on 'parking-it' monetary policy rules.

Accordingly, interest rates are not seen as a way of influencing economic
activity through traditional channels (which rely on seeing interest rates as
a cost variable), or as an equilibrium price between saving and investment,
or between lending and borrowing. Rather, this approach sees the rate of
interest itself as an income-distributive variable directly (see, for instance,
Rogers, 1999; Lavoie, 2014) or acting on the distribution of wealth and income
indirectly – that is, relying on a view that sees interest rates as the source of
an income stream to the rentier class. In this sense, it places income or social
groups at the heart of the discussion over monetary policy.

For instance, emphasizing specifically the limited effectiveness of
fine-tuning (see also Rochon, forthcoming), Lavoie (1996, p. 537) explained
this alternative post-Keynesian view:

> It then becomes clear that monetary policy should not so much be designed to
> control the level of activity, but rather to find the level of interest rates that will be
> proper for the economy from a distribution point of view. The aim of such a policy
> should be to minimize conflict over the income shares, in the hope of simultane-
> ously keeping inflation low and activity high.

A few years later, Lavoie and Seccareccia (1999) would further explore this
view by relying on the work of Pasinetti, and discuss what they called the
'fair' rate of interest, that is the 'rate of interest that will leave unchanged
the DISTRIBUTION OF INCOME between interest and non-interest
income groups, regardless of lending and borrowing activities' (Lavoie and
Seccareccia, 1999, p. 543; emphasis in original) – what Rochon and Setterfield
(2008, 2012) would later call the Pasinetti Rule.

However, before the groundbreaking work of Lavoie and Seccareccia, we
should mention the work of Niggle (1989), which has been unfortunately
largely ignored. Yet, it contains amazing insights into the impact of monetary
policy and income distribution. In particular, Niggle argues that:

> The processes connecting monetary policy to changes in the distribution of per-
> sonal income through the transmission mechanism of the level of interest rates are
> complex, with at least three causal sequences operating: 1) changes in interest rates
> can affect the functional distribution of income, and thus the personal distribution;
> 2) changes in interest rates change the market values of financial assets, effecting

capital gains or losses; 3) interest rates influence investment, aggregate demand, employment and income. (1989, pp. 818–819)

These effects can be seen in Figure 7.1.

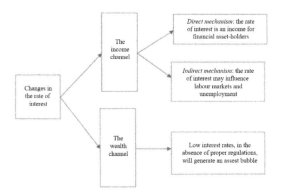

Source: Rochon and Seccareccia, 2021.

Figure 7.1   Income distribution channel of monetary policy

Figure 7.1 considers ways in which monetary policy can impact income distribution. The income channel is divided into a revenue channel (the direct mechanism) and a cost channel (the indirect mechanism). According to the first channel, interest rates themselves are an income-distributive variable by nature: changes in interest rates represent an income to the rentier class. Any increase in rates will redistribute, from a monetary policy perspective, income away from the working class to the rentier class. This is why Smithin (1996) has called the years of high rates the 'revenge of the rentier class'.

Moreover, changes in interest rates may have consequences on labour markets and unemployment through an indirect channel. Here rates are seen as the cost of borrowing or lending: increases in rates may discourage borrowing and lending and lead to predictable outcomes on labour markets, which in turn will impact wages, and the wage share. While this is a legitimate channel, its robustness has been called into question, as evidenced in the above quote by Cynamon et al. (2013).

The second channel, the wealth channel, focuses on the consequences of low interest rates on asset prices. Rossi (2020) is among those in heterodox circles who has discussed the issue in some details. Within the mainstream, the relationship between monetary policy and asset price inflation has received increased attention, in particular since the 2007 financial crisis (see Alonso-Rivera, et al., 2019; see also Filardo, 2004).

The above discussion suggests that there are two sources of distribution from the perspective of monetary policy: the policy on the one hand, by which we mean changes in the rate of interest and their impact on economic activity, and the rate of interest itself.

Hence, the parking-it approach places social classes and groups, and therefore conflict, at the heart of the discussion of monetary policy, leading Seccareccia (2017) to ask, 'Which vested interests do central banks really serve?', similar to Rochon's (forthcoming) emphasis on the 'inherent biases' of monetary policy.

However, the story does not end here, as it is possible to further discuss the impact of monetary policy on specific groups, like women or racialized minorities. Indeed, as far as the issue of gender is concerned, mention should be made of 'ladder effects' (Blanchard, 1995; Braunstein, 2013) related to the distributive nature of monetary policy: for instance, women in a precarious professional and/or family situation are likely to be more affected by varia-tions in aggregate demand caused by variations in a central bank's interest rate (Thorbecke, 2001). The same is true with regard to the position of women in economic sectors sensitive to variations in the exchange rate and terms of trade (Braunstein and Heintz, 2008). These factors are of utmost importance to women, as employment and access to real-estate ownership have become decisive elements of their empowerment (Vallet, 2020).

Moreover, and most importantly, and this cannot be emphasized enough, these impacts may not be temporary, but rather have long-lasting effects. It appears, therefore, that the conclusions drawn from this heterodox research go in the opposite direction to what some central banks have claimed, in two important ways. First, it shows how money is not neutral, not even in the long run. Indeed, post-Keynesians have been advocating how these income-distributive effects are long-lasting, and how this may lead to impor-tant structural change. Second, rather than benefiting all members of society, monetary policies dedicated to fighting inflation seem to serve first the inter-ests of some, specifically capitalists and the wealthy. This is what was recently called the 'reverse Robin Hood effect' (Casiraghi et al., 2018; see also Rochon and Rossi, 2006). Rochon (forthcoming) has referred to the 'inherent biases' of monetary policy.

If what we discuss above can be verified empirically, then it raises important questions about central banks' power and its relation to democracy.

3.   THE INCOME-DISTRIBUTIVE NATURE OF MONETARY POLICY AND THE EXERCISE OF CENTRAL BANK POWER IN A DEMOCRACY

Given the discussion above, two important lines of inquiry are followed here: the relation between central banks and power on the one hand, and the relation between central bankers and power on the other.

3.1   The Relation between Central Banks and Power

With respect to the first relation, the distributive feature of monetary policy comes down essentially to the exercise of power, both of central banks as institutions and of central bankers, and the dynamics of how such power is exercised. This approach remains largely underdeveloped, especially in economics, although interesting work has emerged in sociology and political science (Dietsch et al., 2018; Pixley, 2018; Riles, 2018).

In a democracy, the power of the central bank is seen as legitimate because it is alleged to serve the people, by delivering a public good. Specifically, central banks are the institutions performing the social mission of producing a public good – macroeconomic stability and prosperity, and inflation-targeting – by achieving their targeted macroeconomic objectives. Central banks are the 'agent' of a 'principal' (society) and its political representatives (generally politicians) (Walsh, 1995; Alesina and Tabellini, 2008). Such a framework has embodied the dynamic evolution of democracies for over a century: the growing separation between the political and the administrative, without completely abandoning the existing relationship between the two (Tucker, 2018).

Because monetary policy claims to be 'mechanistic' or even scientific, central banks are seen as specialized, rationalized and efficient institutions capable of delivering the expected public good for all, while being neutral in the sense that their policies do not favour any specific group.

Hence for the mainstream, central banks would be independent of any perceived favouritism toward any specific group, thereby legitimizing their power. It is in this sense that we described monetary policy above as 'mechanistic'. However, the distributive nature of monetary policy erodes the very notion of an independent central bank. After all, how can you have independent institutions if their policies have the power to frame society's functioning, and worse profit specific groups? As Adolph (2013, p. 103) concludes, 'as long as monetary agents aspire to further wealth or office, paper autonomy alone cannot guarantee the insulation of monetary policy from outside interests'.

However, the income-distributive nature of monetary policy challenges such a legitimacy. Indeed, through their policies central banks have the power to shape economies and societies (Braunstein and Seguino, 2018), particularly through the 'income distribution channel', as explained above. In other words, they exert 'structural power' (Strange, 1994), capable of favouring some groups more than others. Likewise, central banks' 'structural power' on income distribution is visible through their quantitative easing (QE) programs, where central banks become creditors to specific economic agents: not only are such programs likely to increase the effectiveness of the aforementioned 'wealth channel' by stabilizing the price of financial assets, but these programs give power to central banks as bondholders. Indeed, being an important bondholder is associated with the power to influence the management of the creditors' economic resources – in order to be paid back – thus modifying the creditors' income distribution policies. In that sense, central banks also exert a distributive impact on the macroeconomic income of countries.

In the eurozone, for example, even though the recent massive purchasing programs – such as the Pandemic Emergency Purchase Programme (PEPP) and the Public Sector Purchase Programme (PSPP) that have been implemented since March 2020 – by the ECB have been officially without conditionality (unlike previous programs, the PEPP now also includes Greek debt) so far, it is certain that as a bondholder of European public debt the ECB will have a word to say on the economic policies implemented by the eurozone countries in the future, in order to get reimbursed. The Governor of the Banque de France, François Villeroy de Galhau, has already warned that 'all of this will have to be paid back' (Marsh, 2020).

To sum up, the rise in central banks' power related to income distribution, particularly visible with the recent two crises, can be explained by three reasons (Tucker, 2018, p. 16):

•   Central banks have become part of the fiscal state (through QE programs in particular);
•   Central banks have become part of the emergency state (through their role of lender of last resort);
•   Central banks have become part of the regulatory state (they have the power to supervise and to create norms that rule the life of the everyday person; for instance, in the banking system).

Therefore, such a power questions central banks' but also central bankers' actions vis-à-vis the democratic life, to which we now turn.

3.2   The Relation between Central Bankers' Power and Democracy

In line with the increasingly 'bureaucratic' role of central banks in a democracy discussed above, central bankers who implement monetary policy are supposed to serve democracy through their particular expertise. So far, their expertise has been twofold: 'regulatory expertise' and 'testimonial expertise' (Dietsch et al., 2018). This double expertise is alleged to give central bankers a legitimate power (namely their authority, from a Weberian perspective) since they would be appointed for their skills only. For that reason, their power is alleged to be politically neutral.

However, the distributive nature of monetary policy gives central bankers a type of power they are neither supposed nor prepared to exert in a democracy, because of the political dimension of such a power. To expound this idea, we should consider the following two points.

First, the majority of central bankers are economists (Diouf and Pépin, 2017). Although they have to build ties with politics (either as simple citizens or also because they have ties with politicians due to their remit – the cases of the careers of Christine Lagarde and Mario Draghi, the current and former president of the ECB respectively, come to mind here), central bankers claim that their skills and their mandate put them outside of political debates (Vallet, 2019). The status of independent central banks is the official framework justifying such a stance and thus conferring a legitimacy to their power (Downey, 2020).

Second, a contradiction appears with respect to democratic life: central bankers are not elected by the people, but they have the power to shape the people's everyday lives. In other words, the power to implement monetary policy is ultimately in the hands of unelected central bankers, who instead are appointed by politicians on the basis of their competencies (Farvaque et al., 2016) and their ability to reach the targets defined by the 'principal' (Walsh, 1995; Alesina and Tabellini, 2008).

More problematically, despite the official reference to the 'transparency model' implying regular public communications (their above 'testimonial expertise'), central bankers rest on a type of expertise that is not fully understandable by the average citizen.

Such a feature addresses serious concern about central bankers' power in a democracy. Specifically, central bankers should always have in mind that they serve the people when they implement monetary policy. They ought to ensure people place confidence in their actions, and central bankers must demonstrate that they are not elites disconnected from the will of people (Pixley, 2018; Riles, 2018).

This is a basic condition, but it is not enough: as a delegated power, citizens should always have the opportunity to not only control such a power, but also to participate in its exercise, especially because of the distributive nature of monetary policy. To expound, there could be no power of regulation without representation (Tucker, 2018), and central bankers, as elites, must not be a closed-off social group. On the contrary, the social group of central bankers should be open to society in its recruitment from a sociological perspective.

4.   CENTRAL BANKS SHOULD NOT BE THE 'ONLY GAME IN (DEMOCRATIC) TOWN' TO DEAL WITH INCOME DISTRIBUTION: THE KEY ROLE OF FISCAL POLICY

If monetary policy does have important distributive effects that stray from the intended (or alleged) neutral inflation-targeting mission of central banks, this raises a number of issues about the intent of monetary policy. Of course, while central banks have acknowledged the income-distributive effects, they have argued that these are simply the unintended results – side effects – of sound policy (i.e., inflation fighting), and are short-lived and transitory. As a result, they can be ignored in setting monetary policy. For instance, Ampudia et. al (2018, p. 3) have argued that 'The overall effects of monetary policy on income inequality are modest, compared to its observed secular trend.' Similarly, as quoted above but worth repeating here Cœuré (2013) has argued that central banks

> should refrain from engaging in income redistribution, which should be sanctioned by parliaments. This does not imply that monetary policy actions do not have distributive consequences – in fact, they always have. But these are the side-effects of a strategy that aims to ensure price stability, which is by essence neutral as regards income distribution.

Adam Posen from the Bank of England was clear: income distribution should be ignored by central banks. 'What matters is that the committee is pursuing a policy that is not clearly motivated or traced to a distributive effect as a goal.' Similarly, Mersch (2014) has echoed the same sentiment: 'The ECB has a clear mandate to deliver price stability – and that mandate does not involve policies aimed at the distribution of wealth, income or consumption ... These distributional side-effects then need to be tolerated.'

However, central banks should not deny their role in income distribution, since there is a political dimension to monetary policy, on two levels.

First, the central bank is in interaction with other macroeconomic institutions holding a political power and implementing other policies, which is the case with fiscal policy. Although there could be cooperation between monetary and fiscal policies, they could also diverge – which has been modelled through the famous 'game of chicken' for instance (see Buiter, 2010). Whether cooperating or not, the nature of the relation between monetary and fiscal policies affects income distribution.

Indeed, fiscal authorities could implement specific policies aimed at off-setting the negative consequences of monetary policies, in reference to a collective definition of social justice. For example, such a situation has occurred frequently in the eurozone since 1999 between the ECB and the European governments, in spite of the official rules alleged to curb public spending. In reaction to the tightening of monetary policy, government authorities have undertaken a more expansionary fiscal policy. This is what some economists called a 'strategic substitutability' (Debrun and Wyplosz, 1999; Créel et al., 2002). But in return, the ECB set up monetary policies that were more restrictive to counteract the alleged negative effects of 'loose' fiscal policies – consistent with the ECB's monetarist philosophy, and the need to impose 'monetary dominance'.

In this case, there is an 'indirect' political dimension to monetary policy, even if the income-distributive effects are short-lived and transitory. The possible non-cooperation between monetary and fiscal authorities, which could result from the tension between elected politicians and non-elected experts of independent institutions, can distort the distribution of income according to the balance of power given the political structure in place. As the European case exemplifies, if governments are politically 'stronger' than the ECB, they succeed in imposing their policies and expansive fiscal policy may favour non-rentiers. Conversely, if the ECB has more power than the governments, 'monetary dominance' becomes the rule and low-inflation-targeted monetary policies favouring rentiers can be implemented.

Symmetrically, central banks can be compelled to take the lead in the hope of restoring growth and thus to exert income distribution in favour of the people. Defenders of 'helicopter money', for instance, have insisted on this potential role recently (Couppey-Soubeyran, 2020). However, as the limited impact of QE programs has demonstrated, central banks cannot replace fiscal stimulus, and expansive so-called unconventional monetary policies should be seen as 'Hail Mary' policies (Rochon and Vallet, 2019).

Second, there could also be a 'direct' political dimension to monetary policy. Indeed, if central bankers are aware of serving some groups rather than others when setting up and implementing monetary policy (they already admit to the existence of income-distributive consequences to monetary policy, though short-lived), then this is conscious choice related to the exercise of their power to (re)distribute resources. In other words, relying on both personal interests and values, they make the choice to channel the distribution of resources; this is a clearly political choice.

Moreover, we believe that it is not simply monetary policy that has a 'political' dimension, but also the central banker. Indeed, we must remember that central bankers are chosen from elite groups – groups that share similar values to central banks: fighting inflation to protect net asset values. In other words, central bankers are chosen for their adherence to this ideal, and for their 'culture' and 'regulatory expertise' (Johnson, 2016; Dietsch et al., 2018; Vallet, 2019):

> Because central bankers linked to the financial sector care about their prospects after leaving the bank, they have strong incentives to cater to this industry's preferences. The consequences of these findings are devastating for the naive view of central banks as neutral technocrats that use their independence only to be isolated from the myopic pressures of partisan politics. (Fernandez-Albertos, 2015, p. 25)

However, the post-Keynesian conclusions lead to two important sets of questions:

1. Which segments of the population do central banks really serve? Why do central banks keep implementing such policies in the name of the common good when there is increasing evidence about the impact of their own policies?
2. If indeed monetary policy is alleged to exert long-lasting effects on particular social groups, why are these independent institutions not subject to greater accountability?

Indeed, accountability refers here to the existence of both 'internal' and 'external' norms, where the former refers to norms and rules produced/defined by central banks themselves to help them fulfil their mission: internal organization, forecasting, communication of policies, hiring of orthodox researchers, communication of policy, reinforcement and protection of the message of the evil of inflation. This amounts to the internal culture of central banks, or what Johnson (2016) refers to a 'closed off group'. It is about the self-preservation, which requires institutional independence.

'External norms' refer to norms defined and controlled by society and its representatives to ensure central banks fulfil their mission. In their actual form, external norms deal with 'regular reassessment' of central banks' policies by the legislature (Downey, 2020). Up to now, such a 'regular assessment' has only taken the form of nomination/revocation of governors, as well as speeches of governors pronounced in front of parliament or political representatives of a people – namely other elites – consisting of explaining monetary policies *ex post*. This was well summed up by Paul Volcker, a former chairman of the Federal Reserve: 'Congress created us and the Congress can uncreate us' (Stiglitz, 1998, p. 222).

But more importantly, we agree with Tucker and acknowledge that major distributional power should remain in the hands of politicians in charge of implementing fiscal policy, who are elected and thus representative of the people. In other words, central banks' power should be mitigated through the aforementioned regular reassessment of their policies, but also through the limitations of their prerogatives that imply an income-distributive impact. Central banks should not be the only game in town to deal with such an issue, which should refer mainly to fiscal policy. The increases in central banks' power, visible through the 'monetary dominance framework', that have occurred for 40 years can also be understood as the outcome of the recoiling by politicians and some scholars against the positive role given to fiscal policy. In addition to their status of independence, such a framework is likely to increase the risk of atrophy, bias and even usurpation of power by central bankers. With respect to the dynamics of democracy, this is problematic since fiscal policy relates to the people's choices and needs, as explained earlier.

However, the previous arguments have emphasized that there is a de facto power given to central banks and central bankers to influence income distribution. For that reason, we explain in the next section why such a feature requires a new framework for central banking, implying a need for central banks and central bankers to turn to social responsibility.

5. THE RELATIONSHIP BETWEEN CENTRAL BANKS, CENTRAL BANKERS AND THEIR SOCIAL RESPONSIBILITY: TOWARD A NEW FRAMEWORK

In contemporary capitalism, there is a growing literature that considers the need for firms to adopt models of social responsibility, which emphasizes the social consequences of their economic actions with the aim to promote the common good. In the age of climate change, for instance, such a model has gained ground. However, not only is such a model disputable with respect to firms' profit-seeking as their main objective, but private companies are also not compelled by law to be really engaged in social responsibility, particularly because their role regarding this responsibility is not carved into constitutions.

By contrast, as underlined in the introduction, central banks are alleged to exert such a role with respect to their constitutional missions. Nevertheless, a smaller body of literature has studied the relationship between central banks' power and their social responsibility, and this topic deserves more attention. Here our aim is to fill this gap.

Indeed, in considering the social responsibility of institutions such as central banks in a democracy, we need to question their relation to the political will of a given people, who are at the core of the dynamics of democracy. The political will of the people, embodied by their specific culture (implying specific norms and values), materializes in a tangible way through economic and social policies until the common good is reached. As Janet Yellen, a former governor of the American Federal Reserve system, argued, 'in every phase of our work and decision-making, we consider the well-being of the American people and the prosperity of our nation' (quoted in Dietsch et al., 2018, p. 1).

This is why the common good in a democracy can change according to the changing will of the people: 'Human good is not the good of rest in a permanent status, but of adaptation in a moving process' (Small, 1903, p. 143). This is also why institutions in charge of reaching the common good should be controlled by the people. In totalitarian regimes, the common good decided by a single person is not the common good.

Therefore, we think that institutions that take seriously their social responsibility follow a Weberian 'ethics of responsibility' (Weber, 1963) consistent with the above framework. To elaborate on this idea, let us mention that although it is not possible to connect ethics to a universal truth, 'ethics' refers here to the mediation toward a common good and general interest, which is identifiable in a community through its culture, values and norms. Therefore, 'all particular moral judgments are implied estimates of the usefulness of the actions concerned with reference to ends contemplated as desirable' (Small, 1903, p. 122). 'Desirable' refers here to valuations that stem from moral standards, and broadly encapsulates all moral deeds within a community.

Moreover, the ethics of responsibility rests on the following three principles underpinning individuals' actions (Weber, 1963):

- To be aware of the foreseeable consequences of the action and to be accountable for it;
- A strong commitment to an objective – here the common good;
- To assume the 'sense of proportion' – this refers to a pragmatic and practical action, in opposition to the strict respect of rules in the name of a certain moral. On the condition that his or her sole objective is to serve the common good, an individual must have the liberty to choose the best options offered to him or her.

In light of this discussion, we can now address three lines of enquiry with respect to central banks' and central bankers' actions in a democracy:

1. The independence of central banks should be rejected because it rests on the assumption of a strong opposition between the government and the public; the framework is 'opportunistic government vs unified public (with unified preferences)'. But 'this is not the way real politics is structured. Instead, government is a contested space and the public is divided, with the conventional division between capital and labor' (Palley, 2019, pp. 11–12). Therefore, central bank independence can lead central bankers to take part of this division, and be either close to capital or labour. Likewise, economic (and political) actors have different preferences regarding the use of monetary policy.

Consequently, we should remember that 'central banks' independence involves politics' (Palley, 2019, p. 12). Specifically, we agree with Palley (2019) when he argues that central bank independence – in high-income countries in particular – should be understood in terms of class conflict, and even social conflicts taken in a broader sense (including gender, for instance). Conflicts at large are the core of democracy's life, since they trigger debates on what the common good should be (Touraine, 1994).

Shifting to this framework leads us to reject the idea of an 'optimal' monetary policy à la Friedman, which in this specific context is 'optimal' for some social groups only. With this framework the debate is less about the efficiency of monetary policy and more about the control over monetary policy: if we agree that central banks can have an impact on the inflation rate (especially through the independence framework in developed countries; see Balls et al., 2018), then controlling monetary policy – even through independence, which could lead to lower inflation – is a political issue reflecting social conflicts.

Specifically, as Palley (2019, p. 18) claims, 'capital is interested in achieving its optimal inflation target, not in pushing inflation ever lower'. Therefore, the status of independence can serve central bankers if the latter are close to financial groups: 'Independence creates a form of focal point which financial markets can use to discipline monetary and fiscal policy' (Palley, 2019, p. 22). In other words, independence is likely to generate a form of policy lock-in in favour of capital that can be maintained even when democratic elections produce a change in government. Even through financial supervision, independence could be a means for capital to capture central banks.

By the same token, the distributive nature of monetary policy is supposed to get rid of monetary rules à la Friedman (including the inflation-targeting framework). Indeed, such rules are a lure and even a denial of democracy: not only are these monetary rules strictly aimed at targeting low inflation not preferable with respect to discretionary monetary policies, but they are also harmful to democracy for two reasons.

First, if we acknowledge the distributive nature of monetary policy, the alleged neutrality of these rules is wrong since they serve some groups. Monetary rules should exist only on the condition they participate in improving the common good, which supposes that central banks turn to social responsibility with the 'sense of proportion' exposed previously. Note that what Rochon and Setterfield (2007) call 'parking-it' rules go a long way in improving the common good; i.e., a better distribution of income from the perspective of monetary policy. This approach is consistent with monetary policies aiming to rest on the aforementioned 'fair' rate of interest.

Second, in addition to our development on the political underpinnings of independence, the actual rules à la Friedman serve also central bankers, since their career success depends on respecting these rules. In other words, rules à la Friedman participate in framing a specific culture of central bankers through the social worship of their 'regulatory expertise' (Dietsch et al., 2018), leading them to function as a closed-off social group (Johnson, 2016) and to implement policies not understandable for people. Indeed, many studies have emphasized the overlapping connections between central banking and the financial and monetary sector (Diouf and Pépin, 2017; Vallet, 2019). The more central bankers are labelled as 'hawks' (implying that they are fully committed to price stability during their remit), the better their reputation and the higher the probability of getting good positions in financial and monetary institutions after their mandate (Adolph, 2013). With respect to the required 'ethics of responsibility' followed here, such evidence is not consistent with a strong commitment to the common good democratically framed.

2.   Therefore, a crucial question should be addressed: are central bankers sufficiently controlled, and if not, should the democratic control exerted over monetary policy be redesigned? Specifically, should this control be enlarged to include the terms and conditions of the delegation of power to central banks, which would involve new democratic bodies of supervision (including those in central banks' inner organization; see Vallet, forthcoming). Moreover, this would ensure the people retain a credible threat to change this delegated power (Downey, 2020).

To elaborate on this idea, two points should be emphasized. First, the existing framework of accountability (communication procedures by central bankers) and control over central bankers' decisions (speeches and reports to parliament or government associated with the status of independence) are not enough to fully cope with the challenges associated with the distributive nature of monetary policy. This existing framework is oriented externally of central banks (from central banks to society) and does not counterbalance the power associated with central bankers' 'regulatory' and 'testimonial' expertise (from society to central banks).

In order to exert an effective democratic control over central bankers' monetary policies, we believe that central banks should be transformed through their inner organizations. Indeed, we should consider central banks not as 'black boxes' (Adolph, 2013) but, on the contrary, as 'mobilization structures' aiming to serve the common good from their inner organization (Vallet, 2020). Resting on this framework of central banks as 'mobilization structures' enables us to take into account the social embeddedness of central banks: each central bank's organization has its own features because each monetary zone it embodies, and its objective, history, culture, and so on are different from other banks'. To follow the aforementioned ethics of responsibility compels central bankers to take into account such cultural features: because of the differing contexts, to reach the common good in Switzerland is not the same as reaching the common good in the UK. Therefore, dealing with the distributive nature of monetary policy differs according to the contexts.

From this, we suggest the creation of new bodies in central banks, in particular a body devoted to the discussion of the devising of monetary policy. Such a body would gather individuals embodying the social diversity of a given society, which is supposed to open central banks to a wide range of different personalities and culture. It would be a political body in charge of ensuring central bankers consider the common good when they design monetary policies. Although such a body would not be a 'small parliament' since its role is not to supersede that of the parliament nor to discuss fiscal policy, it would avoid 'from the inside' the risk of atrophy and concentration of power by central banks and central bankers. Regarding crucial topics such as income distribution, such a body could discuss the choices of monetary policy.

This type of body already exists to some extent in some central banks. For instance, the so-called 'Conseil de Banque' within the Swiss National Bank (SNB) supervises and controls the management of the affairs of the SNB. Nominated either by the SNB itself or by the Federal Council, the members of the 'Conseil de Banque' are selected for their trustworthiness and their recognized knowledge in the fields of banking and financial services, business management, economic policy or science. In particular, there is always a representative of Swiss industry.

Our idea of creating a new body in charge of supervising and controlling monetary policies goes beyond that. As underlined above, the composition of this body should reflect diversity on a larger scale, including people differing in gender, age, ethnicity, sexual orientations and sexual identity[2] as well as representatives of unions or other social movements.

3. In addition to the necessary aforementioned changes aimed at improving central banks' social responsibility, new personnel with new skills should be hired. Indeed, an increased diversity among the personnel is required to enhance creativity and to cope with new challenges that central banks are facing (Haldane, 2016). It is essential to promote profiles with new skills, capable of having a managerial expertise on income distribution. This implies recruiting people with academic backgrounds differing from just economics, such as sociology.

In addition, increasing central banks' personnel diversity is needed regarding the reality of central bankers' culture: the latter is related to the domination by the 'powerful' (male, white, highly educated in macroeconomics or econometrics). This is conspicuous regarding the academic profile of central bankers or their social origins (Johnson, 2016; Vallet, 2019), which influence the distributive nature of their monetary policies defending the value of capital and thus can make them close to rentiers' interests (Smithin, 1996).

Such a change will foster the 'circulation' of elites, which is a key condition of the democratic life: everyone should have the opportunity to directly participate in the decision-making process promoting the common good.

6.   CONCLUSION

As we have demonstrated throughout this chapter, central banks should take seriously their social responsibility. The latter is a matter of economic but also social and political consequences of central banks' monetary policies for the economy and society. These consequences refer to several issues that overlap sometimes: unemployment and financial stability, but also income distribution, gender and sexual preferences, the environment and social inequalities, among others. These issues demonstrate that neither monetary policies nor central banks as institutions are politically neutral, and this reality must be acknowledged by the 'world of central banking', which includes central bankers themselves.

This is of utmost importance regarding the current state of democracies: an increasing number of people, in several countries worldwide, have become mistrustful toward elites, sometimes rejecting them. Elites are viewed as confiscating power to the detriment of people. Such a sentiment is not consistent with democratic principles, which rest on the ideas that, first, one individual equals one voice, and second, everyone can participate in the democratic life. For these reasons, even though central banks should not be the only game in town to deal with the buoyant issues of today's democracies, they are directly concerned because they are institutions of power, and because their members are unelected by the people.

Such major changes occurring in central banking also challenge the scientific analysis of central banks and monetary policy. The time is ripe to rethink the understanding of central banking with new tools and new approaches (see Kappes, Rochon and Vallet, forthcoming).

NOTES

1.   This work has been partially supported by the Agence Nationale de la Recherche project ANR-15-IDEX-02. A form of this chapter was published first in *PSL Quarterly Review*: https://rosa.uniroma1.it/rosa04/psl_quarterly_review.
2.   Although it should be mentioned that the members of the 'Conseil de Banque' should come from the different geographical parts of the country.

REFERENCES

Adolph, C. (2013), *Bankers, Bureaucrats and Central Bank Politics: The Myth of Neutrality*. Cambridge: Cambridge University Press.
Alesina, A., and G. Tabellini (2008), 'Bureaucrats or politicians? Part II: multiple policy tasks'. *Journal of Public Economics*, 92, 426–447.
Alonso-Rivera, A., Cruz-Aké, S., and F. Venegas-Martínez (2019), 'Impact of monetary policy on financial markets efficiency under speculative bubbles: a non-normal and non-linear entropy-based approach'. *Análisis Económico*, 34 (86), 157–178.
Ampudia, M., Georgarakos, D., Slacalek, J., Trist, O., Vermeulen, P., and G. Violante (2018), 'Monetary policy and household inequality', *Working Paper Series*, 2179. Frankfurt am Main: European Central Bank. www.ecb.europa.eu/pub/pdf/scpwps/ecb.wp2170.en.pdf.
Balls, E., Howat, J., and A. Stansbury (2018), 'Central bank independence revisited: after the financial crisis, what should a model central bank look like?' *M-RCBG Associate Working Paper Series*, 87. Cambridge, MA: Mossavar-Rahmani Center for Business and Government, Harvard Kennedy Business School.
Blanchard, O. (1995), 'Macroeconomic implications of shifts in the relative demand for skills'. *Economic Policy Review*, 1 (1), 48–53.
Braunstein, E. (2013), 'Central bank policy and gender'. In Figart, D.M., and T.L. Warnecke (eds), *Handbook of Research on Gender and Economic Life*. Cheltenham, UK and Northampton, MA: Edward Elgar Publishing, pp. 345–358.
Braunstein, E., and J. Heintz (2008), 'Gender bias and central bank policy: employment and inflation reduction'. *International Review of Applied Economics*, 22 (2), 173–186.
Braunstein, E., and S. Seguino (2018), 'The impact of economic policy and structural change on gender employment inequality in Latin America, 1990–2010'. *Review of Keynesian Economics*, 6 (3), 307–332.
Buiter, W. (2010), 'Games of "chicken" between monetary and fiscal authority: who will control the deep pockets of the central bank?' *Global Economics View*, 21 July.
Casiraghi, M., Gaiotti, E., Rodano, L., and A. Secchi (2018), 'A "reverse Robin Hood" effect? The distributional implications of non-standard monetary policy for Italian households'. *Journal of International Money and Finance*, 85, 215–235.
Cœuré, B. (2013), 'Outright monetary transactions, one year on'. Speech, Centre for Economic Policy Research, the German Institute for Economic Research and the KfW Bankengruppe, Berlin, 2 September.
Couppey-Soubeyran, J. (2020), 'La "monnaie hélicoptère" contre la dépression dans le sillage de la crise sanitaire'. Institut Veblen. www.veblen-institute.org/La-monnaie-helicoptere-contre-la-depression-dans-le-sillage-de-la-crise.html.
Créel, J., Latreille, T., and J. Le Cacheux (2002), 'Le pacte de stabilité et les politiques budgétaires dans l'Union européenne', *Revue de l'OFCE*, 85 (3), 245–297.

Cynamon, B.Z., Fazzari, S., and M. Setterfield (2013), *After the Great Recession: The Struggle for Economic Recovery and Growth*. Cambridge: Cambridge University Press.

Debrun, X., and C. Wyplosz (1999), 'Onze gouvernements et une Banque centrale'. *Revue d'Economie Politique*, 109 (3), 387–420.

Dietsch, P., Claveau, F., and C. Fontan (2018), *Do Central Banks Serve the People?* Cambridge: Polity Press.

Diouf, I., and D. Pépin (2017), 'Gender and central banking'. *Economic Modelling*, 61, 193–206.

Downey, L. (2020), 'Delegation in democracy: a temporal analysis', *Journal of Political Philosophy*, 29 (3), pp. 305–329. https://doi.org/10.1111/jopp.12234.

Farvaque, E., Hayat, M.A., and A. Mihailov (2016), 'Who supports the ECB? Evidence from Eurobarometer survey data'. *World Economy*, 40 (4), 654–677.

Fernandez-Albertos, J. (2015), 'The politics of central bank independence'. *Annual Review of Political Science*, 18, 217–237.

Filardo, A. (2004), 'Monetary policy and asset price bubbles: calibrating the monetary policy trade-offs'. *BIS Working Papers 155*. Basel: Bank for International Settlements.

Haldane, A. (2016), 'The Sneeches'. Speech, Scottish Business Friends dinner in aid of BBC Children in Need, Edinburgh, 12 May.

Johnson, J. (2016), *Priests of Prosperity: How Central Bankers Transformed the Postcommunist World*. Ithaca, NY: Cornell University Press.

Kappes, S. (forthcoming), 'Monetary policy and personal income distribution: a survey of the empirical literature'. *Review of Political Economy*.

Kappes, S., Rochon, L.-P., and G. Vallet (forthcoming), series on central banking and monetary policies. Cheltenham, UK and Northampton, MA: Edward Elgar Publishing.

Krugman, P. (2018), 'Why was Trump's tax cut a fizzle?' *New York Times* blog, 15 November. www.nytimes.com/2018/11/15/opinion/tax-cut-fail-trump.html.

Lavoie, M. (1996), 'Monetary policy in an economy with endogenous credit money'. In Nell, E., and G. Deleplace (eds), *Money in Motion*. London: Macmillan, pp. 532–545.

Lavoie, M. (2014), *Post-Keynesian Economics: New Foundations*. Cheltenham, UK and Northampton, MA: Edward Elgar Publishing.

Lavoie, M., and M. Seccareccia (1999), 'Interest rate: fair'. In O'Hara, P. (ed.), *Encyclopedia of Political Economy*. London: Routledge, pp. 543–545.

Lavoie, M., and M. Seccareccia (2020), 'Going beyond the inflation targeting mantra: a dual mandate'. Max Bell School of Public Policy, McGill University. www.mcgill.ca/maxbellschool/files/maxbellschool/7_lavoie.pdf.

Marsh, D. (2020), 'French governor suggests wider ECB mandate'. Official Monetary and Financial Institutions Forum, 25 September. www.omfif.org/2020/09/french-governor-suggests-wider-ecb-mandate/?utm_source=omfifupdate.

Mersch, Y. (Member of the Executive Board of the ECB) (2014), 'Monetary policy and economic inequality', keynote speech, Corporate Credit Conference, Zurich, 17 October.

Niggle, C. (1989), 'Monetary policy and changes in income distribution'. *Journal of Economic Issues*, 23 (3), September, 809–822.

Palley, T. (2019), 'Central bank independence: a rigged debate based on false politics and economics'. *Forum for Macroeconomics and Macroeconomic Policies Working Paper*, 49, September.

Pixley, J. (2018), *Central Banks, Democratic States and Financial Power*. Cambridge: Cambridge University Press.

Posen, A. (2012), 'Comments on "Methods of Policy Accommodation at the Interest-Rate Lower Bound", by Michael Woodford', Federal Reserve Bank of Kansas City Economics Policy Symposium on the Changing Policy Landscape. Jackson Hole, Wyoming, 31 August.

Qazizada, W., and E. Stockhammer (2015), 'Government spending multipliers in contraction and expansion'. *International Review of Applied Economics*, 29 (2), 238–258.

Riles, A. (2018), *Financial Citizenship*. Ithaca, NY: Cornell University Press.

Rochon, L.-P. (1999), *Credit, Money and Production: An Alternative Post-Keynesian Approach*. Cheltenham, UK and Northampton, MA: Edward Elgar Publishing.

Rochon, L.-P. (forthcoming), 'The inherent biases of monetary policy'. In Giron, A. (ed.), *Money and Budgetary Policy: Before and After the Global Crisis 2020*. Cuidad de México: Instituto de Investigaciones Económica, Universidad Nacional Autónoma de México.

Rochon, L.-P., and S. Rossi (2006), 'Inflation targeting, economic performance, and income distribution: a monetary macroeconomics analysis'. *Journal of Post Keynesian Economics*, 28 (4), 615–638.

Rochon, L.-P., and M. Seccareccia (2021), 'Un ensayo sobre política monetaria y distribución del ingreso: una perspectiva heterodoxa'. *Ensayos Económicos*, 76 (May), 2–20.

Rochon, L.-P., and M. Setterfield (2007), 'Interest rates, income distribution and monetary policy dominance: post Keynesians and the "fair" rate of interest'. *Journal of Post Keynesian Economics*, 30 (1), 13–41.

Rochon, L.-P., and M. Setterfield (2008), 'The political economy of interest rate setting, inflation, and income distribution'. *International Journal of Political Economy*, 37 (2), 2–25.

Rochon, L.-P., and M. Setterfield (2012), 'A Kaleckian model of growth and distribution with conflict-inflation and Post-Keynesian nominal interest rate rules'. *Journal of Post Keynesian Economics*, 34 (3), 497–520.

Rochon, L.-P., and G. Vallet (2019), 'Economía del Ave María: el modelo teórico detrás de las políticas monetarias no convencionales'. *Ola Financiera*, 12 (34), 1–24.

Rogers, C. (1999), *Money, Interest and Capital: A Study in the Foundations of Monetary Theory*. Cambridge: Cambridge University Press.

Rossi, S. (2020), 'Central banks' contribution to financial instability'. *Bulletin of Political Economy*, 14 (2), 203–217.

Seccareccia, M. (2017), 'Which vested interests do central banks really serve? Understanding central bank policy since the global financial crisis'. *Journal of Economic Issues*, 51 (2), 341–350.

Sharpe, S., and G. Suarez (2015), 'Why isn't investment more sensitive to interest rates: evidence from surveys'. *Finance and Economics Discussion Series*. Washington, DC: Divisions of Research and Statistics and Monetary Affairs, Federal Reserve Board.

Small, A.W. (1903), 'The significance of sociology for ethics'. *University of Chicago Decennial Publications*, 4, 111–149.

Smithin, J. (1996), *Macroeconomic Policy and the Future of Capitalism: The Revenge of Rentiers and the Threat to Prosperity*. Cheltenham, UK and Brookfield, VT: Edward Elgar Publishing.

Stiglitz, J. (1998), 'Central banking in a democratic society'. *De Economist*, 146, 199–226.

Strange, S. (1994), 'The study of international political economy'. In Lehmkuhl, U. (ed.), *Theorien Internationaler Politik*. Munich: R. Oldenburg Verlag, pp. 310–330.

Thorbecke, W. (2001), 'Estimating the effects of disinflationary monetary policy on minorities'. *Journal of Policy Modeling*, 23 (1), 51–66.

Touraine, A. (1994), *Qu'est-ce que la démocratie?* Paris: Fayard.

Tucker, P. (2018), *Unelected Power: The Quest for Legitimacy in Central Banking and the Regulatory State*. Princeton, NJ: Princeton University Press.

Vallet, G. (2019), 'This is a man's world : autorité et pouvoir genrés dans le milieu des banques centrales'. *Revue de la régulation*, 25, spring. http://journals.openedition .org/regulation/14738; https://doi.org/10.4000/regulation.14738.

Vallet, G. (2020), 'Gender diversity as a tool to make central banks progressive institutions: the case of the central bank of Ecuador'. In Yağcı, M. (ed.), *Political Economy of Central Banking in Emerging Countries*. London: Routledge, pp. 151–167.

Vallet, G. (forthcoming), 'The necessary winds of change: empowering women in central banking'. In Kappes, S., Rochon, L.-P., and G. Vallet (eds), *The Future of Central Banking*. Cheltenham, UK and Northampton, MA: Edward Elgar Publishing.

Walsh, C.E. (1995), 'Optimal contracts for central bankers'. *American Economic Review*, 85 (1), 150–167.

Weber M. (1963 [1919]), *Le Savant et le Politique*. Paris: Plon.

8. The past is already gone, the future is not yet here: the case of the Federal Reserve's system of money management

Jong-Un Song

1. INTRODUCTION

Today, central bankers are facing a very confusing situation. Central banks in each country, including the Federal Reserve in the United States (the Fed), responded to the 2007–2008 financial crisis with unprecedented policies. However, for central banks on a path no one has previously trod, central bankers may find themselves in a difficult position regarding carrying out elusive monetary policy responsibilities. In some ways, they may be working with a feeling of desperation. The confession of a researcher at the Fed's board of directors can be seen as coming from this context. "Mainstream economics", Senior Advisor Jeremy Rudd wrote (2021, p. 1), "is replete with ideas that 'everyone knows' to be true, but that are actually arrant nonsense". *The Economist* (2021) criticised Rudd's work as a "pugnacious paper", which surprised all of us. For example, Rudd wrote (p. 1), "everyone knows":

- Aggregate production functions (and aggregate measures of the capital stock) provide a good way to characterise the economy's supply side;
- Over a sufficiently long span – specifically, one that allows necessary price adjustments to be made – the economy will return to a state of full market clearing; and,
- The theory of household choice provides a solid justification for downward-sloping market demand curves.

In Rudd's view, "None of these propositions has any sort of empirical foundation; moreover, each one turns out to be seriously deficient on theoretical grounds" (p. 1). Rudd warns:

> Economists and economic policymakers believe that households' and firms' expectations of future inflation are a key determinant of actual inflation. A review of the relevant theoretical and empirical literature suggests that this belief rests on extremely shaky foundations, and a case is made that adhering to it uncritically could easily lead to serious policy errors. (n.p.)

According to Mitchel Y. Abolafia (2020), the Fed is currently under technical control. The Fed's policymakers are all economists and experts, and also technocrats. People around the world pay attention to every word they say. The market moves according to their thoughts and attitudes. The "scientization" of central banks has allowed them to "gain legitimacy and authority basing their views on, and applying, the language of science" (p. 7). It has allowed their analyses to become objectified and reified in the marketplace. Nevertheless, it has not allowed the control of the money supply to become "scientifically" managed in the sense that the major uncertainties of monetary policy, especially in the midst of financial crises, are now well-understood operations. Rather, the aura of a technical rationality that surrounds central banking disguises the bounds to rationality: a policy process based on a toolkit of cues, concepts and practices that, unsurprisingly, have epistemological limits (Abolafia, 2020).

Whom should we trust in this situation? The surprises do not end here. If one considers the following, one may think that Rudd's words are trivial. At the Federal Open Market Committee (FOMC) meeting of April 30 to May 1, 2013, the US Fed confessed that it was not controlling the financial market in a very technical and academic way:

> several participants raised the possibility that the federal funds rate might not, in the future, be the best indicator of the general level of short-term interest rates, and supported further staff study of potential alternative approaches to implementing monetary policy in the longer term and of possible new tools to improve control over short-term interest rates. (Minutes of FOMC, 2013, p. 10)

Put simply, the Fed confessed that its thoughts were "arrant nonsense", and it had lost control of the financial market. The Fed is an influential global institution. Most people will not believe that the Fed has lost control of the financial market.

We should debate the central banks' societal responsibilities in light of this predicament. It cannot be said that it is good to raise interest in a central bank's social role or responsibility, as the public's interest in this social responsibility increases during social confusion or economic downturns. Periods when the public's interest in central banks grew have been the times of historical upheaval: the Great Depression, the Global Financial Crisis and the secular stagnation we are currently experiencing. The social responsibility of central banks can take different forms depending on economic conditions. In particular, in the current economic downturn, central bankers must pay more attention to social issues to fulfil their social responsibilities.

In this context, our discussion of monetary policy and the social responsibility of the central banks is also evidence that we are living in hard times. Furthermore, asking a central bank to fulfil its social responsibility proves it is not already doing so.

Central bankers may be embarrassed by the growing demand for them to take on responsibilities not discussed when the economy was good. However, they should not avoid taking on the social responsibilities that we expect of them, as these expectations reflect the realities of our times. It is no exaggeration to say that interest in central banks has risen almost explosively since the 2008 crisis. As a result, the role of the central banks is higher than ever. Thus, it can be seen that issues such as the social responsibility of these banks, which have not been the public's primary concern, have begun to be discussed, reflecting this changed reality.

2.   THE FED'S ACHIEVEMENT OF A DUAL MANDATE IS IN TROUBLE

In this section, we would like to clarify that the social responsibility of the central bank established by US capitalism is undergoing a significant change.

The Fed responded to the crisis with unprecedented strength and scope. However, the Fed's successful assessment of its crisis response did not last long. The Fed did not carry out normalisation according to its original plan. Unrest again escalated once the Fed tapered as planned, and financial markets are on the brink of turmoil. The Fed's original strategy was to shrink the size of financial institutions' assets on its balance sheet and absorb the excess reserves granted to the banking system back into the Fed, which it believed would be hard to accomplish owing to financial market volatility. Instead, the Fed was trying to normalise its assets by leaving its asset side of the balance sheet intact. However, the revised normalisation plan was not easy to implement as planned. So, the Fed confessed that the situation involved a loss of control over the financial markets, which is quite surprising. This has never happened in the history of the Fed. However, it also means that the 2008 crisis could have led to the Fed's loss of control.

The Fed has contributed to the growth of the US economy. In the United States, the central bank's social responsibility was price stability and maximising employment. The policy instrument used by the Fed was the open market operation. However, this is not just a policy tool, but requires a suitable financial market environment. Paradoxically, the Fed's policy tools in its response to the 2008 crisis caused it to lose control of financial markets. In this context, the 2008 crisis is quite different from the general crisis the Fed has experienced since its establishment. The 2008 crisis also changed the policy environment of the US system of money management and caused the Fed to lose control.

Since the pursuit of profits is the best approach in a capitalist society, social considerations or responsibilities are only sporadically reflected in the economic policy of capitalist society, which is determined by the superiority of power among the social forces surrounding economic policy at the time. Thus, social responsibility reflected in economic policy inevitably varies from time to time and from country to country. In addition, the level to which social responsibility is reflected in economic policy is determined by the superiority of social forces and the objective environment of economic policy. In this context, the social responsibility of the central bank should also be understood in a historical dimension. The Fed's responsibilities regarding US capitalism, determined at the historical level, are price stability and maximisation of employment, a "dual mandate" that Congress has delegated to the Fed. In this context, price stability and maximisation of employment are the social responsibilities of the central bank created by the United States in the historical compromise of post-war capitalism.

The great transformation that the US central bank is experiencing stems from the policy implemented by the Fed during the 2008 Global Financial Crisis, changing the structural conditions of the social compromise accumulated by US capitalism. Above all, the Fed's response to the 2008 global crisis changed the size and composition of its balance sheet. In particular, attention should be paid to:

1. Changes in the composition of the asset side of the balance sheet; a large number of derivatives from financial institutions flowed into the asset category of the Fed's balance sheet.
2. Changes in the composition of the debit side of the balance sheet; the bank excess reserve has increased rapidly.
3. Changes in the environment of policy implementation, which means that serious difficulties have arisen for the Fed in achieving its dual mandate through monetary policy measures.

The Fed's monetary policy operation requires a robust policy framework in addition to raising and lowering the benchmark interest rate. Critical conclusions follow from this analysis; it is what the Fed's crisis response undermined, and as a result, the Fed's achievement of the dual mandate is in trouble.

BOX 8.1   THE FED'S MONETARY POLICY

The term 'monetary policy' refers to the actions undertaken by a central bank, such as the Federal Reserve, to influence the availability and cost of money and credit to help promote national economic goals. The Federal Reserve Act of 1913 gave the Federal Reserve responsibility for setting monetary policy.

The Federal Reserve controls the three tools of monetary policy – open market operations, the discount rate, and reserve requirements. The Board of Governors of the Federal Reserve System is responsible for the discount rate and reserve requirements, and the [FOMC] is responsible for open market operations. Using the three tools, the Federal Reserve influences the demand for, and supply of, balances that depository institutions hold at Federal Reserve Banks and in this way alters the federal funds rate. The federal funds rate is the interest rate at which depository institutions lend balances at the [Fed] to other depository institutions overnight.

Changes in the federal funds rate trigger a chain of events that affect other short-term interest rates, foreign exchange rates, long-term interest rates, the amount of money and credit, and, ultimately, a range of economic variables, including employment, output, and prices of goods and services.

Source: Board of Governors of the Federal Reserve System (2022).

3.   THE FED'S BALANCE SHEET AND SURGE IN EXCESS RESERVES

This chapter will empirically analyse the framework of the Fed's open market policy. As mentioned earlier, the change in prerequisites of this policy has made it difficult for the Fed to achieve its dual mandate. This was caused by the change in liquidity on the reserve market from scarcity to abundance, and it is none other than the Fed's open market policy that led to this. However, it was inevitable that the Fed would change its policy environment to cope with the 2008 financial crisis. During this crisis, the most vital interest for the Fed was stabilising the financial market and protecting financial institutions' interests.

This chapter will analyse the meaning of the Fed's balance sheet by explaining US capitalism's system of money management. In addition, we will analyse the implications of the situation in which the Fed has abundant reserves caused by supplying enormous liquidity to the banking system.

Let us look at US capitalism's system of money management. It can be analysed through the Fed's balance sheet. The majority of the Fed's balance sheet assets (credit side) are Treasury-bills (T-bills), and most of its liabilities (debit side) are dollars. For this reason, T-bills are the basis for dollars' issuance, and the value of the dollar is affected by T-bills. In contrast, the government's balance sheet assets include the taxes of US households and corporations, and

Table 8.1   *Changes in the composition of the US government's and the*
                Fed's balance sheets

Government		Fed	
Pre-2008 US government's and Fed's balance sheets			
Asset	Debit	Asset	Debit
– Taxes	– Treasury securities	– Treasury bills	– Dollars – Reserve requirements
Post-2008 US government's and Fed's balance sheets			
Asset	Debit	Asset	Debit
– Taxes	– Treasury securities	– Treasury bills – Mortgage-backed securities, etc.	– Dollars – Reserve requirements – Excess reserve

Source: Board of Governors of the Federal Reserve System, www.federalreserve.gov/
monetarypolicy/bst_fedsbalancesheet.htm.

its liabilities include US Treasury bonds. The characteristic of the monetary
system of US capitalism revealed by the synthesis of the Fed and the government's balance sheets is the structure in which US economic performance
(taxes of households and companies) and the dollar's value are linked through
the T-bill. So, the government and the monetary policy of the Fed are structurally linked. Therefore, when the composition of assets and liabilities on
the Fed's balance sheet changes, the structure linking the government and the
Fed's monetary policy has changed, and in the end, the US capitalist monetary
system has changed. Furthermore, the change in the composition of the Fed's
balance sheet can be seen as a crack in the compromise between the postwar
US social forces reflected in the Fed's balance sheet.

The Fed's money management system was created when the Fed was
launched in 1913, but Meltzer (2003) says that it was not a modern central
bank at the time. Instead, the Fed became a "modern central bank" from
1951–1953 when its chairman William McChesney Martin systematically
implemented open market policies.

The core of Martin's systematised open market policy was to hold the
T-bill as a critical asset on the Fed's balance sheet, an idea called "the T-bill
doctrine".

Table 8.1 shows the changes in the composition of the US government's and
the Fed's balance sheets. The introduction of new derivatives from financial
institutions, such as mortgage-backed securities, and the influx of excess
reserves into credit, have transformed the Fed's balance sheet structure.

Next, Figure 8.1 shows how the total volume and provision of T-bills
(2007–2014) changed. First, the most noticeable change is a decrease in
the proportion of T-bills. Before the crisis, the T-bill reached 90 per cent.

However, when the Fed's assets reached $4.489 trillion on October 22, 2014, the Fed's T-bill holdings decreased to 8.0 per cent. What this change means is an increase in the credit risk of the Fed's balance sheet.

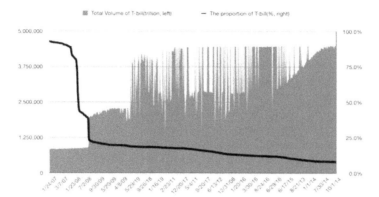

Source: New York Fed.

Figure 8.1   T-bills' total volume and proportion of the Fed's balance sheet (2007–2014)

Second, the "Purchase of Federal Institutions and Mortgage Loans" total has increased significantly. This proportion represents the purchase of mortgage securities from federal agencies (Ginnie Mae, Freddie Mac and Fannie Mae, guaranteed by the US government) and the market; the assets purchased from them were bad financial assets (mortgage securities) that helped trigger the subprime crisis. That is, the Fed took on the financial institutions' credit risks. Finally, the Fed introduced loans to the credit market (starting on July 2, 2008) and purchased long-term government bonds (starting on March 18, 2009).

Put simply, the Fed's purchase of US government bonds and financial institutions' assets led to massive liquidity flowing into the market, while the Fed's credit risk increased significantly. However, other risks can be added. For example, such diversification of balance sheet assets exposes central bank balance sheets to risks such as exchange rates, asset price fluctuations and emergency policies.

Our interest is in a problem related to the surge in excess reserves on the debit side of the Fed's balance sheet due to changes in open market operating conditions. In addition, excess reserves are related to the demand for the open market of financial institutions. In short, the Fed's open market policy cannot be expected to play its role in a state where excess reserves are abundant.

First, for a clear understanding of the increase in excess reserves, let us examine the operation and frame of the open market policy and the relationship with the reserve market.

The Fed performs open market operations with the benchmark interest rate (Federal Fund Market Interest Rate) and RP (Repurchase Agreements) as policy instruments, thereby achieving the central bank's social responsibility. In order for open market operations to be successfully carried out, it is most important to maintain a stable framework for policy operations; that is, to maintain a slightly lower supply than demand. Even if the Federal Reserve boosts or decreases the Federal Fund Market Interest Rate, financial institutions will not respond sensitively if the reserve market supply exceeds demand. In other words, if the banking system's excess reserves are plenty, financial institutions may obtain liquidity without relying on the Fed's liquidity supply; hence the Fed's mechanism for managing reserve market liquidity through the benchmark interest rate is ineffective. In this case, the Fed will lose control of the reserve market (a banking system). Thus, in the end, the scarcity of liquidity in the reserve market is an appropriate policy environment for the Fed to operate the open market, and at the same time it is a decisive condition for the Fed to achieve the central bank's social responsibility.

We will confirm these changes in the policy environment by analysing excess reserves in the debit side of the Fed's balance sheet. Because of the Fed's shift in policy, it was difficult for the US central bank to achieve price stability and maximise employment as mandated by Congress while failing to fulfil its social responsibilities. Furthermore, this is not due to the temporary economic recession but to the structural policy environment of the Fed. As a result, a bubble in the stock market, worsening employment and deepening social inequality can appear.

As shown in Figure 8.2, the excess reserves on the Fed's balance sheet increased slightly from September 1, 2008, and exploded from November 1, 2009.

Next, let us look at how the Fed's supply of reserves and demand for financial institutions changed after the excess reserves soared from the fourth quarter of 2006 to the fourth quarter of 2012.

The first time the Fed's reserve supply and the bank system's reserve demand met, as shown in Figure 8.3, was around the fourth quarter of 2009 and the first quarter of 2010. Since then, the supply and demand for reserves have shifted multiple times, but the financial system's reserve shortage has been eliminated since 2012.

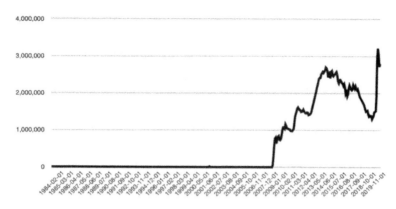

Source: New York Fed.

Figure 8.2   *Changes of excessive reserves of the Fed (1984–2019, million dollars)*

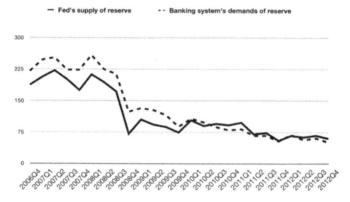

Source: New York Fed.

Figure 8.3   *The supply and demand of reserves (2006Q4 to 2012Q4, billion dollars)*

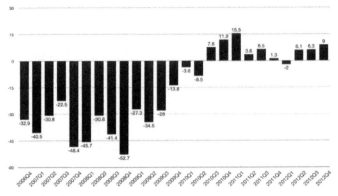

Source: New York Fed.

*Figure 8.4   The Fed's capacity to intervene in the banking system
            (2006Q4 to 2012Q4, billion dollars)*

Now, let us see what changes have occurred to the Fed's capacity to intervene in the banking system.

Figure 8.4 was created by deducting the federal fund market's demand
from its supply. As indicated in the graph, the federal fund market's reserve
supply was less than demand before the second quarter of 2010, but it was
more than demand starting in the third quarter of 2010. In other words, as of
the third quarter of 2010, the Fed's open market operation conditions shifted
from scarce to abundant, and the Fed lost control of the financial system. For
example, if the total transactions of the federal fund market are about $500
billion, the Fed's intervention power regarding that market is about 7 to 8
per cent. However, through the fourth quarter of 2008, the capacity for intervention was significantly reduced, and demand exceeded supply in the third
quarter of 2010. As a result, the Fed's ability to intervene in the federal fund
market entered a negative situation, with it losing its market control. Thus,
there has been a vacuum in the Fed's control of the federal fund market.

How did the Fed respond to these issues? According to a recent New
York Fed statement, the Fed should respond to inequality in ways other than
monetary policy. What the Fed responded to was a change in the federal
fund rate system. Since 2014, it has been trying to solve this problem by
changing a single-benchmark interest rate (the federal fund market rate) to
a multi-benchmark interest rate (the Corridor System) (McGowan and Nosal,
2021, p. 10).

The Fed's policy reaction is based on the requirement for liquidity in the
banking sector rather than the dual mandate. As a result, the Fed altered the

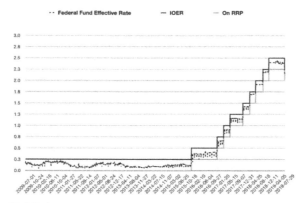

Source: New York Fed.

Figure 8.5   *The Fed's response to the capacity to intervene in the banking system (July 1, 2009 to July 1, 2019, %)*

federal fund rate structure to stabilise the financial market rather than reducing its asset holdings to safeguard financial institution profits. As a result, according to Petrou (2021), the Fed has become the "engine of inequality".

The Fed introduced IOER (interest on excess reserve) and ON RRP (an overnight reverse repurchase agreement) on the assumption that financial institutions will react sensitively to the Fed's adjustment of the benchmark interest rate even when the liquidity is abundant. However, as shown in Figure 8.5, the Fed is not leading the market but is following the movement of financial institutions. Finally, the Fed's control is not recovering even with the new benchmark interest rate system.

Put simply, it can be said that the Fed's response is simply a policy aimed at stabilising the financial market, not achieving the dual mandate. The reason for this may be that the Fed's monetary policy is centred not on the Fed, a government agency, but on the New York Fed, which values financial markets and financial institutions. In this context, former New York Fed President Timothy F. Geithner's word may be noteworthy. Geithner wrote (2014, p. 89), "I basically restored the New York Fed board to its historic roots as an elite roster of the local financial establishment."

4.   CONCLUSION

The Fed is facing two crises simultaneously.

First, from the perspective of the central bank's money management system, the Fed's loss of control over the financial markets due to quantitative easing and large-scale asset purchases is a significant problem. Although the Fed's crisis response was inevitable since the US financial crisis would have jeopardised US capitalism without implementing such a programme, it undeniably destabilised the US capitalist. In other words, when the reserve market grew abundant due to quantitative easing, the management mechanism through which the Fed managed the reserve market via open market operation shifted, and the Fed's influence was weakened. Simply put, there was a problem with the Fed's money management system.

The money supply is subject to state control, which is the money crisis. However, the situation is only genuinely extraordinary, even worse when the central bank does not control the credit market via the money supply (or the benchmark interest rate) due to a breakdown in the capitalist credit management system, the central axis of capitalism. Moreover, 2014 was the year the Fed lost its power, coinciding with the Fed's 100th anniversary.

Second, the Fed's failure to fulfil its dual mandate and accommodate the public has requested new social agenda. The Fed responded to the financial crisis with a monetary policy based on the dual mandate. However, in its response, the Fed prioritises the financial market's stability and financial institutions' profitability above its dual mandate. Thus, the Fed's capacity to fulfil its dual mandate was severely hampered. "What you risk reveals what you value" (Winterson, 1992, p. 91).

So far, the Fed has not fully embraced the dual mandate and new social agendas. The Fed has not yet incorporated new social agendas into its policy considerations. Social justice issues, including inequality, poverty, racial conflict, climate change, gender equality, and empowering all women and girls, have been dismissed as non-central banking issues not discussed when considering central bank policies. However, they are increasingly debated in the context of the central bank's social responsibilities (Vallet, 2020). Therefore, the central bank's future monetary policy should reflect the public's demands and the reality as it has evolved.

In addition, it should not be restricted to just adding social issues' individually concerns but should be a comprehensive redesign that considers the established goal of the central bank, policy measures to accomplish the establishment goal, and the governance of the policy-making process. Of course, changes to specific policy tools are crucial, but the system as a whole must be sophisticatedly recreated to accomplish the public's demands for the social responsibilities of the central bank.

Again, the Fed must completely redesign its system to meet the public's expectations about the central bank's social responsibilities as a steward of the people. The past is already gone, the future is not yet here.

REFERENCES

Abolafia, M.Y. (2020), *Stewards of the Markets*. Cambridge, MA: Harvard University Press.

Board of Governors of the Federal Reserve System (2022), "About the FOMC". www .federalreserve.gov/monetarypolicy/fomc.htm.

Friedman, M., and A.J. Schwartz (1963), *A Monetary History of the United States, 1867–1960*. Princeton, NJ: Princeton University Press.

Geithner, T. (2014), *Stress Test: Reflections on Financial Crises*. New York, NY: Crown.

Minutes of FOMC (2013), April 30 to May 1. www.federalreserve.gov and www .newyorkfed.org.

McGowan, J.P., and E. Nosal (2021), "How did the Fed funds market change when excess reserves were abundant?" *Economic Policy Review*, 26 (1). www.newyorkfed .org/research/epr/2020/epr_2020_fed-funds-functioning_mcgowan.

Meltzer, H.A. (2003), *A History of the Federal Reserve, Volume 1*. Chicago, IL: University of Chicago Press.

Minutes of FOMC (2013), April 30 to May 1. www.federalreserve.gov and www .newyorkfed.org.

Petrou, K. (2021), *Engine of Inequality: The Fed and the Future of Wealth in America*. Hoboken, NJ: Wiley.

Rudd, J.B. (2021), "Why do we think that inflation expectations matter for inflation? (And should we?)". *Finance and Economics Discussion Series* 2021-062. Washington, DC: Board of Governors of the Federal Reserve System.

The Economist (2021), "Does anyone actually understand inflation?" October 9. www.economist.com/finance-and-economics/2021/10/09/does-anyone-actually -understand-inflation.

Vallet, G. (2020), "Gender diversity as a tool to make central banks progressive institutions: the case of the central bank of Ecuador". In Yağcı, M. (ed), *Political Economy of Central Banking in Emerging Countries*. London: Routledge, pp. 151–167.

Winterson, J. (1992), *Written on the Body*. New York, NY: Vintage Books.

9. Precautionary monetary policy and democratic legitimacy: tensions and openings

Rob Macquarie

1. INTRODUCTION

Environmental breakdown raises difficult questions around social responsibility for all actors in the political and economic system. To sustain a good life for citizens, societies must mitigate and build resilience to multiple overlapping processes, including but not limited to climate change and biodiversity loss (Ripple et al., 2020; Steffen et al., 2015). Central banks have been called to action to manage the impact of environmental risks on economic and financial stability and to help mobilise capital for the transition (NGFS, 2020b).

The mainstream approach that many central banks are now considering integrating into their operations emphasises improving information and measurement of novel risks, to 'fix' markets and allow them to reach a sustainable equilibrium (NGFS, 2019, p. 5; Ryan-Collins, 2019). Monetary policy is expected to reflect these measurements and adjustments in a neutral manner. However, the complexity and severity of risks stemming from harm to natural ecosystems and heating in the Earth's atmosphere creates 'radical uncertainty', which frustrates precise measurement of risk or planning for optimal equilibria. An alternative, 'precautionary' approach that recognises this uncertainty would seek to prevent the worst possible outcomes – to achieve good enough outcomes even when policymakers cannot be confident in pursuing optimal ones (Chenet et al., 2021). Under a mindset of this sort, monetary policy tools could be adjusted without waiting until risks can be precisely quantified.

The environmental imperative turns a new page in an existing debate over central banks' exercise of authority, which has varied according to historical and cultural context (Best, 2016; Dietsch, 2020; Goodhart, 2011). In particular, concerns over the compatibility between operational independence and democracy grew following the expansion in central banks' duties and toolkits after the Global Financial Crisis (Fernández-Albertos, 2015; Tucker, 2018).

The mainstream approach to environmental risk inherits ideas from economic theories used to justify operational independence prior to the financial crisis. By contrast, the precautionary approach is in line with a critique of the purported 'neutrality' of monetary policy vis-à-vis longer-term economic effects, especially in light of policies observed during and after the crisis. However, in terms of two forms of legitimacy for central banks identified by scholars and practitioners – related to 'inputs' and 'outputs' – neither approach departs significantly from the account that has been dominant since the turn towards independence, which prioritises good policy outcomes over deep democratic engagement. In other words, the debate over central bank environmental action mainly seeks to bolster output legitimacy, through more effective efforts to reduce environmental disruption (Dietsch, 2020).

Consequently, some tensions with democracy remain. Some of the proposed steps to properly reduce environmental risk may overburden provisions for independent central banks to remain accountable and thus to achieve a sufficient level of democratic input. This chapter argues that a reassertion of democratic authority over aspects of monetary policy related to a just, sustainable transition would defuse these tensions. Its first proposition is that pro-democratic institutional reforms could help policymakers tackle the blind spots in monetary policy – both social and environmental – identified by critics and thus improve democratic legitimacy at both ends of the input–output binary. The second, more theoretical proposition reinterprets the legitimacy of monetary policy operations to move beyond that binary. Examining the 'constructive' value of democracy (Sen, 1999) softens the distinction between inputs and outputs. Under this view, the process by which decisions are reached becomes an important part of the overall outcome. Stressing narrative reasoning and participation, this account of democracy has strong links to the characteristics of successful decision-making under radical uncertainty (Kay and King, 2020) and proves particularly apt for macroeconomic policy in the context of environmental risks, themselves partly a product of public policy.

The next three sections develop this case. The second reviews the history of monetary policy goals, responsibilities and understandings of its democratic legitimacy, including during the COVID-19 pandemic. The third addresses the impact of radical uncertainty and the pressure to consider environmental factors in central bank operations. Contrasting different approaches to environmental risks, it explores the prospects of each for central bank legitimacy, and emerging sources of tension. The final section explores new ways of understanding central bank legitimacy in light of environmental risk, arguing for greater fiscal–monetary coordination and concrete institutional practices to support a precautionary approach formed through a democratic process. The chapter concludes by reflecting on a research agenda to facilitate institutional reform that makes best use of central banks' capabilities.

2.   CENTRAL BANK LEGITIMACY IN HISTORICAL PERSPECTIVE

Democratic legitimacy, while a complex concept, can be understood as 'an ideal for how the members of a democratic constituency ought to make decisions about how to organise their life together' (Peter, 2011, p. 1). Two ways for living up to this ideal are often contrasted, relating in turn to 'process' and 'substance' – in other words, a distinction between *how* decisions are made and their substantive results (Dahl, 1989). In political theory, it is apt to avoid drawing too sharp a differentiation between these concepts. Dahl cautions against searching exclusively in outcomes for what is valuable or good, while ignoring the substantive good that may come from having access to opportunities to act in certain ways, or to disagree (1989, pp. 306–307). In a similar vein, Sen supplements a third, 'constructive' role for democracy which 'helps society to form its values and priorities'; even the idea of 'needs', including the understanding of 'economic needs', requires 'public discussion and exchange of information, views, and analyses' (1999, p. 10).

Nevertheless, in the context of central banking, process and substance have typically been linked to 'input' and 'output' forms of legitimacy respectively (Best, 2016; Buiter, 2014). The balance of these two facets within the exercise of authority by central banks has fluctuated over the decades, as the degree of control elected governments can exercise over central bank decision-making and the specific objectives constructed for monetary policy to pursue have both varied. In the mid-century following the Second World War, central banks were broadly under direct influence from government ministers – whether full-scale nationalisation as in the case of the Bank of England or Banque de France, or general political interference as for the Federal Reserve – and had a wide range of objectives, including full employment and economic growth as well as price stability (Cobham, 2012; Goodhart, 2011). During this period of 'fiscal dominance', where the power of elected officials was felt more or less directly in the monetary policymaking process, input legitimacy for central bank policy would flow from democratic arrangements (or a lack thereof) governing the wider programme of economic policy. Even considered against multiple objectives, output legitimacy too has often been considered satisfied during this period, marked by few banking crises, low inflation and unemployment, and relatively high economic growth (Smith, 1992).

Contrasted with this earlier period, the latter decades of the twentieth century were 'historically abnormal in the degree to which the scope of central banking was narrowed down' (Dow, 2017, p. 1542). The turn in macroeconomics into the 1970s and 1980s brought with it new ideas about the sources of legitimacy for central banks. Firstly, the theory of the neutrality of money vis-à-vis long-term output (Friedman, 1968), formalised in the years to come as the natural rate of unemployment (Hall and Sargent, 2018), restricted stabilisation policy to the short term. It also served to undercut any sense of a real trade-off in terms of democratic sovereignty if monetary policy was removed from the scope of decision-making by an elected government. In addition, the 'Tinbergen rule' was applied to reduce the number of objectives to match the number of instruments used to pursue them (Tinbergen, 1952, 1956), in a one-for-one match between price stability and, at first, the rate of monetary growth, then the rate of interest (Goodhart, 2011). Finally, theories of rational expectations suggested elected decision-makers would be unable to credibly commit to keeping inflation low due to their incentive to stimulate the economy, warranting delegation of monetary policy to an independent agency faced with no such electoral incentive and constrained in policymaking either by rules or reputational concerns (Barro and Gordon, 1983; Kydland and Prescott, 1977).

This set of ideas, which in their later synthesis underpin what Arestis and Sawyer (2008) refer to as 'new consensus macroeconomics', significantly changed how responsibility for monetary policy was understood to be democratically legitimate. Output legitimacy was brought to the fore, with an emphasis on central banks' performance based on a single metric, price stability. Empirical evidence was produced showing that more independent central banks were associated with lower levels of inflation (Alesina and Summers, 1993). Operational independence for setting monetary policy became the norm, characterising approximately nine in ten central banks by 2000 (Garriga, 2016). Input legitimacy was not completely discarded: a certain minimum threshold was considered necessary. Monetary policy could meet this threshold through two channels. Operationally independent central banks were seen as compatible with democracy *ex ante* through the act of delegation itself, to the extent that independence is granted and subject to review by elected politicians (Bernanke, 2017, pp. 29–31). Into the twenty-first century, policymakers increasingly thought of transparent communication, through meeting transcripts, speeches and hearings, as an essential component for ensuring *ex post* accountability for their decisions (Best, 2016; Haldane, 2018).

This widespread shift drew critics, questioning whether the substantive outcomes under independence were really as good as they could be, whether the best balance between objectives had been reached and whether technocratic policymaking was truly 'apolitical' enough to preserve input legitimacy (McNamara, 2002; Stiglitz, 1997). The financial crisis in 2007–2008 sharpened this critique by straining both sides of the equation. Monetary policy tools were now also geared towards providing liquidity and returning the financial system to stability (Guttman, 2012), belying the singularity of the price stability objective. Even then, central banks in major developed economies were unable to return inflation to target levels set before the crisis (Caldara et al., 2020). Meanwhile, unconventional monetary policy interventions, especially asset purchases, put even greater pressure on the assumption that policy is apolitical, by affecting the distribution of income and wealth and the direction of credit (Dietsch et al., 2018; Fernández-Albertos, 2015; Goodhart and Lastra, 2018). Within a wider reassessment of their appropriate scope of action and responsibility (e.g., Akerlof et al., 2014; Blinder et al., 2017), some voices asked directly how to ensure central banks can retain democratic legitimacy and promote social trust in their actions (e.g., Borio, 2019; Tucker, 2018). From a more critical angle, the question has been posed again whether central bank independence 'risks producing inefficient results with regard to our overall social welfare function' (Dietsch, 2020, p. 6). For instance, Aklin et al. (2021) find that central bank independence is also associated with rising income inequality, identifying specific mechanisms in the political logic supporting independence that produce this outcome.

The COVID-19 pandemic embedded unconventional monetary policy even further. Central banks in the United States, Japan, the United Kingdom and the European Union (EU) resumed and deepened their existing asset purchases and extended emergency lending facilities (Mosser, 2020). The unconventional monetary policy response to the pandemic is significant in its scale, spread and scope. Firstly, following the initial signs of financial market panic in March 2020, the decision was made to 'go big' and 'go fast' with asset purchases to avoid tightening market conditions (Bailey et al., 2020, p. 2). For instance, the Federal Reserve vowed to buy any number of assets necessary to stabilise economic conditions (FOMC, 2020). Secondly, several emerging market countries used asset purchases for the first time (IMF, 2020, p. 37). Thirdly, interventions were more varied. Some central banks raised their tolerance for exposing their balance sheets to greater risk; for example, the Fed's decision to buy shares in exchange traded funds holding high-yield debt (Federal Reserve Board, 2020c) or purchases of corporate equity (BoJ, 2020). Other policies began to break down walls between central banks and the wider public sector, such as targeted lending programmes conducted in close coordination with fiscal authorities (e.g., the Bank of England's Covid Corporate Financing Facility; BoE, 2021a) or measures to support state and local governments (e.g., the Fed's Municipal Liquidity Facility; Federal Reserve Board, 2020b).

Meanwhile, institutional change had started before the pandemic. Reviews of monetary policy frameworks were underway at both the Fed and the European Central Bank (ECB) in early 2020. In December 2020, the Bank of Japan followed, announcing its own review in the face of ongoing difficulty to have the desired stimulus on economic conditions and inflation (BoJ, 2021). The main goal in each case is restoring output legitimacy by improving the central bank's ability to achieve economic objectives. However, certain features clearly display a concern for input legitimacy. Coordination with elected policymakers, which can increase democratic sway over targeted programmes or crisis response measures, has received attention (e.g., Lagarde, 2020). Nevertheless, persistent concerns around fiscal dominance (e.g., Bartsch et al., 2020) mean prospects for direct cooperation between monetary and fiscal policies remain limited by historical standards (Ryan-Collins and van Lerven, 2018). In addition, the Fed and ECB have both developed 'listening' events to engage the public and representatives from civil society on the scope of their responsibilities and effects of their policies. These are hoped to increase accountability, offer reflections on what mandated goals mean in practice to citizens and social groups, and suggest ways to improve monetary policy transmission (ECB, 2020; Federal Reserve Board, 2020a). While still nascent, these forms of direct engagement between the central bank and society at large signal a more nuanced approach to legitimacy, which this chapter seeks to build on in later sections.

3. RADICAL UNCERTAINTY AND ENVIRONMENTAL RISK

Broadly, recent changes in monetary policymaking reflect resurging awareness of radical, deep or fundamental uncertainty. Knight (1946) and Keynes (1937) both regarded risk, understood as a form of uncertainty where the probabilities of future events are known or can be calculated in advance, such as a game of roulette, as separate from uncertainty proper, where it is not possible to make such a measurement or calculation. In situations marked by radical uncertainty, identifying a perfectly 'optimal' policy is not possible, and better decision-making makes use of discretion and improvisation to reach a 'good enough' outcome (Kay and King, 2020).

As the new consensus has fractured and central banks have grappled with an increasingly uncertain global economy, the importance of flexibility and discretion has again increased (Best, 2016). Unconventional monetary policy is especially at odds with precise optimisation. Braun characterises asset purchases, an asset swap using the consolidated public sector balance sheet, as a shift to a 'hydraulic' policy style for central banks, closer to Keynesian fiscal policy in its connection to aggregate demand, and away from the 'strategic and performative' framework of monetary inflation targeting by manipulating the short-term interest rate (2018, pp. 201–203). This shift has occurred in tandem with a decline in central banks' 'epistemic authority', despite – or perhaps because of – wider use of forward guidance ostensibly aimed at shaping market expectations of long-term interest rates. Braun argues that 'unconventional monetary policies have been testing the limits of the apparatus of expectation management, and thus of performative macroeconomic governance' (ibid., p. 208; see also Kohn, 2018).

In the twenty-first century, one of the most salient causes of extreme uncertainty is the series of complex, interlocking processes driving environmental breakdown, including climate change, biodiversity loss, biogeochemical flows, land systems change and ocean acidification (Bradshaw et al., 2021; Ripple et al., 2020; Steffen et al., 2015). These processes pose significant threats (here described collectively as 'environmental risks') to economic and financial stability as well as collective wellbeing. Alongside the severe consequences of allowing global temperature rises beyond 1.5°C above pre-industrial levels (Carney, 2015), ecosystem fragility has the potential to cause enormous losses in wealth for a wide range of countries around the world (Schelske et al., 2020), while the pandemic itself is an example of a sudden, severe shock likely related to biodiversity loss (IPBES, 2020). Mitigating these processes demands a sustainable transition to bring about a structural shift in the economy – reducing environmentally harmful activities and scaling up green investments – and implies a role for central banks and financial supervisors to reduce the impact of risks and help mobilise capital (Campiglio et al., 2018).

A mainstream institutional response, embodied by the Task Force on Climate-Related Financial Disclosures (TCFD) and, at least in its initial work programme, the Network for Greening the Financial System (NGFS), has pursued a 'market-fixing' approach (Ryan-Collins, 2019). This seeks to correct informational market failures and emphasises quantitative analysis of risks, enabled by data-sharing and financial disclosures among private companies and financial institutions, which are encouraged to adopt new risk management practices (NGFS, 2019). To employ this information, policymakers and private financial institutions have begun to explore new forward-looking models based on climate-economic scenarios, to replace traditional, backward-looking models which rely on equilibria and perfect markets (Monasterolo, 2020). Although described as an 'epistemological break' with earlier practices (Bolton et al., 2020, pp. 21–22), this approach falls short of a full reckoning with radical uncertainty and is no guarantee of a successful transition. Scenario analysis is replete with methodological variation and outcomes are highly sensitive to particular metrics and parameters, many of which are inherently subjective (Chenet et al., 2019, p. 10). Additionally, private financial institutions using scenario analysis to identify risks does not necessarily mean those actors will perceive divesting from the relevant assets in the short term as the rational response, as they may not think of policy responses as sufficiently robust or credible (Bolton et al., 2020, p. 41).

For these reasons, Chenet et al. (2019, 2021) argue for a 'precautionary approach', which they claim would be more effective at minimising environmental risks when the consequences of inaction would be catastrophic and irreversible and the probabilities of threats themselves are not calculable. The approach would 'actively steer market actors in a clear direction – towards a managed transition – to ensure that a scenario that minimises harm to the financial system and wider economy in the future is the scenario that actually occurs' (Chenet et al., 2019, p. 2). This is presented as an alternative mindset for central bankers to adopt which would enable bolder policy action than a market-fixing approach. Kedward et al. (2020) extend the proposal to advocate a precautionary approach to 'nature-related financial risks' beyond those related to climate change, such as those related to biodiversity decline and ecosystem collapse. To support their case, these authors highlight that policy-making at central banks – especially macroprudential financial regulation and some forms of monetary policy – can already be considered a kind of precautionary response to counter systemic risks under radically uncertain conditions in the macroeconomy and financial system (Chenet et al. 2019, pp. 14–16).

Monetary Policy and Legitimacy

While the environmental risk agenda has addressed financial stability and financial supervision first and foremost, consequences for monetary policy are inevitable. Disruption from environmental breakdown is likely to lead to instability of output and inflation, complicating the pursuit of statutory monetary policy objectives (Batten et al., 2016; Schnabel 2020). The effectiveness of policy may also be affected, in terms of both room to manoeuvre and channels of transmission. To anticipate these trends, the NGFS suggests incorporating integrated assessment models and scenario analysis into monetary policymaking practices (NGFS, 2020a). However, monetary policy can affect environmental outcomes in turn, by affecting the scale and allocation of credit. There is therefore a case for integrating new approaches to environmental risks into asset purchase strategies and collateral frameworks, to prevent environmental risks from intensifying on central bank balance sheets and to avoid exacerbating those risks in the wider economy (Monnin, 2020). Nevertheless, interventions up to and including pandemic response measures have not been designed to align monetary policy with environmental goals (Barmes et al., 2020; Dafermos et al., 2020).

The implications for narratives around democratic legitimacy of monetary policy are complex. Firstly, dwindling capacity to stabilise the macroeconomy and financial system threatens conventional output legitimacy. Yet growing awareness of the necessary scale of the sustainable transition implies a broader view of policy effectiveness may be needed. The incidences of risks that will affect future economic conditions are themselves a function of the overall policy mix, including monetary policy – that is, they are endogenous to the system (Ryan-Collins, 2019). Endogeneity in monetary policy theory and practice is familiar in the practice of forward guidance: central banks set policy conditional on economic actors' expectations, while seeking to manipulate output and inflation by shaping those expectations themselves (Dow, 2017, p. 1546). Monetary policymakers' reports to legislatures are signals which have the potential to move interest rates in financial markets (Connolly and Kohler, 2004) and forward guidance appears to have significant effects on asset prices (Bernanke, 2017, p. 6), despite the fact that its logic runs against the observable, highly complex reality marked by radical uncertainty. So too central banks' decisions on environmental risks are likely to affect market behaviours, not only through interventions in markets but also through communication of the choice of measurement itself. However, the more responsibility central banks take for guiding the sustainable transition, the greater the burden on their relationship to democratic process and input legitimacy.

So far, independent central banks have emphasised their mandated primary objectives – price stability, and in some cases financial stability – as the main rationale for any operational changes to monetary policy from an environmental perspective (NGFS, 2020c). With that said, to the extent that many central banks do have secondary objectives to support the wider economic policies of governments that are increasingly committing to net zero emissions reductions and other ecological goals, a case for aligning with those goals can also be made on grounds of policy coherence (Robins et al., 2021). However, some policymakers worry about creating market distortions or creating conflicts with their primary objectives. For these reasons, market neutrality – implying that interventions are designed so as not to impact relative prices – has been a guiding principle in unconventional monetary policy (Cœuré, 2015; Schoenmaker, 2021). Adhering to the broader sense of monetary policy as a neutral tool to promote common goals and seeking to avoid distributional effects with no basis in democratic decisions, this concept extends the new consensus logic of democratic legitimacy for operational independence.

Both angles have been challenged. On the one hand, evidence on corporate bond purchase programmes shows that interventions designed to be 'neutral' result in a bias in favour of high-carbon or environmentally harmful industries, reflecting the status quo (Matikainen et al., 2017). Therefore, a market-fixing approach that claims to be neutral will be ineffective at managing environmental risks in the longer term. On the other hand, it is misleading to claim that a 'neutral' approach avoids overburdening central banks with inappropriate responsibilities. The design of tools like purchases of corporate securities inherently 'face[s] difficult political questions, which their invocation of market neutrality removes from an overtly political process of deliberation' (van 't Klooster and Fontan, 2019, p. 7). In other words, a market-fixing approach looks inadequate in terms of both forms of legitimacy.

The precautionary mindset would enable more proactive measures. Ongoing asset purchases, collateral frameworks and other novel lending programmes for advancing credit to the private sector can be adjusted with eligibility criteria or conditions based on 'rules of thumb' (such as excluding businesses with a certain level of revenues from environmentally harmful activities) (Chenet et al., 2019, pp. 22–23). These proactive steps may improve the chances for stability and a smooth transition and promote *output* legitimacy more broadly (Dietsch, 2020). Yet what of input legitimacy? Under which conditions can the exercise of still greater discretion by independent monetary policymakers be consistent with democratic process? Dietsch argues that inequalities resulting from differential treatment of environmentally sustainable and harmful industries do not represent the same challenge to technocratic authority as economic inequalities resulting from the wider conduct of monetary policy: 'if we are serious about the need to transition to a more sustainable economy, the idea that we should favour low-carbon industries is not a value judgement but a prudential judgement' (2020, p. 13). If central banks have a legal mandate to protect economic and financial stability (and possibly to support government policy) and take discretionary, precautionary action to those ends, they are acting – the thinking goes – within democratic prerogatives.

This optimistic view overlooks a brimming tension. Considering that supporting the sustainable transition and combating environmental risks will involve novel and contentious policies, there is reason to think that operationally independent policymakers will become de facto political actors. For comparison, Fabo et al. (2020) find that central banks' analyses of quantitative easing programmes find them to be more effective and use more abstract positive language than comparable studies by academic economists. In part, this is because they are organisations with reputations to preserve and composed of individuals with a self-interest (however subconscious) in their own career advancement. But it is also a structural consequence of independence. Central bankers' beliefs about legitimacy and the need to maintain the appearance of political (and market) neutrality affect their outward communication. Braun and Düsterhöft (forthcoming) show that central bankers behave 'politically' in their discourse, keeping a 'strategic silence' around topics which are controversial in their jurisdiction – such as house prices or inequality in the United Kingdom or United States, and exchange rates or climate change in the EU and Japan. Central banks' perception of systemic risks in the financial sector also affects their communication of key issues, such as fiscal policy, with democratic policymakers. Diessner and Lisi develop a nascent view of central bank independence that recognises 'the financial system dynamics that ultimately condition the successful transmission of central bank policies' (2020, p. 318). Focusing on the period after the financial crisis, they highlight 'financial dominance', or concerns over financial instability, as a motivation for ECB policymakers to address fiscal policy in its communications. These examples suggest that it is naïve to expect central banks to adopt a precautionary mindset without their actions becoming politicised in a similar manner. Furthermore, if part of the minimum quid pro quo for independence is *ex post* accountability, it is difficult to envisage credible frameworks to hold independent monetary policymakers accountable for the broad range of environmental impacts (Campiglio et al., 2018). Beyond conventions and interpretations, further institutional change will be needed to deliver a democratically legitimate monetary policy approach to environmental breakdown.

4.   GREEN CENTRAL BANKING BEYOND INPUT AND OUTPUT LEGITIMACY

This section argues that rebalancing responsibilities for aspects of monetary policy related to environmental factors could do much more to confer greater legitimacy. Partly, this solution is proposed to overcome the tension between process and substance created by operational independence. A Keynesian frame for governing the wider macroeconomy, marked by close fiscal–monetary coordination and precautionary measures designed to intentionally shape credit markets to stabilise the financial system and real economy, would modify operational independence to restore democratic sovereignty over certain decisions *and* improve the effectiveness of those decisions.

First, however, returning to democratic theory provides an important insight to go beyond the simple dichotomy of input and output legitimacy. The 'constructive' value of democracy (Sen, 1999) does not fit easily into either form, and even collapses the distinction between process and substance. In the central banking context, this value is implicit in critiques which ask whether independence provides enough opportunity to strike the *right* balance between various economic objectives. The concept of 'comprehensive outcomes' (Sen, 2002) is particularly relevant to recent trends in central banking theory and practice:

> If there is one clearly identified criterion of what is rational or what is a "good" decision then the issue is to find a solution that maximizes the results against this yardstick ... If by contrast there is a debate about the decision criteria, the goals to be pursued and the means to mobilize to this purpose, then the issue is much more complex since no one knows beforehand what (if anything) needs to be maximized; Sen designates this alternative view as the quest for "comprehensive outcomes" which incorporate inter alia the processes through which outcomes are reached. (Bonvin et al., 2018)

This view is especially useful for thinking about the sustainable transition. Democratic procedures, which distribute authority more widely across the political unit, are a superior approach to making decisions in the kind of world characterised by environmental breakdown than those which concentrate authority (Hammond and Smith, 2017). Critics may object that consensus across every political constituency will be unattainable and that introducing democratic plurality into decision-making will prevent policy from changing fast enough to meet the scale of the environmental crisis. But these are hardly reasons to expect bold action in the monetary sphere *without* a democratic process. Even if reducing economic and financial instability from environmental risk could be considered a well-defined goal, it is clear that the means for how to do so are contested. 'Politics' will affect progress and policy capture by interest groups remains a threat whether or not decisions are made behind closed doors – for instance, as policymakers consider convening private financial institutions to develop common approaches. Rather than seeking to measure and manage environmental risks and goals in a depoliticised manner, the approach should itself be a process of social deliberation, part of a democratic society's process of continually 'negotiating preferred futures' (Robinson, 2004, pp. 379–380). That is to say that the overall pathway to a more sustainable economy must be constructed and supported by social participation. For example, measures to align monetary policy with environmental goals should consider that a just transition – a sustainable transformation which is fair and delivers positive social impact – is critical for change to be politically and socially viable (Robins et al., 2021), meaning social as well as environmental factors are salient to decisions about how best to manage risks and ensure a smooth transition.

Indeed, an open and democratic process creates conditions for the most successful form of reasoning under radical uncertainty, relying fundamentally on collective narratives (Kay and King, 2020). Narrative reasoning has two important features. To build a narrative in the first place, decision-makers use 'evolutionary rationality', building 'the best explanation … from a myriad of little details and the knowledge of context derived from personal experience and the experience of others' (ibid., p. 410). Critically, because the human faculty for reasoning in radical uncertainty is a social faculty, 'it is important to open that explanation to challenge and be ready to change the guiding narrative when new information emerges' (ibid., p. 412). This use of 'communicative rationality' in turn 'contributes to our evolutionary rationality' (ibid., p. 272). In fact, monetary policymakers are no strangers to this mode of reasoning. When central banks make monetary policy decisions and present their reasoning to democratically elected representatives for scrutiny, they convey a narrative about the economy and how they believe their tools will affect it (Tuckett et al., 2020; Tuckett and Nikolic, 2017, p. 2017).

In practice, a more democratic and deliberative approach to aligning monetary policy with environmental goals and tackling environmental risks might focus on two features: firstly, policy coordination with fiscal policy-makers to plan for the sustainable transition; secondly, making narrative-based decision-making public to draw on a wider variety of information, communicate reasoning and invite challenge.

Policy Coordination

Central banks have previously worked closely with elected fiscal policymakers to achieve a number of economic objectives, even including monetary financing to finance industrial policy and innovation and direct resources into productive areas of the economy (Ryan-Collins and van Lerven, 2018). Insights from the new consensus view also support greater coordination. For instance, Bartsch et al. (2020) emphasise that monetary policy and fiscal policy provide each other with policy space to respond to crises and are both constrained by secular trends lowering the natural rate of interest. In the context of environmental breakdown, the common goal is a credible, mutually supportive fiscal–monetary pathway that hastens the sustainable transition to reduce overall systemic risks. Policy coordination addresses endogeneity in environmental risk management and evokes the constructive value of democracy: socially constructing the pathway that best delivers a smooth transition and minimises harm in future. Furthermore, history suggests that control over policy makes elected officials more cognisant of the links between monetary policy and real economic developments (Woodruff, 2019). Considering the importance of active industrial policy to accelerate structural change towards more sustainable economic activity (Altenburg and Rodrik, 2017), fostering greater understanding of the financial and monetary dynamics of the transition among finance ministries would encourage synergies between these policy areas.

In what manner can the central bank meaningfully contribute to this partnership? Scenario-building efforts already underway at many institutions demonstrate central banks' capacity to research and plot a course for a credible macroeconomic pathway consistent with a successful transition. While net zero or other concrete public goals should be the anchor (Robins et al., 2021), radical uncertainty means plurality is the essential starting point: for models to be useful to understand the variety of risks that can occur from a slow or disorderly sustainable transition, policymakers should consider a wide range of pathways (Battiston and Monasterolo, 2020) and use a range of methodological approaches. Further research has shown some convergence among scenarios around the assets at either end: the most and least likely to be stranded (Bingler et al., 2020). This is a helpful start: through identifying certain types of companies and assets at the tail end, debt issued by those companies can be excluded from asset purchases, and restrictions or disincentives can be placed on the use of those assets as collateral, on a precautionary basis. However, since scenarios must be furnished with rich narratives to specify policy and technological assumptions and fix certain elements (Köberle et al., 2021), the final choice of pathway – including the environmental alignment of monetary policy tools – is a political question.

In deepening the degree of policy coordination, it is worth exploring the grey areas between full-blooded independence and fiscal dominance. In principle, sensitivity to democratic preferences for the environmental transition might still be able to accommodate operational independence to determine the potency of stimulus. For instance, the volume or rate of change of asset purchases might remain for independent policymakers to decide, while eligibility criteria are agreed and signed off by government officials. What matters is that decisions over the settings of monetary policy tools that relate to interpretation of environmental risk – for example, tolerance of negative environmental impacts within collateral frameworks – remains ultimately at the discretion of elected officials. Scenario planning should also consider the fiscal position, for a democratic fiscal authority to actively communicate to the central bank.

Information and Communication

An important precondition for such a process is to recognise that decision-making facing radical uncertainty can be based on qualitative as well as quantitative factors. This flows from the observation in the precautionary approach that precise quantitative modelling of environmental risk is a chimera and that heuristics are needed to guide urgent decision-making (Chenet et al., p. 2021). There is precedent for taking on qualitative data about economic agents' expectations to make monetary policy, such as the network of 'agents' employed by the Bank of England to survey businesses, local authorities and civil society contacts (Tuckett et al., 2020). Qualitative approaches would allow policymakers to make use of the growing volume of data on the economy's impact on the climate and the wider natural world. For example, efforts by business groups to establish new metrics for a range of environmental, social and governance factors are likely to promote a wider range of disclosures (e.g., WEF, 2020); metrics are included for impacts on the climate (emissions) as well as biodiversity (land use exposed to ecologically sensitive areas). Policymakers could apply rough 'rules of thumb' based on new measures.

Communication is equally essential to the process of narrative reasoning. Central banks' recent responses to macroeconomic uncertainty offer examples. Explaining the Bank of Canada's efforts to help people appreciate the underlying reality of uncertainty while keeping faith in the Bank's ability to make good policy, Poloz (2014, p. 12) noted several important steps such as 'explicitly building forecast ranges or scenario modelling around key assumption variables ... into our public policy dialogue; pointing to key elements ... laying out complementary research ... [and] investing more in consultations'. Central banks grappling with environmental risk in their monetary policy frameworks have also shown they recognise the value of transparency; for example, measuring the climate risk of collateral currently on balance sheets against several different yardsticks and publishing the results (e.g., Oustry et al., 2020). Furthermore, evidence suggests experimentation in explaining monetary policy to the public boosts social trust in key messages (Bholat et al., 2018). Novel institutional mechanisms, like the 'Fed Listens' and 'ECB Listens' events, have potential to promote constructive value and comprehensive outcomes in central banks' approach to their duties. By communicating 'the dilemmas, the grey areas, the trade-offs, and the value judgments' and promoting public engagement, central banks can build the conditions for robust social consensus around monetary policy goals (Riles, 2018, p. 65), leading to greater input and output legitimacy (through enhancing the transmission mechanisms for their policies and pursuit of the right *outcomes* in the longer term).

In the context of the sustainable transition, further innovations could develop the full potential of qualitative information and public engagement. At the Bank of England, information from the agents is gathered and analysed within the Bank in the conduct of its mandate to pursue price stability. Following an update to its monetary policy remit to support the government's objective of achieving net zero emissions (Sunak, 2021), the Bank opened a consultation and presented four tools for greening its corporate bond purchase scheme (BoE, 2021b). Establishing new, standing institutional mechanisms in a similar vein could allow a range of social actors to contribute evidence on a regular basis, considering that these tools may require updating as the transition unfolds and central banks make fresh monetary policy interventions. To improve their democratic features, governance of such procedures could be arranged to represent elected representatives (similar to a Parliamentary inquiry in the case of the UK) as well as permanent central bank officials. A mechanism of this sort would provide a forum to test assumptions in the narratives underlying scenarios developed by macroeconomic policymakers. Again, precautionary action could take shape from the results. For example, a public commission or inquiry might serve as a kind of meta-study to synthesise the best available knowledge and emerging research around ecosystem degradation, on which to base metrics for asset eligibility and collateral frameworks. Considering the importance of bank finance for promoting a sustainable transition in the building sector (GFI, 2020), surveys and events could seek to understand challenges facing business owners and the general public around accessing loans; in turn, this could inform policymakers on monetary policy transmission and on the design of interventions (primed for use on a counter-cyclical basis) aimed at stimulating green bank loans.

5.   CONCLUSION

If the most severe consequences of environmental breakdown are both unfathomable in scale and currently underappreciated in policy (DeFries et al., 2019), the only socially responsible way to treat environmental risks is with an abundance of caution. In the context of monetary policy, rapid action to slim down overweight tails in the probability distribution of future events (Weitzman, 2009) contrasts starkly with new consensus macroeconomics. That body of theory justified operational independence by claiming monetary policy is fundamentally neutral – that its goals are uncontroversial and its conduct apolitical. The veil has been lifted. The reality is far from true neutrality: central banks' very design as independent institutions and the tools they use to affect outcomes within the modern economy both involve distributional impacts and value judgments. Thus, a precautionary approach to environmental risks gains force: if central banks are to be non-neutral, they should recognise radical uncertainty and act to minimise harm.

This chapter interprets central bank legitimacy to give democracy a key role in delivering this superior outcome and resolve an apparent tension between the benefits of proactive measures (outputs) and accountability for independent policymakers (inputs). A research agenda to facilitate this transformation is called for. Central banks can contribute by deepening some of the work already underway: in particular, macroeconomic and macrofinancial research to chart ambitious transition scenarios for the economy and financial sector, engaging fiscal policymakers to coordinate assumptions while leveraging technocratic expertise on both sides. In addition, existing literature on policy coordination can be a point of departure to explore the shades of independence between the extremes – such as whether government control over environmental factors in monetary policy can be reconciled with operational independence for the overall strength of stimulus.

Political science and sociology also have contributions to make. Firstly, excavating details of how fiscal and monetary authorities worked together to achieve development goals during the period of fiscal dominance: which practices worked best, and how can they be adapted for the twenty-first-century financial system? Secondly, theorising and experimenting with new forms of participation and scrutiny for elected politicians, civil society actors and citizens, particularly on consensus-building processes, would help economic policymakers build support for implementing transition pathways through proactive measures. How have initiatives like citizens' climate assemblies been able to distil key areas of agreement and spread understanding of the complicated trade-offs posed by the sustainable transition? Humans make the best decisions under radical uncertainty when they reason socially. Connecting this to the value of democracy might be central banks' best chance of meeting the environmental challenge.

REFERENCES

Akerlof, G., Blanchard, O., Romer, D., and J. Stiglitz (eds) (2014), *What Have We Learned? Macroeconomic Policy after the Crisis*. Cambridge, MA: MIT Press. https://doi.org/10.2307/j.ctt9qf899.

Aklin, M., Kern, A., and M. Negre (2021), *Does Central Bank Independence Increase Inequality?* Policy Research Working Paper, 9522. Washington, DC: World Bank. https://openknowledge.worldbank.org/handle/10986/35069.

Alesina, A., and L. Summers (1993), 'Central bank independence and macroeconomic performance: some comparative evidence'. *Journal of Money, Credit and Banking*, 25(2), 151–162. https://doi.org/10.2307/2077833.

Altenburg, T., and D. Rodrik (2017), 'Green industrial policy: accelerating structural change towards wealthy green economies'. In Altenburg, T., and C. Assmann (eds), *Green Industrial Policy: Concept, Policies, Country Experiences*. Geneva: UN Environment and German Development Institute, pp. 18–36.

Arestis, P., and M. Sawyer (2008), 'A critical reconsideration of the foundations of monetary policy in the new consensus macroeconomics framework'. *Cambridge Journal of Economics*, 32(5), 761–779.

Bailey, A., Bridges, J., Harrison, R., Jones, J., and A. Mankodi (2020), *The Central Bank Balance Sheet as a Policy Tool: Past, Present and Future*. Paper prepared for the Jackson Hole Economic Policy Symposium, August 27–28. Working Paper, 899. London: Bank of England. https://papers.ssrn.com/sol3/papers.cfm?abstract_id =3753734.

Barmes, D., Kazi, D., and S. Youel (2020), *The Covid Corporate Financing Facility: What are the Conditions for the Billion Pound Bailouts?* London: Positive Money. www.positivemoney.org/publications/ccff/.

Barro, R.J., and R.B. Gordon (1983), 'Rules, discretion and reputation in a model of monetary policy'. *Journal of Monetary Economics*, 12(1), 101–121. https://doi.org/ 10.1016/0304-3932(83)90051-X.

Bartsch, E., Bénassy-Quéré, A., Corsetti, G., and X. Debrun (2020), *It's All in the Mix: How Monetary and Fiscal Policies Can Work or Fail Together*, 23rd Geneva Report on the World Economy. Geneva: International Center for Monetary and Banking Studies.   https://voxeu.org/content/it-s-all-mix-how-monetary-and-fiscal-policies -can-work-or-fail-together.

Batten, S., Sowerbutts, R., and M. Tanaka (2016), *Let's Talk about the Weather: The Impact of Climate Change on Central Banks*. Staff Working Paper, 603. London: Bank of England.

Battiston, S., and I. Monasterolo (2020), *On the Dependence of Investor's Probability of Default on Climate Transition Scenarios*. December 6. SSRN. https://papers.ssrn .com/sol3/papers.cfm?abstract_id=3743647.

Bernanke, B. (2017), 'Monetary policy in a new era: prepared for conference on rethinking macroeconomic policy'. Peterson Institute. www.brookings.edu/research/ monetary-policy-in-a-new-era/.

Best, J. (2016), 'Rethinking central bank accountability in uncertain times'. *Ethics & International Affairs*, 30(2), 215–232. https://doi.org/10.1017/S0892679416000095.

Bholat, D., Broughton, N., Parker, A., Ter Meer, J., and E. Walczak (2018), *Enhancing Central Bank Communications with Behavioural Insights*. Staff Working Paper, 750. London: Bank of England.

Bingler, J.A., Senni, C., and P. Monnin (2020), *Climate Financial Risks: Assessing Convergence, Exploring Diversity*. Discussion Note, 2020/2. Zurich: Council on Economic Policies. www.cepweb.org/climate-financial-risks-assessing-convergence -exploring-diversity/.

Blinder, A., Ehrmann, M., de Haan, J., and D.-J. Jansen (2017), 'Necessity as the mother of invention: monetary policy after the crisis'. *Economic Policy*, 32(92), 707–755.

BoE (Bank of England) (2021a), 'Covid corporate financing facility (CCFF)'. www .bankofengland.co.uk/markets/covid-corporate-financing-facility.

BoE (Bank of England) (2021b), *Options for Greening the Bank of England's Corporate Bond Purchase Scheme*. Discussion Paper. London: Bank of England. www.bankofengland.co.uk/paper/2021/options-for-greening-the-bank-of-englands -corporate-bond-purchase-scheme.

BoJ (Bank of Japan) (2020), *Enhancement of Monetary Easing*. Memo, April 27. Tokyo: Bank of Japan. www.boj.or.jp/en/announcements/release_2020/k200427a .pdf.

BoJ (Bank of Japan) (2021), *Minutes of the Monetary Policy Meeting on December 17 and 18, 2020*. January 26. Tokyo: Bank of Japan. www.boj.or.jp/en/mopo/mpmsche _minu/minu_2020/g201218.pdf.

Bolton, P., Despres, M., Pereira Da Silva, L.A., Samama F., and R. Svartzman (2020), *The Green Swan: Central Banking and Financial Stability in the Age of Climate Change*. Basel: Bank for International Settlements and Banque de France.

Bonvin, J.-M., Laruffa, F., and E. Rosenstein (2018), 'Towards a critical sociology of democracy: the potential of the capability approach'. *Critical Sociology*, 44(6), 953–968. https://doi.org/10.1177/0896920517701273.

Borio, C. (2019), *On Money, Debt, Trust and Central Banking*. Working Papers, 763. Basel: Bank for International Settlements.

Bradshaw, C.J.A., Ehrlich, P.R., Beattie, A., Ceballos, G., Crist, E., Diamond, J., Dirzo, R., Ehrlich, A.H., Harte, J., Harte, M.E., Pyke, G., Raven, P.H., Ripple, W.J., Saltré, F., Turnbull, C., Wackernagel, M., and D.T. Blumstein (2021), 'Underestimating the challenges of avoiding a ghastly future'. *Frontiers in Conservation Science*, 1. https://doi.org/10.3389/fcosc.2020.615419.

Braun, B. (2018), 'Central bank planning: unconventional monetary policy and the price of bending the yield curve'. In Beckert, J., and R. Bronk (eds), *In Uncertain Futures: Imaginaries, Narratives, and Calculation in the Economy*. Oxford: Oxford University Press, pp. 194–216.

Braun, B., and M. Düsterhöft (forthcoming), *From Delegation to Contestation: Central Banks and Technocratic Politics*. Paper presented at Council for European Studies, 27th International Conference of Europeanists, June 2021.

Buiter, W. (2014), 'Central banks: powerful, political and unaccountable?' *Journal of the British Academy*, 2, 269–303. https://doi.org/10.5871/jba/002.269.

Caldara, D., Gagnon, E., Martínez-García, E., and C.J. Neely (2020), *Monetary Policy and Economic Performance since the Financial Crisis*. Finance and Economics Discussion Series, 2020-065. Washington, DC: Board of Governors of the Federal Reserve System. https://doi.org/10.17016/FEDS.2020.065.

Campiglio, E., Dafermos, Y., Monnin, P., Ryan-Collins, J., Schotten, G., and M. Tanaka (2018), 'Climate change challenges for central banks and financial regulators'. *Nature Climate Change*, 8(6), 462–468.

Carney, M. (2015), 'Breaking the tragedy of the horizon: climate change and financial stability'. Speech given at Lloyd's of London, September 29. www.bankofengland .co.uk/speech/2015/breaking-the-tragedy-of-the-horizon-climate-change-and -financial-stability.

Chenet, H., Ryan-Collins, J., and F. van Lerven (2019), *Climate-Related Financial Policy in a World of Radical Uncertainty: Towards a Precautionary Approach.* Working Paper Series, IIPP WP 2019-13. London: UCL Institute for Innovation and Public Purpose. www.ucl.ac.uk/bartlett/public-purpose/wp2019-13.

Chenet, H., Ryan-Collins, J., and F. van Lerven (2021), 'Finance, climate-change and radical uncertainty: towards a precautionary approach to financial policy'. *Ecological Economics*, 183, 106957. https://doi.org/10.1016/j.ecolecon.2021.106957.

Cobham, D. (2012), 'The past, present, and future of central banking'. *Oxford Review of Economic Policy*, 28(4), 729–749. https://doi.org/10.1093/oxrep/grs023.

Cœuré, B. (2015), 'Embarking on public sector asset purchases'. Speech given at the Second International Conference on Sovereign Bond Markets, Frankfurt, March 10. www.ecb.europa.eu/press/key/date/2015/html/sp150310_1.en.html.

Connolly, E., and M. Kohler (2004), 'News and interest rate expectations: a study of six central banks'. In Kent, C., and S. Guttman (eds), *The Future of Inflation Targeting.* Sydney: Reserve Bank of Australia, pp. 108–134.

Dafermos, Y., Gabor, D., Nikolaidi, M., Pawloff, A., and F. van Lerven (2020), 'Carbon bias in the ECB's collateral framework'. New Economics Foundation, October. https://neweconomics.org/2020/10/decarbonising-is-easy.

Dahl, R. (1989), *Democracy and its Critics.* New Haven, CT: Yale University Press.

DeFries, R., Edenhofer, O., Halliday, A., Heal, G., Lenton, T., Puma, M., Rising, J., Rockström, J., Ruane, A.C., Schellnhuber, H.J., Stainforth, D., Stern, N., Tedesco, M., and B. Ward (2019), *The Missing Economic Risks in Assessments of Climate Change Impacts.* London, New York, NY, and Potsdam: Grantham Research Institute on Climate Change and the Environment, Earth Institute, Potsdam Institute for Climate Impact Research. www.lse.ac.uk/granthaminstitute/publication/the -missing-economic-risks-in-assessments-of-climate-change-impacts/.

Diessner, S., and G. Lisi (2020), 'Masters of the "masters of the universe"? Monetary, fiscal and financial dominance in the Eurozone'. *Socio-Economic Review*, 18(2), 315–335. https://doi.org/10.1093/ser/mwz017.

Dietsch, P. (2020), *Legitimacy Challenges to Central Banks: Sketching a Way Forward.* Discussion Note, 2020/2. Zurich: Council on Economic Policies. www.cepweb.org/ legitimacy-challenges-to-central-banks-sketching-a-way-forward/.

Dietsch, P., Claveau, F., and C. Fontan (2018), *Do Central Banks Serve the People?* Cambridge: Polity Press.

Dow, S. (2017), 'Central banking in the twenty-first century'. *Cambridge Journal of Economics*, 41(6), 1539–1557. https://doi.org/10.1093/cje/bex051.

ECB (European Central Bank) (2020), 'Strategy review: ECB listens portal'. www.ecb .europa.eu/home/search/review/html/form_questions.en.html.

Fabo, B., Jančoková, M., Kempf, E., and L. Pastor (2020), *Fifty Shades of QE: Conflicts of Interest in Economic Research.* Working Paper. Chicago, IL: Becker Friedman Institute. https://bfi.uchicago.edu/working-paper/fifty-shades-of-qe-conflicts-of -interest-in-economic-research/.

Federal Reserve Board (2020a), 'Fed listens: perspectives from the public – part of the Federal Reserve's review of monetary policy strategy, tools, and communication practices'. www.federalreserve.gov/monetarypolicy/review-of-monetary-policy -strategy-tools-and-communications.htm.

Federal Reserve Board (2020b), 'Municipal liquidity facility'. www.federalreserve .gov/monetarypolicy/muni.htm.

Federal Reserve Board (2020c), 'Secondary market corporate credit facility'. www .federalreserve.gov/monetarypolicy/smccf.htm.

Fernández-Albertos, J. (2015), 'The politics of central bank independence'. *Annual Review of Political Science*, 18(1), 217–237. https://doi.org/10.1146/annurev-polisci -071112-221121.

FOMC (Federal Open Market Committee) (2020), *Federal Open Market Committee Statement.* March 23. www.federalreserve.gov/monetarypolicy/files/ monetary20200323a1.pdf.

Friedman, M. (1968), 'The role of monetary policy'. Presidential address delivered at the 80th Annual Meeting of the American Economic Association. *American Economic Re*view 58(1), 1–15.

Garriga, A.C. (2016), 'Central bank independence in the world: a new data set'. *International Interactions*, 42(5), 849–868.

GFI (Green Finance Institute) (2020), *Financing Energy Efficient Buildings: The Path to Retrofit at Scale.* London: Green Finance Institute. www.greenfinanceinstitute.co .uk/report-financing-energy-efficient-buildings-the-path-to-retrofit-at-scale/.

Goodhart, C. (2011), 'The changing role of central banks'. *Financial History Review*, 18(2), 135–154. https://doi.org/10.1017/S0968565011000096.

Goodhart, C., and R. Lastra (2018), 'Populism and central bank independence'. *Open Economy Review*, 29, 49–68. https://doi.org/10.1007/s11079-017-9447-y.

Guttmann, R. (2012), 'Central banking in a systemic crisis: the Federal Reserve's "credit easing"'. In Rochon, L.-P., and S.Y. Olawoye (eds), *Monetary Policy and Central Banking.* Cheltenham, UK and Northampton, MA: Edward Elgar Publishing, pp. 130–164.

Haldane, A. (2018), 'Folk wisdom'. Lecture for the Bank of Estonia's 100th Anniversary, Tallinn, September 19. www.bankofengland.co.uk/speech/2018/andy -haldane-bank-of-estonia.

Hall, R.E., and T.J. Sargent (2018), 'Short-run and long-run effects of Milton Friedman's Presidential Address'. *Journal of Economic Perspectives*, 32(1), 121–134.

Hammond, M., and G. Smith (2017), *Sustainable Prosperity and Democracy: A Research Agenda.* CUSP Working Paper Series, 8. Guildford: Centre for the Understanding of Sustainable Prosperity. www.cusp.ac.uk/themes/p/no08/.

IMF (International Monetary Fund) (2020), *Global Financial Stability Report: October 2020.* N.p.: International Monetary Fund. www.imf.org/en/Publications/GFSR/ Issues/2020/10/13/global-financial-stability-report-october-2020.

IPBES (Intergovernmental Science-Policy Platform on Biodiversity and Ecosystem Services) (2020), *Workshop Report on Biodiversity and Pandemics of the Intergovernmental Platform on Biodiversity and Ecosystem Services.* Bonn: IPBES Secretariat. https://doi.org/10.5281/zenodo.4147317.

Kay, J., and M. King (2020), *Radical Uncertainty: Decision-Making for an Unknowable Future.* London: Bridge Street Press.

Kedward, K., Ryan-Collins, J., and H. Chenet (2020), *Managing Nature-Related Financial Risks: A Precautionary Policy Approach for Central Banks and Financial*

Supervisors. Working Paper Series, IIPP WP 2020-09. London: UCL Institute for Innovation and Public Purpose. www.ucl.ac.uk/bartlett/public-purpose/wp2020-09.

Keynes, J. (1937), 'The General Theory of Employment'. *Quarterly Journal of Economics*, 51(2), 209–223. https://doi.org/10.2307/1882087.

Knight, F. (1946), *Risk, Uncertainty and Profit*. Boston, MA: Houghton Mifflin.

Köberle, A., Ganguly, G., and A. Ostrovnaya (2021), *A Guide to Building Climate-Financial Scenarios for Financial Institutions*. Briefing Paper, 35. London: Imperial College London, Grantham Institute. www.imperial.ac.uk/ grantham/publications/a-guide-to-building-climate-financial-scenarios-for-financial -institutions.php.

Kohn, D. (2018), 'Central bank talk about future monetary policy: lessons from the crisis and beyond'. In Hartmann, P., Huang, H., and D. Schoenmaker (eds), *The Changing Fortunes of Central Banking*. Cambridge: Cambridge University Press, pp. 65–79. https://doi.org/10.1017/9781108529549.005.

Kydland, F., and E. Prescott (1977), 'Rules rather than discretion: the inconsistency of optimal plans'. *Journal of Political Economy*, 85(3), 473–490.

Lagarde, C. (2020), 'The monetary policy strategy review: some preliminary consider-ations'. Speech at the 'ECB and Its Watchers XXI' conference, September 30. www .ecb.europa.eu/press/key/date/2020/html/ecb.sp200930~169abb1202.en.html.

Matikainen, S., Campiglio, E., and D. Zenghelis (2017), *The Climate Impact of Quantitative Easing*. London: Grantham Research Institute on Climate Change and the Environment. www.lse.ac.uk/granthaminstitute/wp-content/uploads/2017/05/ ClimateImpactQuantEasing_Matikainen-et-al-1.pdf.

McNamara, K. (2002), 'Rational fictions: central bank independence and the social logic of delegation'. *West European Politics*, 25(1), 47–76.

Monasterolo, I. (2020), 'Climate change and the financial system'. *Annual Review of Resource Economics*, 12(1), 299–320. https://doi.org/10.1146/annurev-resource -110119-031134.

Monnin, P. (2020), *Shifting Gears: Integrating Climate Risks in Monetary Policy Operations*. Policy Brief, 2020/1. Zurich: Council on Economic Policies. www.cepweb.org/shifting-gears-integrating-climate-risks-in-monetary-policy -operations/.

Mosser, P.C. (2020), 'Central bank responses to COVID-19'. *Business Economics*, 55(4), 191–201. https://doi.org/10.1057/s11369-020-00189-x.

NGFS (Network for Greening the Financial System) (2019), *First Comprehensive Report: 'A Call to Action'*. Paris: Network for Greening the Financial System. www .ngfs.net/en/first-comprehensive-report-call-action.

NGFS (Network for Greening the Financial System) (2020a), *Climate Change and Monetary Policy: Initial Takeaways*. Technical Document. Paris: Network for Greening the Financial System. www.ngfs.net/en/climate-change-and-monetary -policy-initial-takeaways.

NGFS (Network for Greening the Financial System) (2020b), 'Origin and purpose'. www.ngfs.net/en/about-us/governance/origin-and-purpose.

NGFS (Network for Greening the Financial System) (2020c), *Survey on Monetary Policy Operations and Climate Change: Key Lessons for Further Analyses*. Technical Document. Paris: Network for Greening the Financial System. www.ngfs .net/en/survey-monetary-policy-operations-and-climate-change-key-lessons-further -analyses.

Oustry, A., Erkan, B., Svartzman, R., and P.-F. Weber (2020), *Climate-Related Risks and Central Banks' Collateral Policy: A Methodological Experiment*. Working

Paper, 790. Paris: Banque de France. https://publications.banque-france.fr/en/climate-related-risks-and-central-banks-collateral-policy-methodological-experiment.

Peter, F. (2011), *Democratic Legitimacy*. London: Routledge.

Poloz, S. (2014), *Integrating Uncertainty and Monetary Policy-Making: A Practitioner's Perspective*. Discussion Paper, 6. Ottawa: Bank of Canada. www.bankofcanada.ca/2014/10/discussion-paper-2014-6/.

Riles, A. (2018), *Financial Citizenship*. Ithaca, NY: Cornell University Press.

Ripple, W.J., Wolf, C., Newsome, T.M., Barnard, P., and W.R. Moomaw (2020), 'World scientists' warning of a climate emergency'. *BioScience*, 70(1), 8–12. https://doi.org/10.1093/biosci/biz088.

Robins, N., Dikau, S., and U. Volz (2021), *Net-Zero Central Banking: A New Phase in Greening the Financial System*. Policy Report. London: Grantham Research Institute on Climate Change and the Environment. www.lse.ac.uk/granthaminstitute/publication/net-zero-central-banking-a-new-phase-in-greening-the-financial-system/.

Robinson, J. (2004), 'Squaring the circle? Some thoughts on the idea of sustainable development'. *Ecological Economics*, 48(4), 369–384.

Ryan-Collins, J. (2019), *Beyond Voluntary Disclosure: Why a 'Market-Shaping' Approach to Financial Regulation Is Needed to Meet the Challenge of Climate Change*. Policy Note, 61. Vienna: SUERF, The European Money and Finance Forum. www.suerf.org/docx/f_a821a161aa4214f5ff5b8ca372960ebb_4805_suerf.pdf.

Ryan-Collins, J., and F. van Lerven (2018), *Bringing the Helicopter to Ground: A Historical Review of Fiscal-Monetary Coordination to Support Economic Growth in the 20th Century*. Working Paper Series, IIPP WP 2018-08. London: UCL Institute for Innovation and Public Purpose. www.ucl.ac.uk/bartlett/public-purpose/wp2018-08.

Schelske, O., Wilke, B., Retsa, A., Rutherford-Liske, G., and R. de Jong (2020), 'Biodiversity and ecosystem services: a business case for re/insurance'. Swiss Re Institute, August. www.swissre.com/institute/research/topics-and-risk-dialogues/climate-and-natural-catastrophe-risk/expertise-publication-biodiversity-and-ecosystems-services.html.

Schnabel, I. (2020), 'Never waste a crisis: COVID-19, climate change and monetary policy'. Speech given to INSPIRE research network, July 17. www.ecb.europa.eu/press/key/date/2020/html/ecb.sp200717~1556b0f988.en.html.

Schoenmaker, D. (2021), 'Greening monetary policy'. *Climate Policy*, 21(4), 581–592. https://doi.org/10.1080/14693062.2020.1868392.

Sen, A.K. (1999), 'Democracy as a universal value'. *Journal of Democracy*, 10(3), 3–17. https://doi.org/10.1353/jod.1999.0055.

Sen, A.K. (2002), *Rationality and Freedom*. Cambridge, MA: Harvard University Press.

Smith, D. (1992), *From Boom to Bust*. London: Penguin Group.

Steffen, W., Richardson, K., Rockström, J., Cornell, S.E., Fetzer, I., Bennett, E.M., Biggs, R., Carpenter, S.R., de Vries, W., de Wit, C.A., Folke, C., Gerten, D., Heinke, J., Mace, G.M., Persson, L.M., Ramanathan, V., Reyers, B., and S. Sorlin (2015), 'Planetary boundaries: guiding human development on a changing planet'. *Science*, 347(6223), 1259855. https://doi.org/10.1126/science.1259855.

Stiglitz, J. (1997), 'Central banking in a democratic society'. *De Economist*, 146(2), 223–224.

Sunak, R. (2021), 'Remit for the monetary policy committee – March 2021'. Letter to the Governor of the Bank of England. HM Treasury, March 3. www.bankofengland.co.uk/letter/2021/march/mpc-remit-2021.

Tinbergen, J. (1952), *On the Theory of Economic Policy.* Amsterdam: North-Holland.

Tinbergen, J. (1956), *Economic Policy: Principles and Design.* Amsterdam: North-Holland.

Tucker, P. (2018), *Unelected Power: The Quest for Legitimacy in Central Banking and the Regulatory State.* Princeton, NJ: Princeton University Press. https://doi.org/10.2307/j.ctvc7789h.

Tuckett, D., Holmes, D., Pearson, A., and G. Chaplin (2020), *Monetary Policy and the Management of Uncertainty: A Narrative Approach.* Working Paper, 870. London: Bank of England. https://ssrn.com/abstract=3627721.

Tuckett, D., and M. Nikolic (2017), 'The role of conviction and narrative in decision-making under radical uncertainty'. *Theory & Psychology,* 27(4), 501–523. https://doi.org/10.1177/0959354317713158.

Van 't Klooster, J., and C. Fontan (2019), 'The myth of market neutrality: a comparative study of the European Central Bank's and the Swiss National Bank's corporate security purchases'. *New Political Economy,* 25(6), pp. 865–879. https://doi.org/10.1080/13563467.2019.1657077.

WEF (World Economic Forum) (2020), *Measuring Stakeholder Capitalism: Towards Common Metrics and Consistent Reporting of Sustainable Value Creation.* White Paper. Geneva: World Economic Forum. www.weforum.org/reports/measuring-stakeholder-capitalism-towards-common-metrics-and-consistent-reporting-of-sustainable-value-creation.

Weitzman, M. (2009), 'On modelling and interpreting the economics of catastrophic climate change'. *Review of Economics and Statistics,* 91(1), 1–19.

Woodruff, D.M. (2019), 'To democratize finance, democratize central banking'. *Politics & Society,* 47(4), 593–610. https://doi.org/10.1177/0032329219879275.

10. The social sources of "unelected power": how central banks became entrapped by infrastructural power and what this can tell us about how (not) to democratize them

Timo Walter

1. INTRODUCTION: PROFITEERS OF THEIR OWN FAILINGS – HOW THE GLOBAL FINANCIAL CRISIS HAS MADE CENTRAL BANKS INDISPENSABLE (AGAIN)

The period since the 2007–08 (global) financial crisis (GFC) must have felt to central bank(er)s like a particularly bumpy roller coaster ride. The crisis threatened to put an abrupt end to the modern myth of inflation targeting, on whose success story the power, prestige and autonomy of central banks had been founded since the 1980s. The failure to see the portends of financial fragility despite multiple warning signs (Fligstein, Stuart Brundage and Schultz, 2017) dealt a blow to central banks' claims that their scientific expertise gave them superior ability to manage finance and the economy, and warranted the far-reaching autonomy they had been granted in the pursuit of price stability. Indeed, it was not least this principle of central bank independence that was faulted for having encouraged a narrow technocratic focus on price stability, cultivating a "strategic ignorance" (McGoey, 2012) to other matters such as the endogenous expansion of credit and build-up of fragilities in the financial system. Central banks turned this threat into an opportunity: seizing charge of the crisis response has allowed them, if anything, to strengthen their (already central) role in macro-economic governance. "Unconventional" measures such as quantitative easing, as well as the stretching of central banks' mandate to accommodate the issue of financial stability, have led to significant expansion of the scale and scope of monetary policy. Initially intended as temporary derogation, the continued failure to restore the "orderly conditions" (Mehrling,

2011, p. 48) required for the operation of (and thus a return to) the sturdy script of inflation targeting has turned this provisional solution into a new normal.

While central bankers have generally embraced the greater power and greater responsibility, they have also shown considerable unease with the greater scrutiny that this transformation has brought down on them, to the point where even the hallowed principle of central bank independence no longer seems sacrosanct. "Unconventional" monetary policy has created a funda-mental predicament for central banks. The larger the scope of their "uncon-ventional" measures grew and the longer they were maintained, the clearer it became that central banks' agency can in fact reach (quite considerably) beyond the pursuit of just price stability, despite their continuous insistence this must be the only, or primary, focus of monetary policy. To the chagrin of (many) central bankers, the quest for orderly conditions (that would permit a return to safe, conventional ground) has exhibited an expansionary, even centrifugal logic, drawing monetary policy into dealing with an ever-wider range of particular distortions, as if by osmosis or capillarity. However, the more central banks demonstrate a manifest ability to influence a wide range of prices, the more they cast doubt on the carefully maintained fiction of the allocative/distributional neutrality of monetary policy. Thus, central banks are fighting a two-front war: while on the one hand they continuously stretch mon-etary policy beyond their official mandate of price stability in order to restore "orderly conditions," on the other they insist on retaining the (exclusive) right to decide where to transgress it. Quite unsurprisingly, both among the public and an increasingly influential expert community, this has only fueled debates arguing that monetary policy needs to be democratized. Given that central bank agency increasingly appears as a highly fungible resource, it seems that the decision of what ends it should be deployed for should be wrested from the hands of technocratic and power-hungry central bank(er)s (e.g., Jacobs and King, 2016), and be restored to the public as their principal.

In this chapter, I do not want to weigh in directly in this perennial debate on how much central bank independence is necessary and how much democratic accountability is necessary (or vice versa).[1] Instead, I will argue that the expan-sion of the scope and range of monetary policy over the last decade has led to a deeply problematic narrowing of this debate to the question of which ends central banks should pursue. I propose that it is profoundly misleading to con-ceive of central banking as a fungible means or resource, whose deployment towards competing, alternative ends or goods is what needs to be democrati-cally controlled. Drawing on arguments from Science and Technology Studies (STS) as well as Organizational Sociology (OS), I show how this debate and the impression of central bank agency as a highly fungible form of power rests on a deeply problematic analytic distinction between technical-scientific agency itself, on the one hand, and its *control* by competing socio-political interest towards specific ends, on the other. In contrast, I argue that whatever "autonomous power" formal organizations (such as central banks) wield is in fact derived from social institutions such as (financial) markets which serve as infrastructures through which it can be projected. Like any (social) technology, central bank agency is "co-produced" (Jasanoff, 2004b) by creating durable amalgamations of its (scientifically instructed) organizational scripts (akin to codified procedural knowledge) and these infrastructures.

Through a brief analysis of the historical process of co-producing modern central banking, I show how this agency depends on a particular "investment in form" (Thévenot, 1984) that has allowed monetary policy to massively expand its precision, range and effectiveness – but which effectively binds it to the system of market-based finance on whose institutional forms it is thoroughly dependent for influencing economic outcomes. I suggest that the remarkable expansion of central bank agency since the 1980s owes less to an improvement in central banks' intrinsic technical or scientific know-how or capacities, and more to the massive global diffusion and deepening of market-based finance, which has in equal measure expanded central banks' "infrastructural power" (Mann, 1984). This sociological perspective on the *social* sources of central banks' *technical* agency and its apparent fungibility allows us to see that the effectiveness of "unconventional" monetary policy since the 2007–08 financial crisis was made possible by relying on the very same (infra-)structures that helped generate the crisis in the first place. Indeed, the evolution of central bank agency since 2007–08 highlights that the extension of this agency is not possible without a parallel extension of the scope and depth of its infrastructures. Much as has been described by the literature on the so-called "risk society" (Beck, 1986), deploying technical agency such as contemporary central banking towards ends beyond its initial "investment in form" involves extending its infrastructures to subsume these ends to its organizational scripts and technologies. In doing so, one increases the complexity of those infrastructures and thus amplify the potential externalities and risks generated by them. It also means that in further extending the scope of central banking by adding objectives to its mandate, we risk increasing our collective dependence on this infrastructure, crowd out alternative instruments for macro-economic governance (such as, in particular, fiscal policy), and undermine our collective ability to limit financialization and counteract its multiple, and consequential, externalities. I conclude by suggesting that if our goal is to democratize central banking, we need to think about loosening its symbiosis with and dependence on financialized market infrastructures rather than burdening central banks with additional demands that will only push them to intensify this symbiosis.

2.   THE SOCIAL SOURCES OF CENTRAL BANKS' ORGANIZATIONAL AUTONOMY

The drawn-out financial and economic troubles of the last decade have done much to relativize the "Whiggish" narrative according to which the perfection of central banks' technical control had ushered in an era of unprecedented macro-economic stability and steady growth (the so-called "Great Moderation"; see Bernanke, 2004). The myth of central bank independence (Polillo and Guillén, 2005) as the (necessary) foundation of these successes has been shaken as it has become clear that the increasing formalization of monetary policy has to some extent "dis-embedded" (Granovetter, 1985; Barber, 1995; Polanyi, 2001) central bank agency, and encouraged a technocratic bias that has facilitated its "capture" (Kwak, 2013) by technocratic rationalities, financial interests or, simply, organizational self-interest. And yet, while many early critiques in the aftermath of 2007–08 targeted what was perceived as excessively technocratic formalization and scientization of central banking, subsequent debates have zeroed in on the principle of central bank independence as the main obstacle to democratizing monetary policy and making it more responsive to the broader public's concerns. Thus, it appears that the decisive turn to "unconventional" monetary policies in the aftermath of the GFC has shifted the discourse on central banks' scientization: their technical and scientific expertise is increasingly depicted as a "multi-purpose tool" (Braun and Downey, 2020) whose utility has unduly been restricted to pursuing price stability, but whose macro-economic agency can be wielded for many other purposes once central banks as organizations learn to overcome their technocratic inhibitions and are made more responsive to the public as their "principal." However much central bankers may insist on the provisional and emergency character of "unconventional" monetary policy, after a decade it has not only become normalized, but it also serves as a continuous reminder that monetary policy, by altering the conditions of access to (re-)finance for particular economic sectors or actors, could in fact be used to pursue various ends beyond the narrow mandate of price stability.

Despite the resonance between the visibly increased scope of central banking and the growing need for macro-economic governance by states (many of whose other instruments have atrophied) to fight multiple economic and social crises, the assumption that central bank agency constitutes a highly fungible resource or power ignores a number of fundamental sociological insights into the nature of formal organizational[2] agency (such as central banks'). As recent work in the fields of historical (economic) sociology and political economy (e.g., Krippner, 2011; Braun, 2018; Walter and Wansleben, 2020) has pointed out, a *systematic* understanding of the nature and the limits of contemporary central banks' agency requires situating it in the historical social, political and economic conditions under which it has been constructed. This work has shown how contemporary central banking continues to bear the traces, or "inscriptions" (Joerges and Czamiawska, 1998), of its origins in the "contradictions of the welfare state" (Offe, 1984), and the global de-centering of state power(s) and agency through which "state managers" (Block, 1981) attempted to cope with the legitimacy crisis of the 1970s. As in particular the literature on the crisis of Fordism as a mode of accumulation (and its regime of macro-economic governance) has highlighted (Aglietta 2000), the welfare state's legitimacy began to erode as the structural macro-economic conditions on which its coherence as a mode of socio-economic organization and govern-ance rested began to dissolve (Offe, 1984; see also Habermas, 1977). As the stable growth rates on whose allocation among social interests the legitimacy of the Keynesian state depended subsided over the 1960s, the centralized appa-ratus of Keynesian macro-economic governance was faced with multiple con-testations. While for some time these strains could be mitigated through fiscal (and monetary) expansion, this strategy eventually backfired, as it transformed multiple *local* distributional struggles into a *global* problem of inflation whose distributional implications even more severely undermined state legitimacy.

It is now widely accepted that the institutional transition to and "rise of neo-liberalism" (Campbell and Pedersen, 2001) are not well described as a process of "releasing" market dynamics and formal economic rationality from their embeddedness in social and political institutions that channeled their operation towards substantive social values.[3] Rather, what occurred was an extensive reconfiguration of state power aimed at exploiting social and economic insti-tutions "beyond the state" for purposes of governing (Rose and Miller, 1992), and which involved a substantive re-working of these (potential) institutional infrastructures in line with the purposes or "rationalities of governing" pursued by state agencies (see, for example, Konings, 2010). Despite these insights into the entanglements in particular between market infrastructures and (the exer-cise of) state power, most existing accounts of the nature and origins of central bank agency continue to "black box" (MacKenzie, 2005[4]) the ways in which its fungibility is intrinsically constrained by the need to align the rationalities or purposes of governing with the "institutional logics" (Thornton, Ocasio and Lounsbury, 2012) of the social and economic infrastructures through which specific forms of *political* governing and control seek to operate.

To appreciate how this widespread habit of treating technical agency as inherently operationally autonomous from its socio-political context (that is, as autonomous in its technical means, but "embeddable" in terms of the ends to which these are deployed) affects our ability to understand the nature and limits of central bank agency, we can turn to Greta Krippner's (2011) seminal and magisterial study of the *"political* origins of the rise of finance." Focusing on the case of the US as a forerunner of similar institutional transformations elsewhere, Krippner argues that the rise of finance was "engineered" by the state's attempt to turn the nascent ability of global "market-based finance" (Hardie and Howarth, 2013) to endogenously expand credit into a tool for boosting the US economy and remove constraints on public expenditure. In examining the Fed's role in this process, Krippner argues that it deliberately embraced the de-regulation of finance in the 1980s as a vehicle for breaking free from *political* constraints that prevented it from employing its *technical* expertise and control over the interest rate to break inflationary dynamics (ibid., chapter 5).

Indeed, the Fed had found itself in a profound predicament since the 1970s. The attempt to fight the legitimacy crisis of the Keynesian welfare state through fiscal expansion had transformed a multitude of *local* distributional conflicts into a *global* distributional conflict over inflation. Having been given nominal autonomy in pursuing price stability through the Fed-Treasury Accord of 1951, the Fed found itself unable to effectively do so,[5] as its agency (in particular its control over the interest rate) was hemmed in by political resistance to the (deflationary) costs and externalities of doing so. Following Krippner's account, the Fed sought to evade these constraints by "capitalizing" on the dis-embedding of financial markets instigated by US policy-makers. Under Paul Volcker, the Fed attempted to use the de-regulation of financial markets to foreground the role of market forces and processes in determining the interest rate ("letting the market show through"), thus obscuring the Fed's agency in setting the interest at a level sufficient to break inflation, and its responsibility for the deflationary shock that followed. Krippner's explanatory narrative is sophisticated, and it provides an intuitively plausible account of how central banks strategically engineered the organizational autonomy needed to translate their scientific expertise into effective agency against inflation. However, it identifies the Fed's (and, by analogy, other central banks') considerable goodwill towards "self-regulating markets" and financial rationalities and interest as not intrinsic to the nature and functioning of its agency, but simply as the consequence of a strategy of shifting responsibility for certain effects of using this agency away from central banks.

Despite its resonance with widely shared intuitions that more and better scientific knowledge enhances the scope and range of agency, and that "politics" interferes with and distorts scientific expertise, what this and similar accounts black box is the profound reconfiguration of the nature and "social sources" (Mann, 1984) of their power that central banks and other state agencies had undergone over the course of the 1970s and 1980s. Entrapped in multiple distributive conflicts, the state apparatus sought to counter the erosion of its legitimacy by dis-entangling the exercise of its power from conflicts between competing social values and interests, or "orders of worth" in the useful terminology developed by Boltanski and Thévenot (1991). The Keynesian welfare state had relied on generating global (output) legitimacy which it achieved by laterally coordinating its different policy agencies (in particular, fiscal and monetary) to generate (and evenly allocate) economic growth throughout society. As shrinking growth rates made this form of "organized capitalism" unsustainable, the state reacted with institutional transformations towards what has been called a "dis-organized capitalism" (Offe, 1986; Lash and Urry, 1996). Instead of seeking global output legitimacy, the state sought to break down socio-economic governance into more manageable and clearly delineated "public goods" to be entrusted to independent agencies tailored to deliver these goods, with scientific expertise at once increasing efficacy and adding scientific or procedural legitimacy to the output legitimacy generated. This de-centering of state agency thus produced the so-called "rise of the regulatory state" (Majone, 1994) or "rise of regulatory capitalism" (Levi-Faur, 2005), of which central bank independence constitutes maybe the best-known example (see Wansleben, 2020).

To capture the distinctiveness of the new form of organizational agencies that emerged from this process, a few insights from OS and STS will be useful. As Michael Mann's (1984) seminal work has shown, state agencies have "autonomous power" to the extent that they are able to influence particular outcomes "at a distance"; that is, by "conducting the conduct" of a variety of social actors in a way that achieves regularized control over specified (aggregate) outcomes (Latour, 1988; Rose and Miller, 1992). While the "power" over particular outcomes (means) becomes centralized with distinct agencies and bound to specific ends, it depends and operates through existing institutions that serve as its infrastructures. Organizational power is thus what Mann calls "infrastructural power," that is the ability to make use of and mold *existing* social institutions to shape and produce regularities in agents' conduct. Mann's arguments are corroborated by research in the field of STS showing that (technical) means and (social and political) ends are "co-produced" (Jasanoff, 2004b). To transform complex socio-political problems into "public goods" that can be pursued (purely) "technically," without eliciting (significant) contestation (by the socio-political interests concerned), both infrastructures and the rationalities of governing need to be aligned and "formatted" (Callon and Law, 1982) to work smoothly together. As a result, an organization's agency is "autonomous" to the extent and for as long as it is wielded or exercised within a frame constrained *simultaneously* both from above (political legitimacy of ends) and from below (infrastructural means). Social order is thus inscribed or built into (Jasanoff, 2004a; see also Habermas, 1969) the "programmes" and "technologies" of governing, defining a space of legitimate combinations of ends and means for organizational agency (Miller and Rose, 1990).

What all this suggests is that the institutional transformation of central banking since the 1970s and which peaked in the 1980s is not adequately understood as a dis-embedding from political constraint (which paved the way for a more sophisticated technical agency to be developed). In Krippner's (and many others') account, the technical modifications to the Fed's monetary policy procedures are depicted as primarily cosmetic changes that did not alter the basic nature or modality of monetary policy (control over the interest rate), but were primarily meant to hide responsibility for the deflationary shock needed to break inflation. However, if we abandon the tendency to think in terms of dichotomous and separate social/political and technical dimensions or logics, we can begin to see that the Fed's strategy of acting through the market and its infrastructures was not simply a temporary ruse (replaced later on by more scientifically grounded organizational learning), but heralded a fundamental shift in the modalities of central bank power and agency.

If we bear in mind how organizational agency is co-produced, a subtly but consequentially different picture emerges. Despite the 1951 agreement according the Fed nominal autonomy, its organizational agency remained aligned *laterally* to function as part of a Keynesian state ensemble centered *jointly* upon producing evenly allocated and balanced economic growth. As the Fed's rationality gradually shifted to a more *direct* and *vertical* responsibility for price stability, it needed to reconstruct its organizational script with a view to effectively and efficiently pursuing a more distinctly delineated technical purpose. Doing this required not only reviewing its programme of governing, by undoing the programmatic entanglements with other agencies and organizational purposes, in particular fiscal policy.[6] These programmatic revisions also required reconfiguration at the level of technologies of governing, since until the eventual repeal of Regulation Q and similar regulations, the implementation of monetary policy passed through a complex system of interest rate ceilings (and ancillary regulations to enforce these) on different categories of financial products and institutions, geared towards *lateral* balancing rather than *vertical* efficiency. As it proved exceedingly difficult to produce a *global* effect targeted on inflation through this "dispersed" infrastructure, in which every global policy impulse experienced multiple *local* resistances intrinsic to the infrastructure itself, the Fed (like many other central banks at the time) faced a fundamental incongruence between the nascent programme of governing it was developing and the infrastructures on which its technologies for implementing this programme depended.

This experience highlights very clearly that central banks acquire technical agency and "autonomous" power relationally,[7] as a function and to the extent that their *global* programmes and technologies of governing (their "script") are well aligned with the *local* institutional logics and "orders of worth" (Boltanski and Thévenot, 1991) of its infrastructural basis[8] – if they encounter or provoke resistances in these infrastructures, they lose control over outcomes, and thus the ability to effectively achieve their ends. Scientific knowledge is crucial in such a process of institutional transformation, providing instruction for designing a well-aligned and thus technically efficient combination of programmes and technologies of governing; that is, an organizational script (Meyer et al., 1997). However, technical efficiency (and thus the scientific or procedural legitimacy it provides) at the programmatic level (read: "in theory") is worth nothing if not well aligned to available infrastructures and the technologies that can be constructed through it. This means that, once a functioning alignment has been constructed, central banks need to protect their "investment in form," which is the basis of their autonomous power, and continuously work to monitor and maintain the "isomorphism" between their "organizational script" (the "programme and technologies of governing"), its infrastructures and the scientific rule book for evaluating technical efficiency (Meyer and Rowan, 1977, p. 348).

3. INVESTING IN MARKET-BASED INFRASTRUCTURES TO CONSTRUCT "AUTONOMOUS POWER"

In the knowledge society that has developed in the second half of the 20th century, scientific and technical knowledge has become crucial to the design and legitimation of the "investments in form" on which formal organizational agency is built. An increasingly globalized and standardized body of scientific knowledge and professional expertise has come to constitute a body of "global rationalized structures and rules" (Meyer and Rowan, 1977, p. 343f.) which instruct the construction of formal organizational agency and public authority (Rose, 1993; Meyer et al., 1997). Scientific knowledge thus provides criteria and techniques that help autonomous agencies and organizations such as central banks to "identify various social purposes as technical ones" (Meyer and Rowan, 1977, p. 343f.); that is, to articulate public goods that can be unequivocally differentiated and defined. Scientific, in our case economic, knowledge (e.g., theories, models or measurement techniques) also helps organizations "specify in a rulelike way the appropriate *means* to pursue these technical purposes rationally" (Meyer and Rowan 1977, p. 343f.; emphasis added); that is, to operationalize and implement public goods according to scientific criteria of technical efficiency. However, by conforming to scientific knowledge and criteria in designing its organizational script, an organization also gains scientific or procedural legitimacy: "by designing a formal structure that adheres to the prescriptions ... in the institutional environment, an organization demonstrates that it is acting on collectively valued purposes in a proper and adequate manner" (Meyer and Rowan, 1977, p. 349).

Scientific knowledge thus helps organizations to secure the internal coherence of their investment in form, ensuring that their organizational rationality (the public good to be pursued), the programme operationalizing and the technologies making it implementable are vertically aligned, creating a clear-cut hierarchical "formal structure" in which ends and means, purpose/function and techniques and their relations are well-defined (allowing action to be efficient and its efficiency to be evaluated).[9] However, internal and scientific consistency of an organizational script are insufficient for establishing autonomous organizational agency if this "formal structure" does not align (well) with the "relational networks" (Meyer and Rowan, 1977) of the actors and institutions making up the infrastructures which any such formal structure needs to operate through. This need for ensuring the vertical compatibility and isomorphism of the organizational "software" with its infrastructural "hardware" on which it can be implemented and operated is crucial for understanding the intrinsic limitations on the fungibility of central bank agency, which result from the processes of "co-production" through which this mutual compatibility is constructed (over time).

Because we are used to thinking of the social/political and technical as separate and autonomous from one another, (even many sociological) accounts of modern central banking tend to overlook the persistent path-dependencies that can be inscribed into a hardware–software architecture even after certain programming languages that have shaped their design fall out of fashion. For instance, Krippner interprets the fact that Monetarist "vocabularies" (Meyer and Rowan, 1977, p. 349) for designing and describing central bank agency disappeared over the course of the 1980s as an indication that they were a temporary and primarily politically motivated rhetoric intended to obscure central banks' true intentions. This allows her to portray the Fed's support for "self-regulating" markets as an ideological ruse, extrinsic to the operation of central banks' scientifically informed technical agency proper.

On the perspective developed here, a much deeper path-dependency and entanglement of central bank agency with its market-based infrastructure becomes visible – which fundamentally restricts the fungibility of this agency and the possibilities for its democratization. As we saw in the last section, over the course of the 1970s' Great Inflation, the Fed and other central banks faced an incongruence as their organizational rationality shifted from *lateral* alignment within the state apparatus towards the *vertical* definition of price stability as the public good to be autonomously pursued by monetary policy. In this context, Monetarism helped the Fed (and other central banks) to re-programme its organizational script to create a vertical coherence of its programme and technologies of governing and the infrastructures provided by the emerging global system of "market-based finance" that allowed it to render the inflation problem governable. Instead of controlling *global* credit expansion through multiple interventions in *local* contexts, Monetarism allowed for conceiving of price stability in terms of *global* monetary quantities, and for operationalizing it in terms of control over the longer-term trajectory of monetary growth by the central bank[10] (Walter and Wansleben, 2020).

Despite considerable experimentation, the Fed under Volcker (but also other central banks, with the possible but disputed exception of cases such as the Bundesbank or Swiss National Bank, where bank-based finance still dominated) failed to achieve a robust "isomorphism" between its script and its (tentative) infrastructure(s), producing multiple control failures, over-shoots and endogenously generated market squeezes in the process (Walter and Wansleben, 2020). However, this should not lead us to conclude that Monetarism constitutes only a temporary, ideology-driven deviation from sound (and timeless) principles of monetary policy implementation to which central banking returned soon after (as Krippner claims). Rather, the fact that it proved impossible to bring market-based finance "under the jurisdiction of institutional meanings and control" (Meyer and Rowan, 1977, p. 351) points to a fundamental infrastructural constraint on monetary policy that not only extrinsically limits its fungibility, but which since the 1980s has been inscribed into the very modalities of central bank agency through processes of co-production.

The failure of the Fed's tentative Monetarist script illustrates particularly clearly the nature of infrastructural power, and the constraints it imposes on central banks.[11] The technical framework developed under Paul Volcker was premised on the possibility of setting a rigid, longer-term trajectory for monetary (and thus credit) expansion. However, its infrastructure of market-based finance required (considerable) elasticity of monetary quantities and reserves, because the "shiftability" of assets already established in extending credit needed to be ensured at all times as a condition of continuous market liquidity and stability (Mehrling, 2011). In other words, an organizational script which, in accordance with Monetarist vocabulary, made controlling inflation dependent on rigid control over monetary quantities was incompatible and incongruent with the available infrastructure of market-based finance, making it impossible to construct technologies of governing that at once aligned with the infrastructure *and* scientific criteria of technical efficiency (in Monetarist terms).

As the Fed, and other central banks experimenting with Monetarist ideas, proved unable (and quite unwilling) to reverse the transition to market-based finance and endogenous credit (see Krippner, 2011; Walter and Wansleben, 2020), they had only one choice: they needed to find a way to "decouple" (Meyer and Rowan, 1977, p. 358) or "dis-entangle" (Callon, 1998) their organizational scripts from monetary quantities, re-working both programme and technologies of governing in a way that would no longer require them to contain endogenous credit (over which no effective, rigid control was possible in market-based finance). As long as price stability (as the public good to be pursued) remained defined in terms of controling money aggregates, the endogenous monetary expansion intrinsic to market-based finance would continuously generate anomalies and perturbations, eroding the central bank's claim to technical efficiency and scientific/procedural legitimacy. The Monetarist episode is thus best understood not as a heavy-handed deviation from the timeless principles of technically sophisticated and efficient monetary policy triggered by the need to overcome political and social obstacles to its operation. Rather, it constitutes the birthing problems of the co-production of a (partially) novel modality of central bank agency, culminating in an organizational script that developed from the Fed's (and other central banks dealing with market-based financial structures) experience until it was sufficiently standardized globally to be given the name of "inflation targeting" (Bernanke and Mishkin, 1997), with a whole new scientific vocabulary that did not figure monetary quantities as relevant categories anymore (Woodford, 2003).

To make inflation "targetable," central banks needed to rework their organizational scripts in ways that did not conflict with the institutional logics of market-based finance, and in particular the requirement for elastic monetary policy to stabilize a system of market liquidity now increasingly premised on the shiftability of assets. Instead of governing market expectations by setting a (rigid) trajectory of monetary quantities, it "worked" by manipulating the relational system of asset (classes') prices: under the influence of Rational Expectations economics, it re-purposed the "term structure of the interest rate," a heuristic device that the Fed had already used since before World War 2 (although for a different purpose and within a different technology of governing), and substituted it for the trajectory of monetary quantities as a "frame" in terms of which the effects of policy interventions would become visible. From the term structure, essentially a global ("summarizing" other assets') yield curve(s), the central bank could thus "read off" not only the intertemporal structure of market expectations (regarding inflation) but also indications for how to configure its policy interventions to achieve particular effects (see, for example, Frankel and Lown, 1994; Zaloom, 2009; Christophers, 2017). The yield curve thus allowed for observing and evaluating the (scientific and technical) efficiency of monetary policy actions, constituting a condition of normalcy or "orderly conditions" required for efficient and effective agency to be conducted (Walter, 2019).

This investment in form has helped co-produce a script for monetary policy that has proven immensely efficient in operating through an infrastructure of market-based finance, and which has underwritten a period of unparalleled autonomy and legitimacy for central banking. However, if central banks around the world have since the 1980s shown consistent sympathy for, and often been active proponents of, developments that have extended and deepened the institutional logics of market-based finance as it has developed in the US and the UK, this is not just a coincidence, or due to some ideological or technocratic capture separate from how monetary policy functions. Rather, the co-production of inflation targeting and market-based finance since the 1980s has inscribed this complicity into the very form and organizational script of modern monetary policy – or, to use a different but more common vocabulary, it has "embedded" central banks deeply and firmly in the institutional logics of market-based finance as the infrastructure on which their agency (and thus legitimacy and autonomy) depends. Since the 1980s, central banks have been "co-producing" market infrastructures that (they thought would) stabilize and amplify the forms and script of monetary policy in which they had invested, leading them into an ill-understood complicity with the "finance-led growth regime" (Boyer, 2000) and the significant externalities that it has generated.

As Perry Mehrling (2011) has shown, central banks have thoroughly normalized and displayed considerable strategic ignorance towards the (uncontrolled and uncontrollable) endogenous credit growth of the last decades, securing a continuous and elastic supply of reserves and, effectively, becoming "market-makers of last resort" in order to secure the "orderly conditions" in markets on which the smooth functioning of their agency (and thus their organizational autonomy and legitimacy) depends. They have also supported reforms that would "enhance" the functioning of market-based finance (and thus monetary policy), in particular the commensuration and shiftability of assets (see Carruthers and Stinchcombe, 1999), within and across the boundaries of particular markets – such as the emergence of futures and derivatives markets, which many central bank(er)s considered as a way to improve the transmission of policy signals through markets' systems of relationally defined prices.[12] They have also looked quite kindly upon the diffusion of financial techniques that were seen to improve markets' abilities to carry credit, use reserves more "efficiently" and thus stabilize market liquidity, such as repo markets and certain forms of shadow banking (Gabor, 2016; Wansleben, 2018; Braun and Gabor, 2019). It has been by relinquishing their ability to control and substantively shape the expansive dynamics of market-based finance, and instead aligning their organizational script and form of agency to it, that central banks have been able to harness it as a source of infrastructural power. Thanks to the structural repression of non-financial inflation in this regime of finance-led growth, central banks could focus on fine-tuning their *microscopic* control over the yield curve and "inflationary expectations," while honing the myth that their state-of-the-art science allowed them to exercise extensive *macroscopic* macro-economic control over finance and the economy.

From this perspective, it is not very surprising that inconvenient questions such as how transmission of the central banks' (increasingly precise and sophisticated) manipulations of the artefact of the yield curve to the real economy is actually achieved have remained sidelined (Blinder, 2004, p. 80). Indeed, just as Meyer and Rowan have suggested, when "technologies are institutionalized [as scripts] ... [they] become *myths* binding on organizations" (1977, p. 344; emphasis added) – myths that encourage and require organizations to remain strategically ignorant to anomalies and problems whose exclusion made the construction of a functioning organizational script possible in the first place. Indeed, to protect their investments in form, organizations quite routinely resort to "building gaps between their [novel] formal structures and actual work activities" (Meyer and Rowan, 1977, p. 341), justifying inactivity in cases that could be construed as within the remit of their agency but which may conflict with the logics of their (co-produced) institutional infrastructures and scripts (such as when central banks decided not to "prick" asset bubbles in the late 1990s and early 2000s). Such myths and the strategic ignorance they breed can become remarkably resilient, reinforced by the conventional organization-studies wisdom that organizations will generally react to problems or externalities by re-constructing them in ways that can (comfortably) be governed by their existing "repertoires" of action (their scripts) and well-established technologies and instruments (Weick, 1979, p. 26).

However, once these strategically ignored externalities of unchecked credit growth "suddenly" erupted into the 2007–08 GFC, central banks suddenly faced a new predicament. The crisis, and their failure to see it, not only shattered their carefully constructed myth of macro-economic control through superior scientific expertise, but ruptured the very institutional infrastructures on which their organizational autonomy and agency had been built. To restore market liquidity, shiftability of assets and, more generally, the "orderly conditions" on which their agency depends, central banks were forced into extensive "unconventional" policy measures. As suggested at the beginning of this chapter, this forced them to cross some of the boundaries drawn some 30 years ago to delineate monetary policy as the neutral pursuit of a "public good." The various forms of quantitative easing that central banks have engaged in to restore orderly conditions in markets have not only directly forced them into overtly (rather than by omission), if retroactively, validating the endogenous expansion of private credit; they have also implicated them directly in allocational struggles, by demonstrating that monetary policy is capable of shaping the (re-)financing conditions for specific assets or asset classes quite voluntarily, even against market opinion. "Whatever it takes" has thus created a situation in which the more central banks insist that the extensive projection of their infrastructural power beyond the narrow control of inflationary expectations (for which it has been scripted) must only be temporary, and not be used to interfere in distributional patterns (to be left to "the market") although clearly benefiting the financial sector, the more "populist" (Goodhart and

Lastra, 2018) critiques of the "unelected power" of central banks are gaining the upper hand (Tucker, 2018).

Thus, this extension of central bank activity since 2008–09 may, at first sight, create the impression of a highly fungible agency which hitherto had been artificially restricted – and which needs to be made more democratically accountable now that its scope and potency have become visible. This overlooks, however, the fact that what appears as variation(s) observed at the level of visible agency (a shift from conventional to "unconventional" policy, whose ends are distinct from the narrow objectives of inflation targeting) is in fact superposed on a fundamental continuity at the level of the modalities of this agency. Increasingly, central banks are mobilizing the technologies of intervention constructed through the infrastructures of market-based finance in an attempt to quell or neutralize externalities that *globally* emanate from these very infrastructures, although they manifest themselves initially *locally* – i.e., as sectorally or geographically concentrated[13] – before becoming amplified by the fragilities inherent in market-based finance. How inherently restricted central bank agency *really* is becomes visible through the fundamental continuity at the technological and infrastructural level: rather than develop truly novel forms of agency (in relation to market-based finance, from which they currently draw infrastructural power), central banks have attempted to deploy the infrastructures of market-based finance against the very externalities that have emanated from infrastructure, and have attempted to expand the reach of their agency by extending and deepening the infrastructures through which this "power" is projected (see Mann 1984, p. 208ff., for a lucid depiction of this dynamic).

Indeed, the need to deal with externalities linked to the unbridled credit expansion to which they have become (infra-)structurally complicit has forced central banks to deploy their agency in ways that irritatingly overflow the technical (and depoliticized) frame of inflation targeting through its openly quantitative complexion, to the extent of evoking "hydraulic" associations among observers (e.g., Braun, 2016). Thus, their own attempts to restore "orderly conditions" allowing a return to an uncontroversial targeting of inflation threatened to implode the frame that guaranteed their autonomy. Central banks react to this looming threat by attempting to embellish the formal continuity of unconventional with the modalities of conventional monetary policy. For instance, the foregrounding of "forward guidance" straightforwardly permits central banks to render the attempt to restore "normality" to the yield curve (i.e., "orderly conditions") by committing to temporally extended forms of quantitative easing as a continuation of the management of expectations under inflation targeting. In addition, as central banks have mobilized market-based infrastructures in order to neutralize the externalities produced by those same infrastructures, they have also attempted to deepen and strengthen these

infrastructures in order to render the projection of their "agency" more efficient and effective (Braun, 2018; Gabor and Vestergaard, 2018). At the same
time, where central banks have been given novel tasks or "ends" to deal with
externalities of market-based finance that threaten to interfere with (the internal coherence of) their dominant organizational script, they have reacted by
"building gaps between their [novel] formal structures and actual work activities" (Meyer and Rowan, 1977, p. 341), protecting the integrity of their policy
script (programme and technologies) and rendering their pursuit of those novel
"ends" assigned to their agency largely "ceremonial" (ibid.). Thus, the supervision and regulation of "shadow finance" (Vestergaard and Quorning, 2020) as
well as the widely debated shift to a "macro-prudential regulation" (Coombs,
2017) that would restore control over credit cycles has been sidelined in favour
of an emphasis on increasing the resilience of the financial system essentially
continuous with the "previous" microprudential paradigm (Thiemann, 2019).

Thus, the very externalities that the infrastructural foundations of central
bank agency have produced have placed additional demands on central bank
agency which have led central banks to *deepen* their dependence on these very
infrastructures in an attempt to *strengthen* their agency to fight its externalities.
Paradoxically, then, the very infrastructures from which contemporary central
banking draws its (considerable) power and agency help produce the need (or
at least: demand) for this power to be deployed ever more widely. To respond
to this demand, however, central banks are forced to further strengthen the
market-based financial infrastructures, thus amplifying their potential to
generate (the same, and further) externalities and risks. If, as often is the case,
central bank agency is conceived of in separation from the sources of infrastructural power, this process may appear as a sort of rational problem-solving
activity. However, if the infrastructural sources of their agency are given due
consideration, it becomes very dubious indeed whether extending central
banks' scope of activity to novel ends or objectives is indeed the best, or even
most democratic, course of action. To understand more precisely why, in the
conclusion we will have a brief look at how the concept of a "risk society"
(Beck, 1986) can help us highlight how such a vicious cycle is in fact characteristic more generally of the formalization (scientization and technization) of
organizational agency in the knowledge society, posing profound problems to
more traditional ideas about achieving and restoring democratic accountability.

4.   CONCLUSION: CENTRAL BANKING IN A "RISK SOCIETY"

In this chapter, I have attempted to point out that there is a fundamental tension
between the nature of central bank agency, whose autonomous power derives
from an investment in form rooting it in the infrastructures of market-based

finance, and the various projects seeking to re-purpose and re-appropriate this power for pursuing ends that lie beyond the frame of autonomous action inscribed in this form. While the symptoms of this tension, such as central banks' persistent reticence against the scope of their mandate formally being expanded, are widely noted and discussed, for the most part they are readily attributed to other (symptomatic) problems such as the "technocratic" biases of central bankers. What is screened from view and public scrutiny is how (many of) these problems are not simply accidental and extrinsic, but intrinsically inscribed into the very nature of contemporary central banking.

Having reinvented themselves as public agencies around scientifically articulated precise mandates since the 1970s, central banks' autonomous power has come to depend on protecting an isomorphism between these scientifically rationalized rules for defining their rationality and programmes of governing, and the technologies they could carve from the market-based infrastructure that allows them to project power over finance and the economy. While central bankers may not routinely reflect the social mechanisms underlying these pressures, they are quite acutely aware that the persistence of central banks' organizational autonomy depends on preserving a coherent vertical integration of its programme and technologies of governing – a clear, scientifically validated hierarchy of ends and means. As we have seen, central banks will seek to protect the hierarchical form in which they have organizationally invested, aiming to preserve the coherence and integrity of their organizational script by fending off programmatic additions to their "formal structure" and by maintaining and extending their infrastructures.

Certainly, the narrowing of central banks' organizational rationality to the pursuit of price stability, and the co-production of a vertically coherent and hierarchically structured (the isomorphism discussed above) organizational form for doing so in a scientifically legitimated, technicized, precise and efficient way has downsides. Arguably, the argument that monetary policy is neutral with regard to competing social interests is tenuous, even at the best of times. Even if monetary policy probably contributes to these distributive effects (much) more indirectly than central banks' prominence in macro-economic matters may suggest, there is no denying that the socio-technical infrastructures that central banks have created for projecting their agency produce considerable blind spots and strategic ignorance in what central banks can and do "see," and help produce significant externalities and risks in the financial system and the economy.

However, it is crucial to understand that the vertically integrated agency of central banks is not a fungible resource that can unproblematically be laterally projected and deployed towards ends outside its scientifically articulated organizational script. The "unconventional" monetary policies of the last decade, while they may initially convey such an impression of fungibility, in

fact constitute a deployment of central bank agency against a series of externalities arising from the very socio-technical (market-based) structures from
which this agency draws its infrastructural power. In other words, from the
perspective developed here, it is better understood as a form of organizational
maintenance or repair work, in which central banks sought to recondition the
infrastructures on which their technologies of governing depend.

Already the massive political, legal and scientific disputes that have accompanied this maintenance work should warn us that central banking is probably
not the "multi-purpose tool" (Braun and Downey, 2020) and fungible agency
it has been made out to be under the impression of its "unconventional"[14]
elements. It has demonstrated the problems that a functionally differentiated
organizational agency such as a central bank experiences when it is forced to
"overflow" the frame hard-wired into its investment in form. If this happens,
one or both of two things can happen: either the organization will "decouple"
novel ends from its organizational script such as to avoid (mutual) interference; and/or it will seek to extend the reach of its infrastructure (and thus
technologies) to make the novel end(s) compatible with its technological
logics, thus to absorb problems and render them in a way that is amenable to
interventions along familiar technological lines – and, it must be stressed, that
is subject to the same externalities and risks emanating from this infrastructure.

While these feedback loops are rarely discussed at the level of individual
organizations, they have been given an influential formulation at the systemic
or societal level through the concept of a "risk society" (Beck, 1986; Curran,
2017). The concept of the risk society was proposed at around the same time
as central banks began their formalization and scientization in the 1980s. It was
meant to draw attention to the fact that in a society in which general welfare,
livelihoods and multiple social interests depended on complex socio-technical
systems that could not (easily) be dis-assembled or replaced, the stakes of democratic accountability and distributive politics had come to lie primarily with
the question of the externalities produced by these infrastructural forms, which
manifested as unpredictable risks in places that were socially, geographically
and temporally distant from the primary users of such infrastructures.

What this means is that the problem of democratic control and accountability in a risk society cannot and must never be addressed by making further
investments in particular forms of agency (and their infrastructures). The
vertical integration of form that makes the formalized agency of, for instance,
central banks possible in the first place also means that their (only available)
strategy for making externalities and side effects of their infrastructural power
amenable to intervention by their agency (short of decoupling) is to absorb and
subsume this problem to its available tools (or technologies) by extending the
range of the infrastructure of socio-technical system through which it projects
this agency – much as we have seen central banks do since the 2007–08 finan-

cial crisis. This is, however, precisely the opposite of what would be needed to hold organizational actors democratically accountable in a risk society – which requires, above everything else, creating conditions that facilitate organizational learning and, where necessary, reflexive organizational adaptation to manage the risks and uncertainties of complex socio-technical infrastructures. Essentially, by adding purposes to central banks' mission, we induce them to expand their infrastructures laterally, absorbing and integrating heterogeneous functions, institutions and infrastructural technologies – thus increasing the internal complexity of their infrastructures (not least by creating organizational decouplings or ceremonial procedures) and thus the potential for externalities and unforeseen risks.

We would, effectively, *further* increase the weight and centrality of central banking in contemporary macro-economic governance, economies and societies. We would also push central banks into further embracing the "stark utopia" (Polanyi, 2001) of market-based finance, by obliging them to expand its infrastructures in order to be able to deal with the additional tasks given to them. Quite apart from the question of whether it is desirable to further increase the structural power of market-based finance in contemporary societies, the complexity problem pointed out by the risk society literature would caution (strongly) against creating a situation in which one particular infrastructure will crowd out other forms of agency (such as fiscal policy) even further, subsuming and binding its functions to an infrastructure whose externalities and risks we barely managed to cope with during the last crisis.

Under the conditions analyzed through the concept of a risk society, placing all our bets on one particular agency and its underlying infrastructure is a wager we should think twice about. A multi-purpose tool, while certainly versatile, is inherently limited when dealing with complex and distributed problems. Compared with a toolbox of more specialized tools, it will necessarily reduce both the scope and precision of dealing with problems that overflow an agency that is limited to intervening through a single leverage point. This is a simple, but immensely consequential, insight that has taken many forms and shapes over the past decades. Whether it is framed as the need for preserving a "requisite variety" (Ashby, 1958) of solutions when potential problems are uncertain, or for preserving "heterarchical" organizational architectures in which multiple technologies and infrastructure are held available (rather than welding them together into a closed, socio-technical system), we would do well not to ignore it.

NOTES

1.   Even less fruitful, in my view, are attempts to attribute various pathologies or shortcomings of contemporary monetary policy to either a lack of democratic responsiveness or insufficient scientific and operational autonomy, respectively.

2.   "Formal organizations are generally understood to be systems of coordinated and controlled activities that arise when work is embedded in complex networks of technical relations and boundary-spanning exchanges" (Meyer and Rowan, 1977, p. 340).

3.   The distinction between formal and substantive rationality goes back to Weber, who used it to emphasize the tension between *formal* technical or instrumental functions or means (that can be employed towards multiple ends, and compared in terms of their effectiveness for achieving those ends) and the *substantive* values that may be affected by particular instrumental means and thus interfere with their selection (Kalberg, 1980).

4.   The concept of the technical as a "black box" is usually traced to Latour, 1988.

5.   Despite its nominal sovereignty over "monetary" policy, any attempt to restrict the global growth of credit could be thwarted by expansive fiscal policies, thus both exposing the Fed (like other central banks) to charges of ineffectiveness (when inflation soared) and/or making it the eternal scapegoat for the distributional consequences of the fight against inflation.

6.   Despite its nominal sovereignty over "monetary" policy, any attempt to restrict the global growth of credit could be thwarted by expansive fiscal policies, thus both exposing the Fed (like other central banks) to charges of ineffectiveness (when inflation soared) and/or making it the eternal scapegoat for the distributional consequences of the fight against inflation.

7.   Power is relational in the sense and "to the degree to which the structure of relations or ties between actors (where relations or ties can be variously constituted, and actors can be individual or collective) determines the ability of some actors to control or limit the actions of others ... and generally possess the ability to direct social life" (Reed, 2013, p. 293).

8.   Following STS scholar Bruno Latour (1990), the ability to control or "conduct" (aggregate) outcomes at a distance requires (organizational) agents to insert and align themselves to institutional logics and rationalities so as to become what he calls "centers of calculation" that can align multiple actors' conduct to the *global* frames they provide for influencing their local logics and calculations of "rational" action.

9.   It is hardly surprising that this problem was hotly debated by central bankers and economists in this period of institutional transition, often referred to as the "Instrument-Target Problem" (Poole, 1970; Matzner, 1994).

10.   In this sense, indeed, the interest rate would be "determined by the market(s)."

11.   In particular in countries where the development of market-based finance lagged behind, the contradictions were often (much) less pronounced, so that Monetarist scripts functioned (much) better.

12.   Another example would be the diffusion of various "calculative devices" and valuation models that improved commensurability and shiftability of assets (MacKenzie, 2006), or valuation techniques such as "fair value"/mark-to-model as well as value-at-risk.

13.   The subprime crisis or the European Sovereign Debt Crisis come to mind.

14. "Unconventional" primarily at the programmatic level, not so much at the technological and infrastructural level, as we have seen.

REFERENCES

Aglietta, M. (2000), *A Theory of Capitalist Regulation: The US Experience.* London: Verso Classics; New York, NY: Verso.

Ashby, W. R. (1958), "Requisite variety and its implications for the control of complex systems." *Cybernetica*, 1 (2), 83–99.

Barber, B. (1995), "All economies are 'embedded': the career of a concept, and beyond." *Social Research*, 62 (2), 387–413.

Beck, U. (1986), *Risikogesellschaft: Auf Dem Weg in Eine Andere Moderne.* 1. Aufl., Erstausg. Frankfurt am Main: Suhrkamp.

Bernanke, B. (2004), "The great moderation." Remarks by the Governor of the Federal Reserve, presented at the Meetings of the Eastern Economic Association, Washington DC, February. www.federalreserve.gov/boarddocs/speeches/2004/20040220/.

Bernanke, B., and F.S. Mishkin (1997), *Inflation Targeting: A New Framework for Monetary Policy?* NBER Working Paper, 5893, National Bureau of Economic Research.

Blinder, A. (2004), *The Quiet Revolution: Central Banking Goes Modern.* New Haven, CT: Yale University Press.

Block, F. (1981), "Beyond relative autonomy: state managers as historical subjects." *New Political Science*, 2 (3), 33–49. https://doi.org/10.1080/07393148108429531.

Boltanski, L., and L. Thévenot (1991), *De la justification: Les économies de la grandeur.* Paris: Gallimard.

Boyer, R. (2000), "Is a finance-led growth regime a viable alternative to Fordism? A preliminary analysis." *Economy and Society*, 29 (1), 111–145.

Braun, B. (2016), "Speaking to the people? Money, trust, and central bank legitimacy in the age of quantitative easing." *Review of International Political Economy*, 23 (6), 1064–1092. https://doi.org/10.1080/09692290.2016.1252415.

Braun, B. (2018), "Central banking and the infrastructural power of finance: the case of ECB support for repo and securitization markets." *Socio-Economic Review*, 18 (2), 395–418. https://doi.org/10.1093/ser/mwy008.

Braun, B., and L. Downey (2020), *Against Amnesia: Re-Imagining Central Banking.* Discussion Note 2020/1. Zurich: Council on Economic Policies.

Braun, B., and D. Gabor (2019), "Central banking, shadow banking, and infrastructural power." Preprint, *SocArXiv*. https://doi.org/10.31235/osf.io/nf9ms.

Callon, M. (1998), "Introduction: the embeddedness of economic markets in economics." *Sociological Review*, 46 (S1), 1–57. https://doi.org/10.1111/j.1467-954X.1998.tb03468.x.

Callon, M., and J. Law (1982), "On interests and their transformation: enrolment and counter-enrolment." *Social Studies of Science*, 12 (4), 615–625. https://doi.org/10.1177/030631282012004006.

Campbell, J. L., and O. K. Pedersen (eds) (2001), *The Rise of Neoliberalism and Institutional Analysis.* Princeton, NJ: Princeton University Press.

Carruthers, B. G., and A. L. Stinchcombe (1999), "The social structure of liquidity: flexibility, markets, and states." *Theory and Society*, 28 (3), 353–382.

Christophers, B. (2017), "The performativity of the yield curve." *Journal of Cultural Economy*, 10 (1), 63–80. https://doi.org/10.1080/17530350.2016.1236031.

Coombs, N. (2017), "Macroprudential versus monetary blueprints for financial reform." *Journal of Cultural Economy*, 10 (2), 207–216. https://doi.org/10.1080/17530350 .2016.1234404.

Curran, D. (2017), *Risk, Power, and Inequality in the 21st Century*. London: Palgrave Macmillan.

Fligstein, N., Stuart Brundage, J., and M. Schultz (2017), "Seeing like the Fed: culture, cognition, and framing in the failure to anticipate the financial crisis of 2008." *American Sociological Review*, 82 (5), 879–909. https://doi.org/10.1177/ 0003122417728240.

Frankel, J. A., and C. S. Lown (1994), "An indicator of future inflation extracted from the steepness of the interest rate yield curve along its entire length." *Quarterly Journal of Economics*, 109 (2), 517–530. https://doi.org/10.2307/2118472.

Gabor, D. (2016), "The (impossible) repo trinity: the political economy of repo markets." *Review of International Political Economy*, 23 (6), 967–1000. https://doi .org/10.1080/09692290.2016.1207699.

Gabor, D., and J. Vestergaard (2018), "Chasing unicorns: the European single safe asset project." *Competition & Change*, 22 (2), 139–164. https://doi.org/10.1177/ 1024529418759638.

Goodhart, C., and R. Lastra (2018), "Populism and central bank independence." *Open Economies Review*, 29 (1), 49–68. https://doi.org/10.1007/s11079-017-9447-y.

Granovetter, M. (1985), "Economic action and social structure: the problem of embeddedness." *American Journal of Sociology*, 91 (3), 481–510.

Habermas, J. (1969), *Technik Und Wissenschaft Als "Ideologie."* Frankfurt am Main: Suhrkamp Verlag.

Habermas, J. (1977), *Legitimationsprobleme Im Spätkapitalismus*. Frankfurt am Main: Suhrkamp Verlag.

Hardie, I., and D. J. Howarth (eds) (2013), *Market-Based Banking and the International Financial Crisis*. Oxford: Oxford University Press.

Jacobs, L. R., and D. S. King (2016), *Fed Power: How Finance Wins*. New York, NY: Oxford University Press.

Jasanoff, S. (2004a), "Ordering knowledge, ordering society." In Jasanoff, S. (ed.), *States of Knowledge: The Co-Production of Science and Social Order*. London: Routledge, pp. 13–45.

Jasanoff, S. (2004b), "The idiom of co-production." In Jasanoff, S. (ed.), *States of Knowledge: The Co-Production of Science and Social Order*. London: Routledge, pp. 1–12.

Joerges, B., and B. Czarniawska (1998), "The question of technology, or how organizations inscribe the world." *Organization Studies*, 19 (3), 363–385. https://doi.org/10 .1177/017084069801900301.

Kalberg, S. (1980), "Max Weber's types of rationality: cornerstones for the analysis of rationalization processes in history." *American Journal of Sociology*, 85 (5), 1145–1179. https://doi.org/10.1086/227128.

Konings, M. (2010), "The pragmatic sources of modern power." *European Journal of Sociology*, 51 (1), 55–91. https://doi.org/10.1017/S0003975610000032.

Krippner, G. (2011), *Capitalizing on Crisis: The Political Origins of the Rise of Finance*. Cambridge, MA: Harvard University Press.

Kwak, J. (2013), "Cultural capture and the financial crisis." In Carpenter, D., and D. A. Moss (eds), *Preventing Regulatory Capture: Special Interest Influence and How to Limit It*. Cambridge: Cambridge University Press, pp. 71–98.

Lash, S., and J. Urry (1996), *The End of Organized Capitalism*. Cambridge: Polity Press.

Latour, B. (1988), *Science in Action: How to Follow Scientists and Engineers through Society*. Cambridge, MA: Harvard University Press.

Latour, B. (1990), "Drawing things together." In Lynch, M., and S. Woolgar (eds), *Representation in Scientific Practice*. Cambridge, MA: MIT Press, pp. 19–68.

Levi-Faur, D. (2005), "The rise of regulatory capitalism: the global diffusion of a new order." *Annals of the American Academy of Political and Social Science*, 598 (1), 200–217.

MacKenzie, D. (2005), "Opening the black boxes of global finance." *Review of International Political Economy*, 12 (4), 555–576.

MacKenzie, D. (2006), *An Engine, Not a Camera: How Financial Models Shape Markets*. Cambridge, MA: MIT Press.

Majone, G. (1994), "The rise of the regulatory state in Europe." *West European Politics*, 17 (3), 77–101. https://doi.org/10.1080/01402389408425031.

Mann, M. (1984), "The autonomous power of the state: its origins, mechanisms and results." *European Journal of Sociology*, 25 (2), 185–213.

Matzner, E. (1994), "Instrument-targeting of context-making? A new look at the theory of economic policy." *Journal of Economic Issues*, 28 (2), 461–476.

McGoey, L. (2012), "The logic of strategic ignorance." *British Journal of Sociology*, 63 (3), 533–576. https://doi.org/10.1111/j.1468-4446.2012.01424.x.

Mehrling, P. (2011), *The New Lombard Street: How the Fed Became the Dealer of Last Resort*. Princeton, NJ: Princeton University Press.

Meyer, J. W., Boli, J., Thomas, G. M., and F. O. Ramirez (1997), "World society and the nation-state." *American Journal of Sociology*, 103 (1), 144–181. https://doi.org/10.1086/231174.

Meyer, J. W., and B. Rowan (1977), "Institutionalized organizations: formal structure as myth and ceremony." *American Journal of Sociology*, 83 (2), 340–363.

Miller, P., and N. Rose (1990), "Governing economic life." *Economy and Society*, 19 (1), 1–31. https://doi.org/10.1080/03085149000000001.

Offe, C. (1984), *Contradictions of the Welfare State*. London: Hutchinson.

Offe, C. (1986), *Disorganized Capitalism: Contemporary Transformations of Work and Politics*. Cambridge: Policy Press.

Polanyi, K. (2001 [1944]), *The Great Transformation: The Political and Economic Origins of Our Time*. Boston, MA: Beacon Press.

Polillo, S., and M. F. Guillén (2005), "Globalization, pressures and the state: the world-wide spread of central bank independence." *American Journal of Sociology*, 110 (6), 1764–1802. https://doi.org/10.1086/428685.

Poole, W. (1970), "Optimal choice of monetary policy instruments in a simple stochastic macro model." *Quarterly Journal of Economics*, 84 (2), 197–216.

Reed, I. A. (2013), "Power: relational, discursive, and performative dimensions." *Sociological Theory*, 31 (3), 193–218. https://doi.org/10.1177/0735275113501792.

Rose, N. (1993), "Government, authority and expertise in advanced liberalism." *Economy and Society*, 22 (3), 283–299. https://doi.org/10.1080/03085149300000019.

Rose, N., and P. Miller (1992), "Political power beyond the state: problematics of government." *British Journal of Sociology*, 43 (2), 173–205.

Thévenot, L. (1984), "Rules and implements: investment in forms." *Social Science Information*, 23 (1), 1–45. https://doi.org/10.1177/053901884023001001.

Thiemann, M. (2019), "Is resilience enough? The macroprudential reform agenda and the lack of smoothing of the cycle." *Public Administration*, 97 (3), 561–575. https://doi.org/10.1111/padm.12551.

Thornton, P. H., Ocasio, W., and M. Lounsbury (2012), *The Institutional Logics Perspective: A New Approach to Culture, Structure, and Process*. Oxford: Oxford University Press.

Tucker, P. (2018), *Unelected Power: The Quest for Legitimacy in Central Banking and the Regulatory State*. Princeton, NJ: Princeton University Press.

Vestergaard, J., and S. Quorning (2020), "The ECB's half-baked supervision mandate or, how to get serious about shadow banking again." *Journal of Economic Policy Reform*, December, 1–15. https://doi.org/10.1080/17487870.2020.1855177.

Walter, T. (2019), "Formalizing the future: how central banks set out to govern expectations but ended up (en-)trapped in indicators." *Historical Social Research/ Historische Sozialforschung*, 44 (2), 103–130.

Walter, T., and L. Wansleben (2020), "How central bankers learned to love financialization: the Fed, the bank, and the enlisting of unfettered markets in the conduct of monetary policy." *Socio-Economic Review*, 18 (3), 625–653. https://doi.org/10.1093/ser/mwz011.

Wansleben, L. (2018), "How expectations became governable: institutional change and the performative power of central banks." *Theory and Society*, 47 (6), 773–803. https://doi.org/10.1007/s11186-018-09334-0.

Wansleben, L. (2021), "Divisions of regulatory labor, institutional closure, and structural secrecy in new regulatory states: the case of neglected liquidity risks in market-based banking." *Regulation & Governance*, 15 (3), 909–932. https://doi.org/10.1111/rego.12330.

Weick, K. E. (1979), *The Social Psychology of Organizing*. New York, NY: Random House.

Woodford, M. (2003), *Interest and Prices Foundations of a Theory of Monetary Policy*. Princeton, NJ: Princeton University Press.

Zaloom, C. (2009), "How to read the future: the yield curve, affect, and financial prediction." *Public Culture*, 21 (2), 245–268. https://doi.org/10.1215/08992363-2008-028.

Index